CRIPPLING LEVIATHAN

CRIPPLING LEVIATHAN

How Foreign Subversion Weakens
the State

Melissa M. Lee

CORNELL UNIVERSITY PRESS   ITHACA AND LONDON

Cornell University Press gratefully acknowledges receipt of a grant from the University Committee on Research in the Humanities and Social Sciences of Princeton University, which aided in the publication of this book.

First published 2020 by Cornell University Press
Printed in the United States of America

Library of Congress Cataloging-in-Publication Data

Names: Lee, Melissa M., 1985– author.
Title: Crippling Leviathan : how foreign subversion weakens the state / Melissa M. Lee.
Description: Ithaca [New York] : Cornell University Press, 2020. | Includes bibliographical references and index.
Identifiers: LCCN 2019034444 (print) | LCCN 2019034445 (ebook) | ISBN 9781501748363 (hardcover) | ISBN 9781501748387 (pdf) | ISBN 9781501748370 (epub)
Subjects: LCSH: Political stability. | Subversive activities. | Sovereignty, Violation of. | Authority. | State, The. | Legitimacy of governments. | International relations.
Classification: LCC JC330.2 .L43 2020 (print) | LCC JC330.2 (ebook) | DDC 327.12—dc23
LC record available at https://lccn.loc.gov/2019034444
LC ebook record available at https://lccn.loc.gov/2019034445

For Greg

Contents

Acknowledgments

State authority entails the creation and imposition of political order. Ungoverned spaces are said to lack that order. In writing this book, I sometimes felt I had to chart some ungoverned space of my own. But ungoverned spaces are rarely truly ungoverned, and like the nonstate would-be governors of this book, I benefited from considerable external assistance that helped me impose intellectual order onto the chaos of my ideas.

At Stanford University, I was fortunate to have a dream team of mentors. Steve Krasner, Ken Schultz, Jim Fearon, and David Laitin encouraged me to aim high. Steve and David introduced me to the literatures that provoked the central line of inquiry in this book. Ken and Jim pushed me hard on the argument and the evidence. Ken in particular always knew exactly what questions to ask, and he spent many hours helping me think through the answers. I owe much to my friends and colleagues who accompanied me along the way: Jonathan Chu, Kara Downey, Jen Haskell, Aila Matanock, Eric Min, Ken Opalo, Melina Platas, Lauren Prather, and Nan Zhang. I also thank the Center for Democracy, Development, and the Rule of Law for providing an intellectual home in my final year at Stanford.

Although the ideas in this book began to take shape many years ago, they would not have matured without the help of those who attended a workshop for the manuscript at Princeton University. Tanisha Fazal, David Lake, Ken Schultz, Dan Slater, Jack Snyder, David Stasavage, Rachel Stein, and Keren Yarhi-Milo helped me see how to develop the argument and the evidence more deeply. Their generosity and input made this book substantially better. My colleagues at Princeton University also weighed in with their time, advice, and support. I thank Faisal Ahmed, Mark Beissinger, Christina Davis, Joanne Gowa, Helen Milner, and Jake Shapiro. Presentations at seminars and conferences resulted in a treasure trove of useful comments. The participants at these events are too numerous to be listed here, but their feedback enriched and improved this manuscript.

I completed the manuscript while in residence at New York University as a visiting scholar. NYU provided a stimulating and lively intellectual environment, and I am especially grateful to David Stasavage for encouraging me to be ambitious with my ideas.

Several individuals helped me reach the finish line. Brendan Cooley and Jamie Hintson provided research assistance at critical points. Diana Kim and Jim Vreeland encountered pieces of the project late in its development but nonetheless left their mark on the final version. Michelle Jurkovich and Manuel Vogt were there in solidarity and support.

Reo Matsuzaki, Hillel Soifer, and Rachel Stein deserve special recognition. They read the manuscript more times than is reasonably humane and they devoted many hours to discussing and debating my ideas. Every conversation with them made this book much better. I owe them a great personal and intellectual debt for allowing me to so thoroughly abuse their generosity.

Parts of this project drew on fieldwork in the Philippines and Uganda. I thank Julio Amador III, Roland Niwagaba, Melina Platas, Morrison Rwakakamba, and the Agency for Transformation for facilitating my research in Manila and Kampala. I also thank the army of undergraduate research assistants who helped assemble the data that appear in chapters 1, 3, and 5.

Early versions of the ideas in this manuscript were published in "Legibility and the Informational Foundations of State Capacity" (2017), *Journal of Politics* 79 (1): 118–32, coauthored with Nan Zhang, copyright © the Southern Political Science Association; and "The International Politics of Incomplete Sovereignty: How Hostile Neighbors Weaken the State" (2018), *International Organization* 72 (2): 238–315, copyright © the IO Foundation. Revised versions of that material appear with permission from the University of Chicago Press and Cambridge University Press, respectively.

It was a pleasure to work with Roger Haydon and the staff at Cornell University Press. I also thank the two anonymous reviewers for helpful and constructive feedback.

Special thanks goes to David Lake. Without his mentorship, advice, encouragement, and tough love, many things would have turned out differently.

Gerard Lumban kept me grounded throughout this process. He served as a sounding board and gut check at various points in the life of this book, often on short notice. He would like to take credit for nurturing my interest in international affairs, and he is probably not wrong. But that credit must also be shared with my parents, John and Suzanne Lee, who created an environment in which politics was omnipresent and normal. Only with that foundation could I begin to ask why things are the way they are.

No one deserves greater acknowledgment than my husband, Greg Desfor. You followed me to Stanford and Princeton, and you tolerated the long hours, frequent absences, and intellectual self-indulgence. Your patience, kindness, and unconditional love and support during the highs and lows got me through this journey. I am a happier, healthier, and more fulfilled person because of you. Thank you for coming along for the ride.

CRIPPLING LEVIATHAN

THE INTERNATIONAL DIMENSIONS OF STATE WEAKNESS

The central problem facing many developing countries today is not that the state is too strong but that the state is not strong enough. For citizens of the developed states in the West, this claim might seem strange. In the United States and in much of Europe, the state is ubiquitous. In many respects, its impingement on the lives of Western citizens is so complete as to be banal. Most Americans and Europeans drive on publicly funded and publicly constructed roads, register their marriages with government authorities, apply at government offices for business licenses, collect social security payments, sue each other in state courts, and enjoy the benefits of public order and national security. We take for granted the regulatory and service-provision functions of the state. More importantly, this is true whether one lives in Washington, Frankfurt, or London—the centers of political and economic power—or in the geographic periphery of the United States, Germany, or the United Kingdom.

For many countries outside the Western world, the situation is quite the opposite: the state's reach over its territory is highly uneven. The state may regulate, tax, and coerce in the capital, but travel beyond Islamabad, beyond Manila, beyond Tbilisi, and the state's influence and indeed its very physical presence begins to wane. In some places, such as the tribal areas of western Pakistan, the state hardly exists at all except as a distant idea. In other places, such as the southern periphery of the Philippines, the state's authority is deeply contested and resisted. In yet others, such as the unrecognized republics of Georgia, the state cannot even access its own territory. Such states can be characterized as having incomplete state consolidation. They are juridically sovereign but in some places administratively absent.[1] In such countries, whether and how much the state affects one's life for better or for worse very much depends on where one lives.

This book is about the problem of incomplete state consolidation—the failure to govern the entirety of a state's territory—and the role of external states in exacerbating this problem. Consolidation refers to the extension and broadcasting of state authority throughout a state's territory. We can think of state consolidation as the degree to which the state is actually present throughout its territory and, relatedly, the degree to which it governs its territory effectively.[2] As such, state consolidation is an inherently spatial property of states; it refers to the evenness of state authority rather than the intensity of that authority. Incomplete state consolidation is a form of state weakness, but one that differs markedly from traditional understandings of state weakness, defined as a lack of capacity in the state's central administrative and bureaucratic structures, or what I call state institutionalization.

The degree of state consolidation varies considerably across the world. Most states are partially consolidated. Their authority is strong in their political center but not in the periphery. This condition characterizes a great number of states in the international system, including countries as diverse as Turkey, Indonesia, Ukraine, Ethiopia, and Colombia. These are countries with state presence in their capitals, but they nonetheless do not exercise full authority over some parts of their territory. In contrast, developed states such as France and the United States are fully consolidated: they administer, control, and govern their entire territories. At the other extreme, failed states such as Somalia for much of its post–Cold War history lack any degree of consolidation, since the state does not exist in any meaningful way even in the capital. Such places are rare in the international system. Given the prevalence of partially consolidated states, incomplete state consolidation is the statebuilding challenge of our time.

In the 30 years since the end of the Cold War, the problem of incomplete state consolidation has begun to occupy greater prominence in the U.S. foreign policy consciousness. Since the 9/11 terror attacks, the U.S. security community has become increasingly concerned about the negative externalities of "ungoverned spaces"—pockets of territory that are either fully or partially outside the authority of the state. In Pakistan, Ukraine, the Philippines, and beyond, terrorists and rebel groups have established safe havens in the margins of the state that allow them to stage attacks, prey on local populations, perpetuate violence, abuse human rights, and impose alternate systems of rule that supplant the state.[3] Yet the problem of incomplete state consolidation reaches beyond the specter of international terrorism, lawlessness, and violence. For a great many people, the absence of the state is highly consequential in terms of economic development, public goods, and human health and well-being.[4] These pernicious effects of incomplete sovereignty do not remain confined within the national borders of unconsolidated states.[5] The 2014 Ebola outbreak and the 2015–16 refugee crisis in Europe vividly illustrate that even fully consolidated states are not immune from the problems of weak statehood in other parts of the world.

Given the consequences of incomplete state consolidation for security, development, and human well-being, why do such spaces remain without effective authority? This book poses a novel answer to that question. Far from being purely a challenge of a state's own making, incomplete state consolidation also has international determinants. The central argument of this book is that foreign subversion undermines state authority and impedes state consolidation. Subversion is the empowerment of nonstate actors that act as proxies for the sponsor state. As a potent instrument of statecraft, subversion operates by imposing costs on governance in the target state. These costs distract the target, deny it resources, and create bargaining leverage for the sponsor. Subversion's deleterious effects on state authority are considerable: it reduces state presence and allows ungoverned spaces to persist.

Subversion is common in the international system. Russian subversion deprived Ukraine and Georgia of control over significant swaths of their territory; quasi states now govern in lieu of the authorities in Kiev and Tbilisi. In Afghanistan, the site of the longest U.S. war, Pakistani subversion has prevented the Afghan state from consolidating any authority beyond Kabul. During the Cold War, Malaysia deployed subversion against the Philippines, and during the 1990s, Syria undermined authority in southeastern Turkey. Ethiopia and Kenya today contribute to statebuilding efforts in Somaliland, Puntland, and Jubaland, three unrecognized administrations in Somalia. With the exception of Crimea, which Moscow annexed and incorporated into Russian territory, these states outsourced the dirty work to local intermediaries. These proxies proved to be highly effective extensions of statecraft for their external sponsors, with devastating consequences for state consolidation.

By and large, however, academics and policymakers have failed to appreciate the significance of this international factor as a contributor to state weakness in the contemporary world. This book aims to change that view.

Why Incomplete State Consolidation and Its International Causes Matter

The problem of ungoverned space remains a pressing concern for academics as well as policymakers in the security and development communities. To be clear, when scholars and analysts refer to ungoverned spaces, they do not mean that these spaces are literally ungoverned. Rather, these spaces are not governed by the central state. Scholars now recognize a plethora of governing arrangements by authorities other than the state.[6] Yet these deficiencies in state authority over territory are puzzling. When pretenders and competitors to the state govern in lieu of the state, these arrangements violate longstanding norms about sovereignty and the monopoly of force that scholars consider to be integral to our understanding of statehood.

Incomplete state consolidation also matters to policymakers because of the economic and security problems posed by organizations that occupy ungoverned spaces.[7] The linkage between weak statehood and insecurity has guided much post-9/11 policy thinking. Some of these negative security outcomes are primarily internal. The Islamic State, which made no pretense at hiding its ambitions to govern like a state, thrived in the authority vacuum in Syria and supplanted the state in northern Iraq. There, the Islamic State terrorized and enslaved local populations and imposed harsh forms of justice. In the Philippines, the criminal organization Abu Sayyaf has taken advantage of ongoing conflict in the South to engage in kidnapping-for-ransom schemes. In Transnistria, an unrecognized proto-state on Moldova's juridical territory, the human rights situation is poor even compared to that in the government-administered parts of Moldova.[8]

Beyond its internal consequences, incomplete state consolidation matters because its externalities affect other countries. Since 2006, every Worldwide Threat Assessment, an annual unclassified report of the U.S. intelligence community to Congress on threats to U.S. national security, has discussed governance, weak statehood, and their implications for U.S. security interests.[9] Scholars too have shown that terrorism emanates from the borders of states experiencing instability.[10] The robust statebuilding interventions of the post-9/11 period were guided by the belief that states that did not govern themselves produced terrorism and required the "assistance" of outsiders to reconstitute their authority.[11]

Despite these global "public bads," some observers have argued that the United States should not overly concern itself with incomplete state consolidation. Such critics charge that the problem of weak statehood has resulted in what *Foreign Affairs* calls a "decade of distraction" in Washington, DC.[12] They assert that the obsession with weak states is not sound strategic doctrine because most weak states do not threaten the United States. They contend that states lacking full domestic sovereignty are dangers mostly to themselves, and argue that U.S. policymakers should focus instead on traditional national security threats from strong states such as a resurgent Russia and an increasingly assertive China.

This book's emphasis on foreign subversion as a cause of incomplete state consolidation shows that these views are shortsighted. The critics that draw a sharp distinction between threats from the great powers and threats from weak states overlook how the diversity of ways in which states pursue their interests blurs this distinction. When the strong engage in foreign subversion against their adversaries and cause ungoverned and undergoverned spaces to persist, it becomes untenable to treat incomplete state consolidation as an unfortunate problem that weak states made for themselves. Moreover, even if weak state authority does not result in direct attacks on the U.S. homeland, disorder does threaten U.S. interests around the globe. Russian machinations against Ukrainian state authority as a means to influence Kiev and the West more broadly are only the latest manifestation of a foreign policy strategy that has existed since the Cold War and earlier. Similarly, while Pakistan may not directly threaten Western interests and security, its ongoing interference in Afghanistan has posed a serious obstacle to Kabul's ability to assert even a semblance of authority in Afghan territory—a state of affairs that bodes poorly for the U.S.-led effort to stamp out terrorist safe havens.

Not all threats from weak states bear on U.S. security or interests, but appreciating the extent to which such threats do matter requires an understanding of the causes of weak statehood. By showing how conflictual international politics influence domestic state authority, and by demonstrating that the pursuit of state interest against adversaries is what drives foreign subversion, I broaden and deepen what we know about incomplete state consolidation. In doing so, this book can highlight areas potentially amenable to policy influence to mitigate the problem of weak statehood and its consequences for security, order, and development.

To recognize that weak state authority matters is not to ignore the fact that states that are strong enough to govern, protect, and provide are also strong enough to abuse, oppress, and exploit. State authority can be used for good or for ill. How state power gets deployed depends on the nature of political accountability, who is in charge of the state, and how those leaders are chosen. The constraints on state authority, the use of state power, and even the existence of the state itself are deeply normative and political issues. Though many of today's consolidated states have used state power to advance human welfare, the process through which these states were constructed historically were often violent affairs. This book does not advocate for the creation of consolidated states as an explicit policy for the West. Statebuilding as a policy must incorporate political and normative concerns, including an assessment of its feasibility and the obstacles to its success. This book is about those obstacles.

The Limits of Existing Explanations

The enduring existence of ungoverned and undergoverned spaces poses a theoretical puzzle to scholars studying sovereignty and state development. Why would administratively competent states allow such spaces to exist when they generate harmful negative externalities? Existing explanations typically fall into two broad categories: (1) systemic or international factors, and (2) domestic factors. Both literatures have done much to advance our understanding of state development, but suffer from some important limitations.

Systemic explanations focus on the structure and normative environment of the international system to account for changing patterns in state development before and after 1945. A large body of scholarship, most famously embodied by the work of Charles Tilly, suggests that in the pre-1945 period, interstate war had beneficial effects on both state institutionalization and state consolidation in Europe.[13] In other words, war promoted the accumulation of power and capacity in the state's administrative institutions, or what I call state institutionalization, as well as the exercise of authority and control throughout the state's territory, or what I call state consolidation, the subject of this book. War was risky business: because victorious states routinely seized part or all of the territory of the losers, the vanquished were either carved up as spoils or wiped from the world map.[14]

The possibility of dismemberment through annexation or death through conquest had two important implications for statebuilding. First, to extract revenue to fund their militaries, European rulers centralized power and built administrative apparatuses for taxation.[15] These efforts promoted state institutionalization. Second, since external pressures were the primary threat to premodern rulers, the periphery became a crucial first line of defense against foreign adversaries. These pressures promoted state consolidation. Consequently, the international environment generated strong incentives for rulers not only to build their states, but to project authority throughout their territories. Subsequent scholarship has generally refined the bellicist thesis without challenging its overarching claim.[16]

The systemic shift after the end of World War II in 1945 established a new international order, two features of which reduced the imperative of domestic statebuilding. First, the postwar period saw the emergence of new international norms or principles about territorial integrity and international recognition. Violent territorial change has become unacceptable since 1945, and "state death" is now exceedingly rare.[17] Concomitantly, decolonization altered the rules of the game by affording international legal sovereignty and its benefits to new states lacking effective authority over their territory.[18]

Second, the post-1945 order altered the material costs and benefits of warfare as an instrument of foreign policy. States have much to lose from the use of force in the post-1945 period. Powerful members of the international system guarantee the territorial status quo: they punish violators with economic sanctions and armed interventions, and they are loath to abet expansionism even by friendly states.[19] Similarly, economic interdependence between states increases the opportunity costs of engaging in disruptive wars.[20] Nor are the benefits of war as great as they once were. Changing modes of economic production reduce the value of seizing and holding territory, and new institutions help states resolve conflicts without resorting to violence.[21]

For much of the world, the upshot is that successful violent dismemberment through annexation or absorption through conquest by another state is a remote possibility. To the extent that external pressures such as international rivalry continue to threaten states in a more limited way in the post-1945 period, the benefits of statebuilding appear to have accrued only to the state's central administrative apparatuses.[22] Scholars have thus concluded that the absence of war is responsible for today's ungoverned and unconsolidated states.

Perhaps because theories about the effects of external pressures on statebuilding do not generalize easily to the post-1945 non-European world, scholars of state development have turned their attention to domestic factors. This second category of theories consists of explanations that focus on features of the state itself to account for patterns in state consolidation. One branch of the literature examines the legacies of colonial history as a constraint on statebuilding. Distorted, flawed institutions established under colonial rule tended to persist over time, impeding political development in later periods.[23] Similarly, when colonial powers drew artificial borders for Africa's new states during decolonization, these borders divided populations in a way that increased the challenge of state consolidation.[24]

A second branch of the literature on the internal sources of state weakness focuses on the domestic costs and benefits of exercising authority. A number of scholars have argued that the state faces severe challenges administering and controlling territory in places with mountainous physical geography or unfavorable political demography.[25] These factors, however, are static (in the case of physical geography) or slow moving (in the case of political demography); they may explain initial levels of state weakness, but cannot easily explain temporal variation. A separate stream of scholarship has thus examined societal divisions, state-society relations, and intra-elite competition as explanations for statebuilding success.[26]

A third set of domestic explanations, drawn from the literature on civil war, argues that grievance, economic inequality, and political exclusion promote resistance to state authority and make state consolidation more challenging.[27] Some grievances may be the product of historical legacies such as colonial borders, but in other cases are the consequence of conscious political decisions to marginalize or exploit segments of the population.[28] Studies of civil war onset have done much to advance our understanding of the determinants of large-scale political violence. Yet civil war and state failure are symptoms, not causes, of incomplete state consolidation. Nor are these the only symptoms; the failure to exercise authority need not manifest only as civil war. One need only look to the unrecognized proto-states inside the juridical borders of Somalia, Georgia, and Moldova to find examples of territory outside the authority of the central state but nonetheless without political violence. Scholars who wish to understand why ungoverned and partially governed spaces remain without effective authority risk misunderstanding the causes of incomplete state consolidation by focusing narrowly on only one of its symptoms.

The attention to domestic explanations was in part motivated by the sense that the post-1945 world was different, and that the international explanations for the pre-1945 period could not adequately explain variation in state consolidation in the post-1945 period. Even if the postwar era is characterized by a waning of war, it is not the case that policy disputes that once drove interstate conflict have also withered away. This observation is as true for sub-Saharan Africa, a region largely free of interstate war, as it is for other regions elsewhere in the world. States continue to have disputes and incompatible interests. The way in which states resolve those disputes in the contemporary period still has implications for state development when states turn to instruments other than conventional force.[29] By overlooking conflictual international relations, researchers ignore an important factor in contemporary political development and state consolidation.

The Argument in Brief

This book argues that foreign subversion is an important obstacle to state consolidation. I begin with the observation that despite a general decline in interstate warfare, the annexation of territory, and the aggressive use of force after 1945, severe policy disputes between states remain a fact of interstate relations. States still claim the territory of their neighbors. They compete with regional rivals for prestige and influence. They take an interest in the treatment of religious and kin groups and object to the marginalization of those groups.

While states have a number of instruments in their foreign policy toolkits with which to pursue their national interests, the existing literature has failed to appreciate the usefulness or potency of foreign subversion as a strategic tool. Although subversion can in principle apply to a variety of forms of political interference, this book focuses on territorial subversion.[30] I define subversion as the empowerment of third-party proxies—local nonstate groups—with the aim of degrading the target state's authority over its territory. Subversion involves delegation from an international actor, the sponsor, to a domestic actor, the proxy. The existence of a proxy is not equivalent to weak state consolidation; rather, it is the interaction between the sponsor and the proxy that undermines state presence.[31] Interaction and delegation are also key to subversion's strategic benefits. Relative to the conventional use of force, using proxies to subvert state authority is cheap, requires little administrative or military capacity, and is less likely to be detected or attributed to the external sponsor. Ambiguity over foreign involvement, and the precise nature and extent of that involvement, reduces the likelihood that the sponsor will suffer retaliation from the target or the broader international community.

Subversion is not without its risks or constraints, however, and these constraints are important for understanding why states do not routinely deploy it in international relations. Because it relies on delegation, subversion can occur only when proxies are available. Crucially, international actors do not manufacture proxies out of thin air, a point I demonstrate vividly in chapter 4. But even when groups are willing to cooperate with sponsor states, the delegation at the heart of subversion introduces risk through potential loss of control over the proxy. These problems will be more acute when the proxy group's objectives and interests do not align well with the sponsor's, or when the proxy and sponsor are geographically distant.

Despite these challenges, subversion remains an attractive and indirect instrument for weakening target states. Foreign-empowered proxy groups undermine state authority in three related ways. First, these groups eliminate the physical presence of the state. Governments cannot govern without some semblance of state presence. They need bureaucrats and physical infrastructure to administer, regulate, enforce, tax, and provide. Proxies interfere with this exercise of state authority by killing or intimidating bureaucrats and destroying state infrastructure. Second, proxy groups create parallel administrative structures that substitute for those of the state. In some cases these parallel institutions compete alongside state institutions, as in contemporary Afghanistan, where Western-imposed institutions have appeared relatively recently. In other cases they fill the political vacuum left by a void of state authority, as in Georgia's breakaway provinces. Third, proxies can gain citizen loyalties and compliance at the expense of the state. Because governing is fundamentally about making and enforcing rules, this amounts to dislodging the state from its presence in the lives of those it purports to rule. These mechanisms increase the costs of exercising state authority and undermine state control. Subversion thus weakens existing state authority and impedes the consolidation of the state. The result is ungoverned space.

States that engage in subversion increase the likelihood that these proxy groups' efforts to damage state authority will succeed. By providing diplomatic, psychological, political, and, perhaps most important, material support, foreign sponsors enhance the capacity of the proxies to inflict actual damage on the authority of the target. Sponsors also play a crucial role in shielding these groups from the target state's efforts to wipe them out. As I will show throughout this book, external sponsors have proved pivotal to the survival of proxy groups that, once invigorated and empowered as extensions of the sponsor, wreak havoc on state authority.

Damaging state authority can help states achieve their policy objectives in several ways. First and foremost, sponsor states gain a powerful source of bargaining leverage by empowering proxies that undermine domestic sovereignty. This leverage is useful for extorting the target state for concessions in return for the cessation of subversion—even when the sponsor does not admit its culpability in undermining the target. Second, internal disorder can distract or "tie down" the target state and force it to spend resources to deal with the problems of incomplete state consolidation. This reallocation of resources will be most likely to occur when the degradation of state authority produces instability or violence in the target state's territory. Third, by empowering alternative authorities that control and administer territory in lieu of the state, the sponsor can deny the target access to valuable resources, such as tax revenues or natural resource wealth. Fourth, the creation of areas of space outside the target state's authority may be an end in itself. The sponsor may seek influence over the population living in the territory in question, or it may wish to use such spaces as political or geographic buffers.

Subversion reduces state authority by raising the target's costs of administration and control or by reducing the efficacy of those efforts. While many theories about weak statehood in comparative politics concern the costs and benefits of exercising state authority, that literature has largely missed how international factors such as foreign subversion can increase those costs above and beyond those of domestic factors. In view of these elevated costs, some target states may rationally decide that it is not worth trying to counter the sponsor state's meddling. Yet as I argue in chapter 2, even when enemy states target undesirable territory for disruption, few target states will regard chaos or encroachment as politically tenable. The inability to abide attacks on domestic sovereignty is part of what makes subversion valuable as a strategic tool. The target states that do respond to foreign machinations will find it difficult to recapture authority losses due to the active efforts to cripple their authority. The result of subversion, then, is the stunting of state authority.

Contributions

This book's investigation of an international factor's influence on what has largely been considered a domestic phenomenon makes four contributions to the scholarship on state development and conflict. First, it investigates state consolidation over territory as an object of study that is separate and distinct from state institutionalization. Because earlier scholarship did not explicitly differentiate between state institutionalization and state consolidation or simply overlooked consolidation, it was not obvious that these facets of state development may have different causes or may respond differently to the same factor, such as war, conflict, or external adversaries.[32] The political processes of institutionalization and consolidation are theoretically distinct. While the existing scholarship suggests that external adversaries may be beneficial for building capacity in the state's central administrative institutions, this book demonstrates that external adversaries are harmful for state consolidation over territory when they employ subversion.[33] This also implies that greater conflict between states will not be a panacea for the problem of undergovernance, a point I return to in the conclusion.

Second, by distinguishing between institutionalization and consolidation, this book also challenges our understanding of the effects of conflictual international politics on internal state development. Recent literature has suggested that the use of force has dramatically declined as an instrument of foreign policy.[34] For some scholars, this absence of war helps explain the persistence of weak states.[35] This book demonstrates that conflict short of war remains highly consequential for internal political development. It is not an absence of war but rather "war" in another form that is responsible for the persistence of weak states. In the contemporary era, hostile states undermine their adversaries by meddling with their authority. "Fighting" in this manner undermines the state's ability to consolidate authority throughout its territory. This finding enriches and complicates our understanding of the relationship between state development and international politics. Existing work has suggested that external conflict promotes state institutionalization. This book reveals the dark side of conflictual international politics: external adversaries impede state consolidation.

Third, this book confronts the conventional wisdom in comparative politics that state weakness is solely a consequence of internal structural and political conditions that make the projection and consolidation of authority costly. While these domestic variables are important, I show that international factors also perpetuate state weakness above and beyond the effects of domestic factors. It is unlikely that foreign subversion explains initial state weakness, and this book does not make that claim. Rather, I argue that foreign subversion by hostile states is an underappreciated yet important international factor that harms state authority and impedes consolidation. I therefore concentrate on showing the link between subversion and limited state presence. To understand why weak states persist, and why otherwise capable, centralized states fail to consolidate control, we need both domestic and international explanations together.

Fourth, this book's analysis of subversion as an instrument of foreign policy sheds light on evolving practices of statecraft. Policymakers and analysts in the intelligence, diplomatic, and military communities often understand conflict in purely state-to-state terms. This framework made sense in a world in which conflicts used to be fought primarily between state actors using traditional means. Consequently, the security community struggles to think systematically about and respond to "gray-zone conflicts" and "hybrid warfare," threats that always existed in the background of the Cold War and have gained increasing urgency today. These complex forms of conflict blur the distinction between the international and the domestic, and between the state and the nonstate. This book helps unblur that distinction. Subversion crucially depends on this blurring; as a kind of limited unconventional warfare, its pernicious effects on state authority perfectly exemplify that gray zone that so troubles policymakers. At its heart, subversion is a different kind of foreign policy tool that states can use against their enemies—one that is unique for its reliance on delegation, but a tool nonetheless. With this understanding of subversion, this book's value to policymakers is that its theory and empirical analyses offer a rigorous way forward for thinking about the consequences of subversion as a strategy of statecraft, as well as the conditions that make subversion's use more likely.

Empirical Strategy and Plan of the Book

This book shows that foreign subversion undermines the consolidation of state authority over territory. Chapter 1 offers an empirical window into the state of state authority in the world. To do that, I introduce an original measure of state authority that I developed with my colleague Nan Zhang.[36] This measure, the first of its kind for a large number of countries and time periods, proxies for state authority by estimating the accuracy of age information collected in population censuses. The accurate reporting of age data depends crucially on state authority and state presence; inaccuracies are therefore indicative of state weakness. Because the measure is subnational, it allows me to conduct within-country analysis that holds constant other national and subnational factors that affect state authority. I use this measure to examine variation in the spatial extent of state authority over territory both within countries and across countries in the developing world. The chapter then illustrates conditions in ungoverned and undergoverned spaces and contrasts the welfare consequences of weak state authority with consolidated state control. It closes with the observation that many areas of undergoverned space seem to occur in countries with acrimonious relations with other states.

Chapter 2 presents the core theoretical argument of the book. States with incompatible policy interests subvert state authority in the pursuit of foreign policy objectives against their adversaries. This conflictual behavior weakens state authority and impedes state consolidation. I describe the use of subversion as an instrument of statecraft and the political benefits of delegating disruption to local proxies in the target state. I also describe the strategic and operational advantages of subversion, and consider how this foreign policy lever can help states increase the probability that they will prevail in their disputes with adversaries. Because subversion is not costless, I also examine the constraints that would-be sponsors face when considering this tool of statecraft. I then introduce three mechanisms through which subversion undermines state authority, and I show how foreign support plays a pivotal role in these processes. Target states are hardly passive victims of subversion, yet as I discuss in this chapter, their efforts to respond to foreign subversion rarely recapture the authority losses imposed on them by the sponsor state.

Two crucial propositions generated from the theory guide my empirical analyses in the next four chapters. The first implication is that subversion should reduce state authority. This is the central claim of the book. Not all states engage in subversion, however, which produces the second proposition: we should see subversion's effects on state authority when the conditions that make subversion both feasible and desirable are present. These conditions are severe policy disputes or incompatibilities between the sponsor and target, and the availability of proxy groups. We can think of these conditions as motive and means, and both must be present for subversion to occur. From an analytic standpoint, this second proposition is especially important because subversion is difficult to observe systematically, particularly when it is so effective that the target no longer actively contests territory. It also helps us understand why such a powerful tool of foreign policy is not deployed all the time in international relations.

I use quantitative and qualitative methods and cross-case and within-case analyses to test the implications of my theory in three steps. The first step shows that when the factors that favor subversion are present, state weakness suffers (chapter 3). The second step explicitly links those factors to the use of subversion (chapter 4). The third step traces subversion to the degradation of state authority (chapters 5 and 6). These empirical approaches are complementary: the statistical analyses offer breadth while the case studies offer depth.

An unusual feature of this book's empirical strategy is that I eschew a hard dichotomy between statistics/cross-case inference and case studies/within-case inference. In chapter 3 I employ large-n statistical analyses, but rather than compare countries using a measure of state authority aggregated at the national level, I utilize a within-country design, where my comparisons are between provinces for a large number of territorially contiguous countries observed in 1960–2012. The sample covers the states in the middle range of the sovereignty spectrum, and excludes failed states and fully consolidated states. Besides being theoretically appropriate, the middle-range states exhibit the within-country variation that I seek to explain. This cross-national within-country design is unique among studies of state authority, and it is made possible through the use of the state authority measure I introduce in chapter 1. I code policy incompatibility using a measure of rivalry, a type of intense and adversarial interstate relationship. This measure abstracts away from the details of particular policy disputes while also capturing cases where those disagreements are especially severe. I code proxy group availability as the presence of an ethnic group whose homeland is split across national borders. Split ethnic groups are not the only possible kind of proxy, but they are an important potential agent for subversion, and like rivalry, they are easy to observe and code systematically for the large-n analysis.

This chapter offers three tests, all using my measure of state authority, and all conducted at the subnational level. I first look for a simple relationship between state authority and the two factors that condition the use of subversion, and show that state weakness is greatest when both factors are present. Then, using regression analysis, I control for the most likely confounders and show that provinces are less likely to be governed when they border a rival state and when they host a split ethnic group. Then, again using regression but looking within provinces over time, I show that changes in rivalry lead to the expected changes in state authority. The sample spans both the Cold War and post–Cold War periods and all major regions of the developing world, which allows me to generalize my findings to a wide range of countries. The within-country comparisons strengthen the internal validity of my findings, while still permitting me to benefit from cross-country inference typical of large-n studies.

Chapter 4 shifts the focus of the analysis to a more direct investigation of the role of foreign subversion. Because the analysis in the previous chapter does not actually observe subversion and instead infers it from the coincidence of policy incompatibility and agent availability, the primary goal of chapter 4 is to empirically establish the link between these conditions and subversion. I assess the role of the same two conditions considered in chapter 3's statistical analysis through a comparison of Russia's relations with the 14 other Soviet successor states. This design is ideal for examining the decision to subvert because it allows me to overcome the challenge posed by the difficulty of defining and coding policy disputes in a systematic way across countries. I isolate one important axis of policy dispute common to Russia's foreign relations with the Soviet successor states: orientation toward the U.S.-led international order. State positions with respect to this issue area are clear and easy to observe in a systematic way. As I argue in chapter 2, however, the strategy of subversion depends on the availability of local proxies, and not just disputes between states. This chapter confirms that intuition: it is when both motive (policy dispute) and means (local proxies) are available that we observe Russia wielding subversion as a tool of statecraft.

The next two chapters move to a pair of qualitative case studies that investigate how subversion actually results in the degradation of state authority in target states, the core claim of this book. Chapter 5 examines Malaysia's use of subversion as an instrument of extortion against the Philippines during the late 1960s and 1970s. Upon Malaysia's independence, the Philippines asserted a territorial claim over part of Malaysia's territory of Sabah. Malaysia considered this claim to be without merit and a threat to its territorial integrity. Unable to resolve the dispute, Malaysia turned to subversion. It cooperated with Muslim separatists in the southern Philippines to weaken Manila's hold over its periphery as a means to persuade the Philippines into abandoning the Sabah claim. The chapter illustrates the deleterious effects of subversion on Philippine state authority in the South, thus showing the "ground-level" consequences of foreign interference. Its focus on Malaysia and the Philippines also demonstrates that states that are not territorially contiguous can use subversion to undermine state authority—thus serving as an out-of-sample test buttressing the statistical results of chapter 3.

Chapter 6 examines a different logic guiding the strategy of subversion: tie-down. This strategy is evident in Thailand's subversion of Vietnamese-occupied Cambodia in the 1980s. The case traces how Thai fears of Vietnamese aggression after the Vietnamese occupation of Cambodia influenced Bangkok to support the Khmer Rouge to sow chaos inside Cambodia. An interesting and important feature of the Cambodia case is the "tabula rasa"-like state of the country after the Vietnamese imposed a puppet regime in Phnom Penh. That is, although the Vietnamese defeated Cambodia's former leaders, upon victory neither Vietnam nor its new puppet regime exercised any meaningful degree of state authority. Nor was there any state to govern due to the Khmer Rouge's devastation of the country. This blank-slate-like feature mitigates concerns about reverse causality and the influence of initial levels of within-country variation in state authority, and therefore allows me to draw more valid inferences about the effect of Thai subversion on Vietnamese efforts to consolidate state authority in Cambodia. As with chapter 5, this in-depth case study provides a look at the effects of subversion on state authority in a more micro way.

The evidence in the four empirical chapters deliberately draws on multiple world regions. Chapter 3 tests my arguments on a sample of developing countries in the Americas, Africa, Asia, Eurasia, and the Middle East. Chapters 4, 5, and 6 focus on the post-Soviet space and Southeast Asia. The aforementioned methodological considerations in each chapter guide the selection of cases. Because each methodological approach has strengths and weaknesses, I choose cases that offer specific and distinct analytic advantages that allow me to bring complementary forms of evidence to bear on my theoretical argument. Since each approach is distinct and tests different aspects of my theory, together they increase confidence in my overall argument.

I also select cases from regions that are salient for U.S. foreign policy. The post-Soviet space and Southeast Asia are zones of geopolitical contestation where the United States faces a resurgent Russia and an assertive China. They are also regions where some states lack full authority over their territory and where state weakness challenges U.S. interests. To understand the persistence of state weakness, we must look to the role of foreign subversion. To understand foreign subversion, however, we should not limit our attention to the great powers. In the post-Soviet space, Russia is responsible for undermining state authority. In Southeast Asia, it was not a great power that engaged in subversion but rather non-great-power states acting against adversaries in the same region. For scholars, this variation shows that subversion is not a tool confined to the arsenals of the great powers. For policymakers, this variation provides an important lesson for U.S. foreign policy: focusing solely on great powers in the regions important to U.S. interests will cause us to misunderstand why state weakness persists in otherwise capable countries.

The book's conclusion discusses the theory's significance for scholarship and policy. I close the book with implications that result from my central argument about the underappreciated but sizeable role of foreign subversion and its effects on state authority. Importantly, the argument and evidence presented in this book push back against the normatively unsustainable notion that more conflict will yield effectively governed states. They also challenge scholars to rethink the European statebuilding experience, the baseline for much of the state development literature, through the lens of subversion. I also discuss the prospects for third parties to improve state authority and close the gap between juridical sovereignty and domestic sovereignty. Although there may be some room for third parties to reduce the incentives for states to cripple the domestic authority of their adversaries, system-level constraints that operate in the post-1945 world suggest that subversion of state authority is likely to remain an attractive weapon of statecraft for the foreseeable future.

THE STATE OF STATE AUTHORITY

Northern Uganda is a striking place. Bordered by Kenya on the East, the Democratic Republic of the Congo on the West, and what was formerly southern Sudan in the North, the region claims about 35% of Uganda's total land mass and about 20% of its population. Economic activity consists primarily of agriculture and, in the semiarid region of Karamoja, pastoralism centered on cattle keeping. Though it is not rich in exploitable mineral resources, the North is a place of great natural beauty. It is the home of several national parks and wildlife preserves, and is traversed by the White Nile, one of the two tributaries of Africa's most famous river.

Northern Uganda is also severely undergoverned. Those familiar with Uganda's history may not find the unevenness of the state's reach surprising. The country's North-South divide has roots in British policies from the colonial period, which favored the South and marginalized the North. Yet colonial legacies are not destiny. Uganda's first leaders after independence in 1962— Apollo Milton Obote, his more infamous successor Idi Amin, and the short-tenured Tito Okello—all hailed from the North. When Yoweri Museveni and his National Resistance Movement (NRM) won control of the country in 1986 after the five-year Uganda Bush War, the locus of political power shifted to the South. Recognizing the potential political threat of the North to the security of his new government, Museveni and the NRM sought to consolidate state authority throughout the country.[1]

At least in the North, these efforts have largely failed. A report prepared by the World Bank in 1992, six years after the NRM's victory, illuminates the degree of the state authority deficit:

> The affected districts have been to a large extent cut off from the rest of the country since the end of 1986, with the result that line ministry officials have had very limited access to their field staff. It has been difficult for government programs and projects to be implemented in the area, especially where ambushes by rebels and bandits were common. . . . Local authorities have been only able to raise tiny amounts of revenue because of the poverty of the population and the breakdown of marketing, transport, and revenue collection. Many local posts have gone unfilled and many officials have been unable to get out into the field to do their jobs.[2]

As we see in this excerpt, state authority was elusive. Even as the rest of Uganda made impressive strides in consolidating state authority and promoting economic and human development elsewhere, the North languished. In a 2010 interview with the U.S.-based Center for Global Development, Makerere University professor Julius Kiiza noted the ongoing challenges of political and economic development in northern Uganda, pointing to the state's lack of monopoly of violence, lack of fiscal control, and lack of service provision.[3] In short, Uganda continues to be an example of a country with limited state authority over territory.

What is state authority, and what is the state of state authority in the post-1945 era? The goal of this chapter is to address these questions. As I suggested in the introduction, state weakness has often been understood primarily as a deficiency in the capability of the central state's bureaucratic and administrative institutions. This book concerns itself with a different dimension of state weakness: the territorial reach of the state's authority. Because state authority over territory has, until recently, received less attention in the literature, this chapter begins by defining this concept. I then move from the abstract to the concrete, providing an overview of the prevalence of ungoverned and partially governed spaces in the contemporary international system. I then show what life is like in areas where the state's authority is limited or absent, and contrast human welfare conditions in undergoverned spaces with those in governed spaces. As we will see, weak state authority characterizes a large number of states in the contemporary international system. I leave to the following chapter the task of explaining why such spaces persist.

The Exercise of State Authority

To exercise state authority is to govern: to make and enforce rules and regulations, and to provide services. The world's early states did little in administrative terms other than levy taxes, provide a modicum of security, and occasionally conscript soldiers. The modern state, however, is distinguished by a significant expansion in the scope of state activities.[4] Today's states are expected to regulate, enforce, tax, protect, and provide, and to do so evenly across the full extent of their territories. When the state governs all of its territory, its authority is consolidated. When the state's authority is limited, contested, or absent altogether in particular parts of its territory, those spaces are undergoverned or ungoverned from the perspective of the state.

This last point is worth emphasizing: in this book, the term "ungoverned" refers to an absence of *state* authority, not an absence of authority altogether. It is not always the case that spaces devoid of state authority exist in a pure condition of anarchy. For example, in a well-researched study, Zachariah Mampilly documented the phenomenon of rebel rulers, who govern in lieu of the state.[5] If the Hobbesian state of nature is not completely a myth, it is certainly an empirical rarity. This is true even for Somalia after the 1990s, a state that many political scientists and analysts consider to be the prototypical "failed state."[6] Somaliland and Puntland, two of Somalia's unrecognized states, are examples of spaces where alternative authorities administer and control territory. These spaces are governed. They are not governed by the state.[7]

The exercise of state authority requires the presence of the state in the form of state bureaucrats and physical infrastructure such as roads, government offices, and public schools and primary health facilities. A state that is not administratively present cannot govern, because the business of governing requires that the state interact with its population in order to induce or compel their compliance with rules and regulations. Think of the tax assessor, who must have access to taxpayer assets in order to calculate the taxes owed to the state. Historically the work of the tax assessor and his similarly reviled counterpart, the tax collector, required face-to-face interactions with taxpayers. In many developing countries, especially those in which postal and online systems are not well functioning, taxation still entails this kind of interaction. Or consider the beat cop who patrols a neighborhood, or the soldier sent to quell violence and restore order. Even mundane governance activities such as registering births or applying for a construction permit entail some form of interaction between the state and its population.

This definition of state authority, which concerns itself with the territorial penetration of the state, is akin to what Stephen Krasner refers to as "domestic sovereignty." In Krasner's conceptualization of sovereignty, domestic sovereignty is both the organization of public (state) authority and the degree to which it is exercised effectively.[8] There are many ways to think about the meaning of effective state authority. Although there are exceptions, a great deal of the literature on state development and state capacity concerns itself with the quality of the state's central administrative institutions. Administrative institutions hold primacy of place both for scholars who recognize the multidimensionality of state capacity as a concept and for scholars who understand state capacity as a form of power.[9] For them, state weakness is a deficiency in the power and strength of state administrative institutions, or what I call state institutionalization.[10] Denmark has well-developed, high-quality administrative institutions. Uganda does not. Somalia, an extreme case, effectively has no administrative institutions at all.

This book studies effective state authority in terms of its evenness over territory, rather than its intensity or quality. Scholars such as Jeffrey Herbst, Guillermo O'Donnell, and Michael Mann are all interested in understanding the spatial extent of state power.[11] I call this state consolidation. Can the state provide order throughout its territory? Can the state collect taxes throughout its territory? Can the state regulate throughout its territory? The Ugandan state governs, but it does not govern evenly. It is quite effective at ensuring stability in some parts of its territory, but it is quite ineffective at doing so elsewhere, and can be classified as unconsolidated. Its presence in its citizens' lives depends very much on where those citizens live.

Importantly, state institutionalization and consolidation do not necessarily move together. Table 1.1 arrays the possibilities. The countries most people consider to be developed states are both institutionalized and consolidated. Denmark has a high degree of administrative capability and it effectively exercises authority throughout its territory. Countries commonly referred to as failed states, like Somalia, lack administrative capabilities and do not govern the entirety of their territories. The more interesting cases are those in between. Since the end of its civil war, Sierra Leone has scored low on institutionalization but high on consolidation. Its administrative institutions are weak, but weak as it is, the state's reach extends evenly throughout its territory. No doubt the country's small size makes the task of governance easier. In contrast, Georgia since 1999 has scored high on institutionalization but low on consolidation. It inherited bureaucratic institutions from the Soviet period and strengthened these in the 1990s. However, Georgia exhibits marked unevenness in the territorial reach of the state, to the point where alternative claimants to power exclude Georgian state authorities from large swaths of Georgia's territory in the North.

TABLE 1.1   State institutionalization versus state consolidation

		CONSOLIDATION	
		HIGH	LOW
Institutionalization	**High**	Denmark	Georgia since 1999
	Low	Postwar Sierra Leone	Somalia since the 1990s

Both institutionalization and consolidation are constitutive of the state. They are important conceptually and in welfare terms, but represent different approaches to understanding what makes a state a state, and offer different standards of evaluation. They also present different dilemmas for would-be statebuilders, whether foreign or domestic: the causes of weak institutionalization and low consolidation are not necessarily the same, nor are the solutions necessarily the same. Indeed, this book breaks from much of the literature by distinguishing between these aspects of the state and showing that conflictual foreign pressures undermine consolidation.

Measuring Spatial Variation in State Authority

How prevalent are gaps in state authority across space and time? This is not an easy question to answer. To do so, we have to know how to identify incomplete state consolidation when we see it. Political scientists often look for the consequences of state weakness: where the ill effects of weak statehood are present, state authority must be limited or absent. This approach informs the widespread use of infant mortality as a proxy for state authority.[12] Scholars consider infant mortality to be the canary in the state authority coal mine. We know that this measure correlates highly with state weakness and, at least in developing countries, depends on state authority due to the state's central role in providing primary health services. Another common method to identify a lack of state authority is to look at violence. Where we observe political violence, we know that the state is not providing order, and is therefore failing to execute a fundamental state function.

The practice of looking at outcomes of weak statehood is not a bad approach, but it is subject to some important limitations. Most data, for example, are available at the national level. National data are useful for identifying countries with incomplete state consolidation but not for identifying where within those countries the state's authority is limited. Subnational data have only recently become available for many outcomes related to state authority, and are often subject to missingness precisely because state authority is low.

In fact, the state's inability to collect accurate information about its population can actually tell us something about where and to what degree the state exercises authority. All states, including the world's earliest states, seek to gather information about the people the state purports to rule. Information is crucial for the effective exercise of state authority, as states need information for planning, monitoring, and enforcement across a wide variety of domains.[13] In ancient times, this information was often a simple count of the population. The Bible, for example, tells of King David's census of the people of Israel, which was conducted in part to facilitate military conscription. Ancient China and Rome also counted their populations. Census enumeration requires some degree of administrative capacity, as well as a significant mobilization of labor. In modern times, states produce extensive amounts of demographic and economic information, which is used for planning, the levying of taxes, and the allocation of resources. States that cannot gather accurate information about their populations are likely doing little else effectively. Two brief examples illustrate the relationship between information and state authority.

The Republic of Georgia is a useful case to consider because the places where state authority is limited are clear and uncontroversial. One such place is Abkhazia, a breakaway region that does not recognize Georgian rule. Georgian state authority over these rogue provinces was tenuous in the 1990s and essentially absent by the 2000s. An examination of the patterns of missing data in Georgia's official statistical yearbooks supports this conclusion.[14] Georgia has not collected population data for towns and cities in Abkhazia since 1995. In a sign of declining Georgian control, agricultural production statistics and construction data for Abkhazia disappeared from the official Georgian statistical yearbook in 1998. Industry data for Abkhazia vanished in 2006, the same time that trade, hotel, and restaurant data also disappeared. That the Georgian state cannot collect data from Abkhazia is all the more notable because of the depth and breadth of the statistics it collects for the rest of the country. These statistics include everything from national accounts data and educational figures to counts of abortions, fires, sheep and goats, and tons of pollutants released into the air. Nor is the problem due to Abkhazia's formal status as an autonomous republic, for Georgia has a second autonomous republic, Adjara, over which it still exercises authority.

A second illustration of the relationship between information and state authority comes from the practice of census enumeration. In developing countries, censuses are conducted via in-person household interviews, a task that requires access to and interaction with the population. In the most severe cases of state authority deficits, the state's weakness is so complete that it cannot even access its territory to carry out this task. Moldova's 2004 census excluded territories in the unrecognized Pridnestrovian Moldavian Republic, otherwise known as Transnistria, a region that the Moldovan government in Chişinău does not control and cannot enter. Similarly, Georgia's 2002 census excluded most of breakaway Abkhazia in 2002 and all of Abkhazia and South Ossetia in 2014. No census in Pakistan has included the disputed territory of Kashmir. Iraq's 1997 census excluded three provinces in Kurdish areas, which were then outside Baghdad's control. The act of census taking therefore tells us something about state authority: a state that carries out any census at all is more capable than a state that does not. Scholars have therefore used the existence of the population census as a measure of state authority.[15]

As these illustrations suggest, the state's ability to get accurate data about its population and its activities is a function of state authority. This insight allows us to look at variation in the former and infer something about the latter. In a 2017 article, Nan Zhang and I build on that insight to develop a measure of state authority that is based on the quality of census data, and I deploy that measure in this chapter and in the quantitative analyses in chapter 3.[16] We estimate census quality by examining age data. The key idea underlying our measure is that the production of accurate age data is a function of state authority. An important feature of this measure of state authority is that it directly captures activities of states rather than those of their domestic competitors that seek to supplant the state, since only state-produced data are reported in censuses.[17]

Our census indicator captures two sources of census inaccuracy that are intimately related to state authority: enumerator error and respondent error. Enumerator error is error introduced by census interviewers. As previously mentioned, census enumeration in developing countries is carried out almost exclusively via face-to-face household interviews, in which a trained interviewer asks household members a series of questions and records answers on a form. Because these state agents are responsible for gathering information, the quality and accuracy of that information depends in part on whether they shirk their duties. While there are many idiosyncratic reasons to shirk, systematic shirking within countries is heavily influenced by poor conditions related to state authority. These conditions include physical insecurity and inadequate state infrastructure that make it dangerous or difficult for census interviewers to perform their duties. For example, in the 1961 Nepal census, poor infrastructure led some enumerators to skip entire villages. Instead the enumerators sat on hills, looked down at the villages, and made up data.[18] Importantly, interviewers who shirk cannot simply turn in empty census forms to their supervisors, as submitting too few completed forms is evidence of shirking.[19] As the Nepal example shows us, interviewers make up data.

A second source of error is respondent error, which occurs when individuals do not know their precise ages. Knowledge of one's precise age is relevant only in a context in which central state authorities penetrate, organize, and administer society by promulgating rules and collecting population data.[20] The state's exercise of authority increases the likelihood of individuals knowing their own ages in two important ways. First, because rights, responsibilities, and privileges vis-à-vis the state are conditional on age, individuals have an incentive to learn their precise ages. Second, through interactions with the state's administrative apparatus, individuals obtain "artifacts" necessary for proving one's age, such as national identification cards or birth certificates, in order to gain access to state privileges and rights. In the context of a census, identity documents are important for the production of accurate age data, as respondents and enumerators can refer to these papers to determine a respondent's true age.[21] When the state is ubiquitous, as it is in the United States, knowledge of precise age is banal. In contrast, when individuals do not interact with the state administrative apparatus, which is the case in parts of many developing countries, quantitative age has no meaning or social import, and age tends to be reckoned in qualitative terms (young or old). Similarly, the inability of respondents to produce an identity document with their exact year of birth suggests that individuals have little incentive to keep documentation proving their ages. In other words, precise age is not a salient piece of information, implying weak or absent state administration and control. When individuals are asked to give a precise age, as in the case of the census, they estimate.

Crucially, when people make up data, either because they must populate census forms or because they are asked to estimate their age, they do not give random numbers, even when they attempt to be random. Rather, individuals tend to favor (or avoid) certain terminal digits, such as numbers ending in five or zero. This tendency toward digit preference or avoidance appears in aggregate data as an abnormally high number of individuals with certain ages—far more than one would expect to observe in a normal population, and thus indicative of some problem with data accuracy.

To see how enumerator and respondent error can affect census accuracy, consider the following exchange between a census enumerator and respondent during the 1971 Moroccan census:

> ENUMERATOR: "What is your age?"
>
> RESPONDENT: "Who me? Our generation was unrecorded. We didn't have any. No date of birth. Nothing."
>
> ENUMERATOR: "How many (years), how many? Estimate."
>
> RESPONDENT: "How am I going to estimate? *I have nothing to estimate with.* I can tell you that I am 60 years; 70 I haven't reached."
>
> ENUMERATOR: "Have you reached 80?"
>
> RESPONDENT: "I don't think so. Someone who is 80 is . . ."
>
> ENUMERATOR: "*You who still have energy, you are 70.*"
>
> RESPONDENT: "Perhaps that, perhaps it is correct, Sir."[22]

Two points are evident in the exchange. First, the respondent indicates that she does not know her age because her birth was never recorded and because she never received any document to prove her age. Since it is the state's responsibility to record vital information and issue official documents, it is unlikely that the respondent interacts much with the state, which suggests an absence of the state or its unimportance in the respondent's life. Indeed, the researcher observing the exchange notes that respondents in Morocco recognize that they do not know their ages "because they do not work in modern institutions where ages are considered necessary."[23] Despite being ignorant of her exact age, the respondent provides an estimate, albeit one subject to round-number or base-10 bias, the tendency to favor numbers that are multiples of 10. This estimation is an example of respondent error.

Second, we see an example of enumerator error in the enumerator's interactions with the respondent. Initially the respondent indicates that she is not yet 70 years old. Yet, through the intervention of the enumerator, the respondent decides by the end of the exchange that her age is probably 70. In this case the enumerator not only does not attempt to arrive at a more precise estimate of the respondent's age, but in fact inflates her age based on the enumerator's judgment of the respondent's appearance and health. Moreover, the enumerator reveals the same nonrandomness in his estimation of age as the respondent: a preference for numbers that end in zero.

These observations about the state and its relationship to age accuracy in census data provide the foundation for the indicator of state authority that Nan Zhang and I developed.[24] To quantify age accuracy, the indicator exploits a fact well known among demographers: that true age distributions within a population follow a naturally smooth curve. In expectation, the percentage change in the number of individuals in two consecutive single ages is extremely small in a natural population. Deviations from this smooth curve suggest inaccuracies in the age returns. In other words, one would not expect to observe large fluctuations between adjacent ages or clustering on ("preference for") particular ages ending in the same terminal digit.[25]

Figure 1.1 illustrates this phenomenon using data from Mali's 1998 census. The left panel shows the distribution of population for each single age for Sikasso, a region located near the national capital. The right panel shows the distribution for Gao, a region where the state's reach is weak and where militants have contested its sovereignty. Although the underlying age curves are evident in the distributions for both regions, the age curve for Gao exhibits considerable variance ("noise") around the true distribution, which is graphical evidence of age inaccuracy. Building on the insights regarding the sources of census error, I interpret these patterns as evidence of weak state authority.

Our census indicator quantifies age accuracy using a demographic technique called the Myers Index.[26] The Myers Index was initially proposed by Robert Myers, an actuary perhaps best known for his work founding the U.S. Social Security system. To summarize, the index begins with the assumption that in a

A

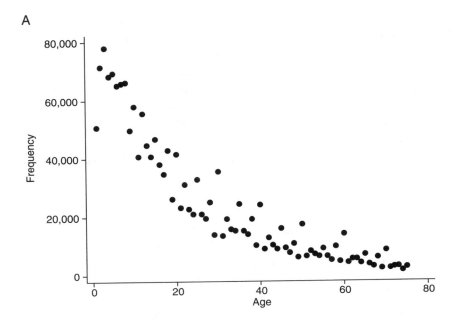

B

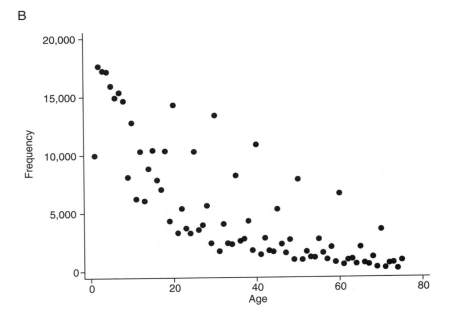

FIGURE 1.1. Two regions in Mali, 1998: (A) Sikasso, Myers score: 12.34; (B) Gao, Myers score: 27.89.

natural population, the number of people whose ages end in each terminal digit (zero through nine) should distribute uniformly. Mortality, however, skews this distribution such that there is a greater number of people with ages ending in the earlier terminal digits than in the later terminal digits. Myers developed a technique to correct for the effects of mortality through what he called a "blending" process; any errors remaining after this correction can be attributed to inaccuracies in the reporting of age.[27] The index has a theoretical range of 0 to 90, and the values have a natural interpretation as the percentage of individuals exhibiting digit preference. For example, 0 indicates no digit preference, while 90 indicates that all respondents reported ages ending in a single terminal digit (since 10% of those respondents should have reported a true age). The index is a useful approach for estimating age inaccuracy in censuses, and even appears in some national census publications and reports. While Myers developed the technique itself, Nan Zhang and I are the first to suggest its application as a means to estimate levels of state authority. Higher values indicate greater age inaccuracy and thus greater state weakness.[28]

The Myers Index has several properties that make it suitable as a proxy for state authority over territory. First, the data are available at the subnational level for a large number of countries over time. This subnational component is a crucial feature of the data, as it allows me to capture the territorial variation in state authority, the key outcome of interest in this book. In this chapter, I also take advantage of the subnational component to link state authority to human welfare and well-being.

Second, the Myers Index is a conceptually valid measure of state authority over territory. I assess its validity by examining the correlation between the index and other measures of state authority with more limited geographic and temporal coverage. The correlation tables and data sources are reported in the appendix. The correlations are relatively strong, which suggests that the index is indeed picking up something about state authority.[29]

Third, the indicator is not sensitive to demographic shocks unrelated to state authority. Consider two types of shocks: (1) the devastation of the youth population due to war, and (2) a sharp increase in births. Both types of shocks change the shape of the age distribution curve but do not on their own introduce significant numbers of discontinuities or noise into the distribution. Recall that systematic errors detectable by the Myers Index manifest as large percentage changes in the number of individuals in consecutive single ages. Graphically, these errors appear as noise around the "true" underlying distribution, typically as spikes in population with ages ending in zeros and fives. It is this noise that is captured by the Myers Index; the overall shape of the underlying distribution is flexible.

A particularly striking example comes from the Île-de-France (the region containing Paris, the French capital) in 1982. Figure 1.2 shows two sharp discontinuities in the age distribution. The discontinuity around ages 60–65 represents the loss of the generation of young men who died in World War II: men who were in their 20s during the war and who would have been in their 60s had they survived to 1982. The discontinuity around age 37 represents the postwar baby boom, as individuals born in 1945 would be in their late 30s and early 40s in 1982. Neither type of shock biases the Myers Index. The score for the Île-de-France is 0.64, indicating very little age inaccuracy and suggesting a high degree of state authority, which one would expect for this part of France. Put differently, it is not the shape of the curve or its discontinuities that indicate weak statehood, but rather noise or dispersion around that underlying distribution.

With the Myers Index in hand, we can now begin to address the question of how prevalent state authority gaps are over space and time. One way to answer that question is to look at patterns in the spatial extent of state authority between countries. Figures 1.3 and 1.4 depict the Asia-Pacific region for the period 1980–89 and the Africa region for the period 2000–2009 using a log-transformed measure of census error. Countries with available data are shown with shaded subnational

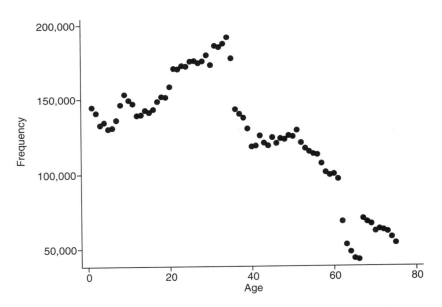

FIGURE 1.2. The effect of demographic shocks on the Myers Index. Myers score: 0.64. The figure depicts the age distribution curve for the Île-de-France in 1982. Despite the discontinuities in the curve, the lack of noise around that curve indicates that this region is an area of strong state authority.

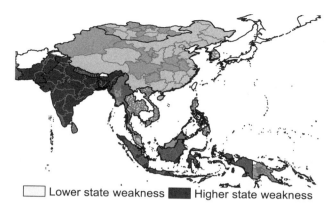

Lower state weakness ☐ ■ Higher state weakness

FIGURE 1.3. State weakness in the Asia-Pacific region, 1980–89 average. State weakness is measured as the inaccuracy of census data (Myers scores). Greater inaccuracy indicates greater state weakness. Myers scores are logged to reduce cross-country skew, but India remains an outlier due to its exceptionally high raw Myers scores; subsequent analyses account for country-level differences. Due to data comparability reasons, depicted internal boundaries may not accurately reflect boundaries as of 1980–89. Countries with missing data during this period are depicted in white.

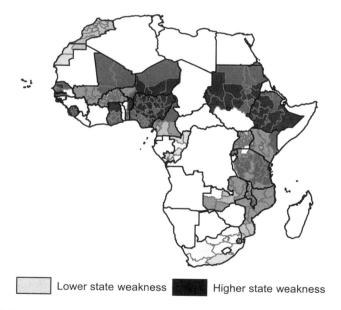

Lower state weakness ☐ ■ Higher state weakness

FIGURE 1.4. State weakness in Africa, 2000–2009 average. State weakness is measured as the inaccuracy of census data (Myers scores). Greater inaccuracy indicates greater state weakness. Myers scores are logged to reduce cross-country skew; subsequent analyses account for country-level differences. Due to data comparability reasons, depicted internal boundaries may not accurately reflect boundaries as of 2000–2009. Countries with missing data during this period are depicted in white.

units; the darker the unit, the more error we detected in that country's census, which indicates a greater degree of state weakness relative to other units.

What are immediately apparent are sharp differences between countries. The data suggest that India has overall worse levels of state authority than China, and that Ethiopia has overall worse levels than South Africa. That such strong differences exist between countries is not very surprising, though India's status as an extreme outlier is unexpected. These cross-country differences have their origins in national-level factors that I account for in subsequent analyses. Still, it is striking that two regions as different as Asia and Africa should show such variation in state authority over territory, a fact that points to the commonality of undergoverned and ungoverned space.

The patterns in figures 1.3 and 1.4 offer a high-flying view of state authority across broad world regions, and in doing so trade off the ability to perceive interesting within-country patterns. The Myers Index's subnational coverage offers a key advantage over alternative measures because it allows me to examine patterns of state authority within countries that the cross-country differences mask. The Philippines in 1960 is an instructive example of uneven state reach. Figure 1.5 depicts the extent of state authority between Philippine provinces. As before, darker areas indicate higher levels of state weakness. Perhaps not surprisingly, the light-colored areas in the map cluster around Manila and its surrounding provinces on the northern island of Luzon. The dark-colored areas in the southern part of the map include Sulu and Basilan, two islands that make up the region then called Western Mindanao. Mindanao, the large island group in the South, is the most geographically distant part of the country, and state authority was especially tenuous in the provinces in the western and central regions. The northern island Luzon also has one dark-colored province. This province is part of the Cordilleras, a difficult-to-penetrate region of Luzon known both for its rugged terrain and for the stunningly beautiful rice terraces that the indigenous population carved into the mountains. Given these characteristics, it is not surprising that the state has a relatively more difficult time obtaining information about the population of this region.

Ungoverned and partially governed spaces also vary in their prevalence over time. As should be evident from the previous figures, incomplete state consolidation is not a problem confined to either the Cold War or post–Cold War periods. We can see this more clearly in the example of Turkey. Figure 1.6 shows the extent of Turkish state authority over territory for four snapshots in time straddling the Cold War/post–Cold War divide. The maps indicate an improvement in state authority; much of the unevenness in governance that existed in 1975 appears to have declined by the year 2000. Yet the maps also point to the puzzle of enduring state weakness—and uneven improvement—in southeastern Turkey. Though this region fared no worse than other parts of eastern Turkey in 1975, it failed to secure the same kinds of state authority gains as the rest of the country.

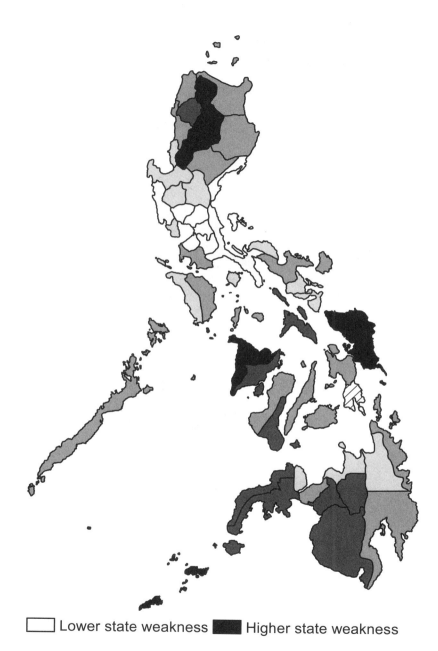

☐ Lower state weakness ■ Higher state weakness

FIGURE 1.5. State weakness in the Philippines, 1960. State weakness is measured as the inaccuracy of census data (Myers scores). Greater inaccuracy indicates greater state weakness. The dark area in Luzon, the northernmost island in the Philippines, corresponds to the Cordilleras, a rugged region of historically low state authority that is populated mostly by indigenous people. The hatched area indicates a province with no data.

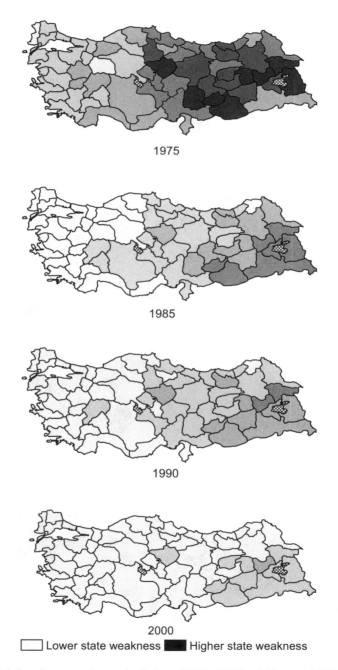

1975

1985

1990

2000

Lower state weakness ▪ Higher state weakness

FIGURE 1.6. State weakness in Turkey: 1975, 1985, 1990, and 2000. State weakness is measured as the inaccuracy of census data (Myers scores). Greater inaccuracy indicates greater state weakness. The crosshatched areas indicate Lake Van and Lake Tuz.

Not all countries struggle with persistent incomplete state consolidation. Indonesia, an archipelago state of more than 15,000 islands, exhibited considerable unevenness in state authority in 1971 (see figure 1.7). Yet unlike Turkey, Indonesia overcame this challenge. By 2010, the state's reach extended throughout the archipelago. By no means does this mean that the quality of life in Indonesia's governed spaces is the same as the quality of life in Denmark's governed

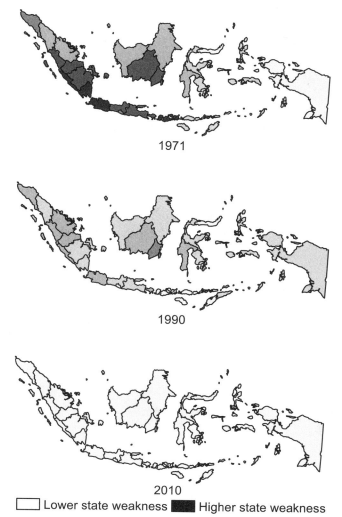

1971

1990

2010

☐ Lower state weakness   ■ Higher state weakness

FIGURE 1.7. State weakness in Indonesia: 1971, 1990, and 2010. State weakness is measured as the inaccuracy of census data (Myers scores). Greater inaccuracy indicates greater state weakness.

spaces. What it does mean is that governance gaps can be closed, even in countries with exceptionally difficult geographic conditions.

The Human Consequences of Uneven State Authority

Whether and where the state exercises its authority is not an esoteric matter. When governments do not exercise state authority, they do not govern. Because the scope of state activity is so broad in the contemporary period, the failure to govern can bear on human lives in a number of ways, including in the domains of security and stability, health, and education. For individuals living in undergoverned and ungoverned spaces, weak or absent state authority is not an abstraction but a fact of life that has serious and sometimes deadly consequences for welfare and well-being. While it is beyond the scope of this book to do a comprehensive worldwide analysis of the relationship between state weakness and human development, abundant anecdotal and systematic evidence points to an important connection.

The ill effects of the absence of state authority are easiest to see when the state fails to maintain order. Scholars refer to this area of state activity as maintaining the monopoly of force: excluding other actors that also claim to be the legitimate wielders of coercion. Providing order is so fundamental to what states do that scholars often define the state as the entity that wields the monopoly of force. Yet the reality is that some states fall quite short of this standard. States that lack the monopoly of force are populated with rival claimants to authority. For example, in the last three decades of the twentieth century, militant secessionist groups fought both the state and each other in the western and central parts of Mindanao and its associated islands. On the Indian side of the Line of Control that divides the disputed region of Kashmir, a rebel group refused to acknowledge Indian sovereignty and made this refusal known via a wave of violence in the 1990s. A 2007 RAND study described the entire East African corridor that stretches from Somalia through Sudan and as far south as Mozambique as beset with rivals to the state.[30]

The presence of alternative authorities in the ungoverned peripheries of states sometimes inspire states to attempt to reassert their domestic sovereignty over the territories in question. This is why many ungoverned and partially governed spaces are in fact sites of violent contestation between state and nonstate actors. Contestation implies efforts by the state to assert authority in places where its authority is incomplete. Violence may well be a part of statebuilding, but for ordinary civilians caught in the crossfire, this violence is both disruptive and dangerous.

An account of civilian life during the Kashmir insurgency in the 1990s on the Indian side of the Line of Control illustrates the hazards of a lack of order:

> The losers of the insurgency against the Indian government are the Kashmiris. In 1995, the city of Srinagar was dusty and dirty, with uncollected rubbish dumped on the roadside for dogs and cows to forage through. The streets were full of potholes. The charred remains of once revered buildings, such as the library next to the mosque at Hazratbal, were a visual reminder of past battles. Dal lake was thick and stagnant with weeds. The lives of the Kashmiris have been convulsed by bomb attacks, reprisals, crossfiring, and curfew.[31]

Clearly, to call this situation adverse would be to understate the impact of India's lack of state authority on Kashmiri lives and livelihoods.

The welfare consequences of the state's failure to provide order are also clear in cases in which civilians find themselves the intentional targets of violence, a phenomenon well known to scholars of civil war and human rights. A 1997 United States Agency for International Development (USAID) report to the U.S. embassy in Kampala, Uganda, cataloged the egregious human rights violations inflicted on civilians living in the ungoverned northern part of the country for the period 1994–97. According to the report, the Lord's Resistance Army (LRA), an armed group opposed to Yoweri Museveni's NRM government in Kampala, committed two types of atrocities against civilians. One type was "well-coordinated brutal attacks and massacres in which the indiscriminate murder or the large-scale abduction of civilians is the object," while the other type consisted of "assaults in remote areas in which civilians are murdered in small numbers, in which boys and girls are abducted, houses looted and burned, and victims mutilated."[32]

When USAID interviewed civilians living in the northern provinces of Gulu and Kitgum, respondents referred "almost immediately" to the human rights violations and the negative impact of the conflict on their lives, expressing "bewilderment about the LRA's purpose in 'killing their own people.'"[33] The violence exacted a psychological toll as well. The report noted that civilians fled exclusively away from LRA territory toward the protection of government-controlled towns—places where the state did in fact exercise authority—yet still remained in a state of terror.[34]

Violent contestation between the state and its domestic rivals does not characterize all ungoverned spaces. However, this does not imply an absence of violence altogether, nor does it imply stability or security. The Donbas region of eastern Ukraine after the ejection of Ukrainian authorities provides a compelling illustration of this point. A general state of disorder prevails in Donetsk, a

once-thriving city in the East under the control of rival claimants to state authority. In 2015, a local restaurant owner described Donetsk as a lawless city where
even police that supported the unrecognized separatist government were power-
less to provide security.[35] Two police officers with the Donetsk People's Republic,
who agreed to be interviewed by journalists from USA Today, agreed with this
assessment. "Civilians have been killed, and executions happen here," said one of
the officers, before admitting that any attempt to bring order to the city would
result in his own execution.[36] The parts of Ukraine under Kiev's authority are
certainly not pinnacles of well-governed space, but they are more safe and more
stable for ordinary civilians than Donetsk.

Weak state authority also affects human development in terms of health and
education. In many developing countries, governments are responsible for providing health and education services. In Uganda, for example, medical workers
and teachers are civil servants. Similarly, the Philippines counts health workers
at all levels of government as government employees. Uganda and the Philippines are not unique in this respect. The World Health Organization's 2006 *World
Health Report* found that in low- and middle-income countries, more than 70%
of doctors and more than 50% of other types of health-service providers work in
the public sector.[37] That more than a majority of health workers in each category
are government employees is indicative of the state's outsized and important
service-provision role. Similarly, in most countries the vast majority of teachers
are civil-service workers. When states are responsible for delivering these kinds of
social services, areas lacking state authority often suffer the welfare consequences
of inadequate provision.

Consider the Philippines, a country that exhibits considerable regional differences in primary health provision and health outcomes. When interpreting these
regional differences, it is useful to compare the four regions of Mindanao, the
southernmost island group in the Philippine archipelago. Although imperfect,
this comparison effectively controls for geography and distance from the capital
region of Metro Manila. The island group also exhibits interregional variation:
in the 1970s, state authority was quite weak in Western and Central Mindanao,
and comparatively stronger in Northern and Southern Mindanao (see table 1.2).

The regional differences in health provision are apparent in terms of access to
health stations. The Philippine health network for the rural population includes
public and private rural health units, as well as local clinics called barangay health
stations. In the 1970s, health units typically counted one doctor, one nurse, one
midwife, and one sanitary inspector among their staff, while the barangay health
stations usually had a resident midwife who worked with trained and untrained
birth attendants.[38] A national report found significant regional disparities in the
coverage of this health network in 1974. In Western Mindanao, one of the regions

TABLE 1.2   State weakness and infant mortality in the Philippines, 1970 and 1990

REGION	STATE WEAKNESS 1970	INFANT MORTALITY 1973	STATE WEAKNESS 1990	INFANT MORTALITY 1993
Western Mindanao	12.85	81.5	7.07	51.8
Central Mindanao	13.07	—	7.95	49.1
Northern Mindanao	9.66	90.3	2.54	37.1
Southern Mindanao	9.28	67.1	2.52	43.1
Metro Manila	5.95	57.8	1.98	27.1
National average	9.36	67.6	2.94	39.7
National average excluding Manila	9.14[a]	69.9[a]	2.96	40.7

Sources: Data are from World Bank 1984, 129; and National Statistics Office Philippines and Macro International 1994, 85.

Notes: State weakness is measured as the inaccuracy of census data (Myers scores). Higher values indicate greater state weakness. Infant mortality is defined as the number of deaths per 1,000 live births.

[a] Excludes Central Mindanao.

with limited state authority, the ratio of rural health units to population was one unit per 26,244 persons, exceeding both the government's target ratio of one unit per 20,000 persons and the countrywide average of one unit per 21,388 persons.[39] The distribution of barangay health stations was more varied, with Mindanao as a whole faring worse than the national average.[40]

Inadequate primary health provision is also evident in terms of access to health workers themselves. The health stations are part of the physical infrastructure of the health network, and they are staffed by skilled health workers. For that reason it is perhaps not surprising that we see similar regional disparities with respect to access to these workers. For example, a 1993 national health survey examined access to medical assistance during birth, which can reduce the incidence of both maternal mortality and infant mortality. The survey showed that mothers who gave birth in Western Mindanao were much more likely to have traditional birth attendants rather than physicians or trained nurses assist with their deliveries. In this region, almost 7 in 10 births were attended by a traditional attendant, compared to the national average of 5 in 10 or the Metro Manila rate of 1 in 10.[41]

These deficiencies in state-provided health care matter for health outcomes. Access to doctors and other trained medical personnel and the facilities where they work can mean the difference between life and death, sickness and health. Infant mortality outcomes are particularly useful for seeing the consequences of a lack of state presence in the realm of health care. Health workers and health facilities in the public sector link the state to health outcomes since access to health care is especially crucial for reducing infant and child mortality rates.[42] This is evident in the data shown in table 1.2, as places in the Philippines where health-care provision is lower are also places where health outcomes are worse. Infants born in Western Mindanao had poor survival rates. Academic and government studies revealed that in 1973, 82 in 1,000 died before reaching their first birthday, compared to the national average of 68 in 1,000.[43] While mortality rates declined over the next 20 years, regional disparities in 1993 continued to correspond to uneven access to health care—and to state weakness (see figure 1.8). In Western Mindanao, 52 infants in 1,000 died before their first birthday, compared to the national average of 40 in 1,000. The correlation is strong ($\rho = 0.90$) and statistically significant ($p < 0.01$). These data point to the very real health consequences for parents and their children in places in the Philippines where state authority is tenuous.

Weak state presence also affects education, another dimension of human development. Where the state cannot provide order, the effect on education is often a direct consequence of conflict and instability. A 2016 UNICEF report,

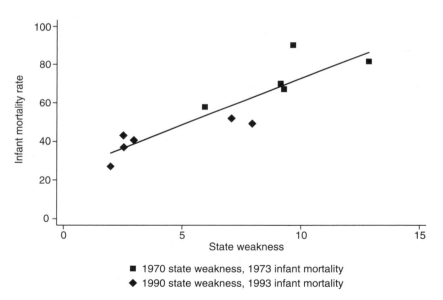

FIGURE 1.8. State weakness and infant mortality in the Philippines, 1970 and 1990. State weakness is measured as the inaccuracy of census data (Myers scores). Higher values indicate greater state weakness. Infant mortality is defined as the number of deaths per 1,000 live births. Data are from World Bank 1984, 129; and National Statistics Office Philippines and Macro International 1994, 85. Observations are taken from table 1.2 and include Western Mindanao, Central Mindanao, Northern Mindanao, Southern Mindanao, Metro Manila, and the national average excluding Manila. $\rho = 0.90$, $p < 0.01$. Observation total: 12.

for example, noted that nearly one in four children in conflict-affected countries are not in school.[44] The 1990s Kashmir insurgency illustrates the linkage between conflict and educational outcomes. The Kashmiri sociologist Bashir Ahmad Dabla, who has written extensively about the social impact of the Kashmir conflict, noted the damage wrought on education: "In many rural areas of Kashmir, many students, particularly girl students, had to drop out of schools due to security-related factors. It happened in the background in which the security forces either took over the school building forcibly or security picket was established near to the school."[45] The military historian Victoria Schofield similarly observed the disruption of conflict: "Since 1950, the number of schools had increased ten times, but many schools have been burnt by 'renegade' militants who the Kashmiri activists believe are working against their cause."[46] In these examples, the deleterious effect on educational attainment is almost mechanical: children cannot go to school if the schools are occupied or destroyed. As I will argue in chapter 2, the physical capture or destruction of the state's infrastructure is one of the mechanisms through which subversion undermines state authority.

Conflict is not necessary for educational outcomes to suffer under poor state authority, however. Let us return to the example of the Philippines. The Philippine National Economic and Development Authority (NEDA) collected literacy data for all regions of the country in 1970. Because the civil war in Western and Central Mindanao did not begin until a few years later, these literacy data allow us to see how the lack of state authority and state presence affects education before direct disruption of foreign-abetted conflict that would later exacerbate the problem of undergovernance. Table 1.3 shows the literacy rates for the four regions of Mindanao and Metro Manila, and the national average with and

TABLE 1.3   Literacy, poverty, and state weakness in the Philippines, 1970–71

REGION	STATE WEAKNESS (1970)	LITERACY (1970)	POVERTY (1971)
Western Mindanao	12.85	65.5	35.1
Central Mindanao	13.07	66.7	17.1
Northern Mindanao	9.66	83.7	55.3
Southern Mindanao	9.28	81.8	36.1
Metro Manila	5.95	95.7	14.9
National average	9.36	81.4	37.6
National average excluding Manila	9.14	80.2	39.5

Source: Literacy and poverty data are from World Bank 1980, 33, which draws on data from NEDA.

Notes: State weakness is measured as the inaccuracy of census data (Myers scores). Higher values indicate greater state weakness. The literacy rate is defined as the percentage of the adult population that completed at least four years of elementary education. The poverty rate is defined as the percentage of the population below the poverty line.

without Metro Manila. Mirroring the patterns from the health case, Western and Central Mindanao exhibit lower literacy rates than Southern and Northern Mindanao. That the two undergoverned parts of Mindanao perform less well than their better-governed counterparts in the same island group is not surprising given the state's role in regulating and providing public education. Indeed, a 1980 World Bank report examined the NEDA data and attributed literacy outcomes to the availability of schools.[47]

One might ask whether these poor outcomes are the result of greater poverty rather than weak state authority. To examine this question, I look at NEDA data on poverty rates in 1971. As one would expect, the NEDA data indicate that high poverty and low levels of literacy are related (see table 1.3). However, Central Mindanao and Northern Mindanao show that poverty is not the whole story. Central Mindanao, a weakly governed region with the largest Myers score, has a low incidence of poverty but a low literacy rate. In contrast, Northern Mindanao, where state authority is stronger, has a high poverty rate (the second highest among all Philippine regions in 1971) but a high literacy rate. The comparison between Western Mindanao and Southern Mindanao is also instructive. Both have similar poverty rates, but Western Mindanao has high state weakness and low literacy, while Southern Mindanao has low state weakness and high literacy. These data suggest that poverty alone does not drive low literacy, and that weak state authority also plays a role in human development.

The relationship between human welfare outcomes and state weakness is not unique to the Philippines. Though a lack of outcome data at the subnational level prohibits a systematic worldwide analysis, I take advantage of an unusual moment of data transparency and availability in Nigeria that provides an opportunity to assess the consequences of state consolidation for human welfare at a more granular level for a single country. To do so, I leverage subnational data collected in the 2008 Nigeria Demographic and Health Survey, which is part of a larger state-of-the-art survey program aimed at understanding health and population trends in the developing world.[48] The survey provides subnationally representative outcome data at the state level, Nigeria's largest subnational administrative unit, for the year 2008. I combine these data with my measure of state weakness using figures from the 2006 census. I also utilize government estimates of state-level poverty rates in 2010 to calculate the residual of state weakness not explained by economic development.[49] Put differently, although the census data and poverty data are not available for the same year, I use the poverty data to estimate a "purer" measure of state authority not contaminated by economic development. This allows me to see whether human welfare is in fact related to state authority rather than to poverty alone.

I examine four important human welfare outcomes. Two indicators are measures of education: the percentage of adults with any education and the percentage of adults that are literate. One indicator comes from the domain of health: the percentage of children aged 12–23 months who were fully vaccinated (infant mortality data are not available at the state level).[50] A fourth indicator relates to energy: the percentage of households with access to electricity. All four indicators depend on state authority. The state provides schools and teachers, and it provides basic public health services, including vaccination services. Electricity directly relates to human welfare because it is essential for adequate shelter, human development, and domestic and economic activity. In Nigeria, electricity provision is an important area of state activity. In 2003, the federal government owned 98% of the installed capacity for electricity generation, and in 2005, the state established a new authority to undertake a massive rural electrification effort.[51] As with education and health, access to electricity provides a window into human welfare and well-being.

Figure 1.9 shows scatterplots that graph the relationship between each human welfare indicator against the residuals of state weakness. They also report the correlation coefficient for that relationship. In each scatterplot, we observe a clear negative and statistically significant correlation between the indicator and state weakness. Nigerian units with low levels of state weakness, such as Lagos State (1.6 standard deviations below the mean), enjoy high rates of educated population, literacy, childhood vaccination, and electrification (see table 1.4). In contrast, Nigerian units with high levels of state weakness, such as Zamfara State (1.9 standard deviations above the mean), perform poorly in these areas. Lagos and Zamfara both appear in the tails of the distributions in figure 1.9, but they are not outliers, nor are they unusual in exhibiting a tight relationship between state weakness and human welfare. Compare both units to Kaduna State, which ranks near the national average on all indicators; the same pattern is evident. Moreover, because I use a residualized measure of state authority, we can be confident that economic disparities between wealthy Lagos, impoverished Zamfara, and average Kaduna are not driving the relationship.

Across the board, the qualitative and quantitative data point to the dismal consequences of weak state authority. The contemporary business of governing involves a variety of activities that directly bear on human welfare. Areas that are governed tend to produce better human development outcomes than those that undergoverned or ungoverned. If one could choose where to be born, one would probably not choose to be born in northern Uganda in the 1990s, Central or Western Mindanao in the 1960s and 1970s, Zamfara State in the 2000s, or the Indian side of the Line of Control during the Kashmir insurgency.

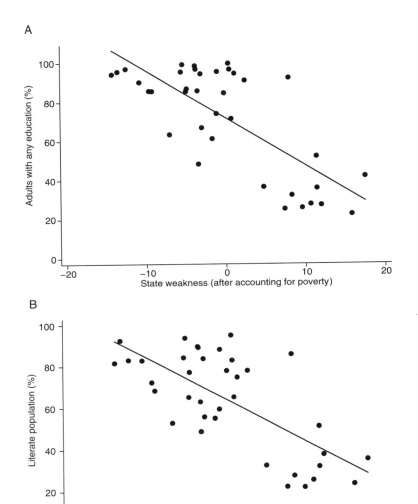

FIGURE 1.9. Human welfare and state weakness in Nigeria, 2006–10:
(A) % adults with any education, $\rho = -0.74$; (B) % literate adults, $\rho = -0.70$;
(C) % fully vaccinated children, $\rho = -0.62$; (D) % population with access to
electricity, $\rho = -0.48$. Education, vaccination, and electrification data for 2008 are
from National Population Commission and ICF Macro 2009, 329, 334–37, 374.
State weakness for 2006 is measured as the inaccuracy of census data (Myers
scores); graphs report the residuals of state weakness not explained by poverty.
Poverty data for 2010 are from *Press Briefing* 2012, 9–10. All correlations are
statistically significant ($p < 0.01$) and signed as expected. Observation total:
37 states (including the Federal Capital Territory of Abuja).

C

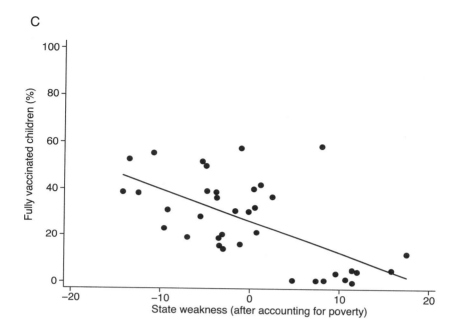

D

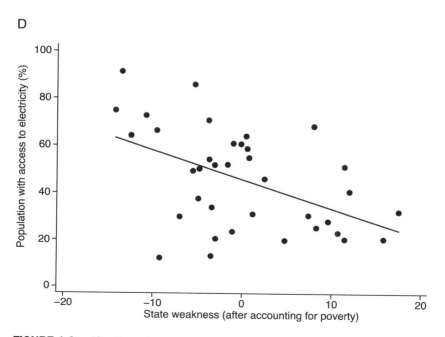

FIGURE 1.9. (Continued)

TABLE 1.4   Human welfare and state weakness in Lagos, Kaduna, and Zamfara, 2006–10

INDICATOR	LAGOS	KADUNA	ZAMFARA	AVERAGE	SD
State weakness (residuals)	−13.5	0.72	15.8	0	8.3
Poverty rate	59.2	73.0	80.2	69.4	10.6
Any education	95.5	71.3	22.4	71.7	27.0
Literate adults	92.6	65.2	23.4	63.6	23.7
Vaccinated children	52.8	21.4	5.4	26.4	18.3
Electrification	91.4	55.1	20.6	45.8	21.1

Sources: Poverty data for 2010 are from Press Briefing 2012, 9–10. Education, vaccination, and electrification data for 2008 are from National Population Commission and ICF Macro 2009, 329, 334–37, 374.

Notes: All data are percentages except state weakness. State weakness for 2006 is measured as the inaccuracy of census data (Myers scores) in 2006. Observation total: 37 states (including the Federal Capital Territory of Abuja).

Human Welfare and the State

One of the most significant long-run changes in human history is the impact that being governed has on human welfare. It has not always been the case that being governed by central state authorities was desirable. As the scholar James Scott has shown compellingly for Southeast Asia prior to the twentieth century, for 2,000 years being governed meant slavery, conscription, taxation, corvée labor, death, and disease. Early states were less interested in providing and more interested in taking. Those who could flee the state's reach did so and developed distinct strategies for remaining outside the state's authority.[52]

The contemporary period could not be more different. The social contract between the governors and the governed is much more extensive. Today's states still extract, but in return they provide. Slavery has been formally abolished everywhere in the world, and most states now are partners in the fight against disease rather than purveyors of disease. The 2000 Millennium Development Goals and the 2015 Sustainable Development Goals reflect the view that states are responsible for providing the kinds of goods and services that make being governed attractive. Even though nonstate actors like nongovernmental organizations and alternative claimants to state sovereignty sometimes provide services in lieu of the state, these situations are normatively undesirable, uncommon in the international system, and unsustainable in the long run. For better or worse, the expectation is that the state should govern, and that it should do so throughout the entirety of its territory.

This chapter has shown that there is considerable variation in the degree to which states meet this expectation. Ungoverned and partially governed spaces are surprisingly prevalent. Thomas Risse and Eric Stollenwerk have called them the default condition in the international system.[53] They exist in a wide variety of countries, world regions, and time periods. They persist in some places, but not in others. Where they remain, they often have harmful—even deadly—effects on human well-being.

Why do such spaces persist? Many of the countries described in this chapter share a common characteristic: they have been or remain embroiled in antagonistic relationships with nearby countries. Uganda and Sudan, India and Pakistan, the Philippines and Malaysia, and Turkey and Syria are all examples of country pairs in which at least one member of the pair fails to exercise authority over territory and has assigned responsibility for that problem to the other member of the pair. The task of the following chapter is to introduce a theory about why and how this foreign meddling affects state authority.

THE STRATEGY OF FOREIGN SUBVERSION

In spring 2014, two new entities joined the world's roster of self-proclaimed quasi states. The Donetsk People's Republic and the Luhansk People's Republic, both located in the Donbas region of eastern Ukraine, each have the trappings of real states: territory, government offices, armed forces, a flag, even a national anthem. They issue identity documents, levy taxes, collect garbage, and have created central banks. But they lack a crucial feature that makes a state a state in the contemporary era—widespread diplomatic recognition—and remain juridically part of Ukraine.

Russia played midwife in the birth of the two republics. Moscow engaged in an extensive campaign of subversion by supplying and supporting the separatist rebels of Donetsk and Luhansk. It has vigorously denied its involvement in cleaving the Donbas from Kiev's grasp, instead framing its assistance as strictly humanitarian in nature. While it continues to pay lip service to Ukraine's sovereignty over the de facto republics, Moscow's ongoing support ensures that the two regions effectively remain outside central state authority. But Moscow has not annexed the breakaway republics, as it did Crimea. Its interference in eastern Ukraine was never intended to expand the territory of the Russian Federation. Rather, Moscow subverted Ukraine to acquire what it really sought: bargaining leverage over Ukrainian foreign policy. These acts resulted in the deconsolidation of the Ukrainian state.

This chapter presents the theory of why and how foreign subversion by hostile states exacerbates state weakness and prevents state consolidation. Foreign subversion is the empowerment of nonstate actors with the aim of undermining territorial state authority. It entails cooperation between an external sponsor state and a nonstate group that acts as a proxy for that sponsor. These proxies undermine authority in a target state by destroying the target's administrative presence and governing in its stead. Foreign subversion is rarely the initial cause of weak statehood, but it is an important factor that explains why some countries are unable to consolidate their authority—a point that the literature on state development has largely missed. Importantly, foreign subversion requires both motive, in the form of deep policy disputes or incompatibilities between the sponsor and target, and means, in the form of proxy groups on the ground. Without both conditions in place, foreign subversion will not occur, and in those cases we must look to other explanations for incomplete state consolidation.

To make these arguments about foreign subversion and its effects on state authority, I first discuss why states interfere in state authority over territory as a means of pursuing their foreign policy interests against their adversaries. I consider how subversion increases the likelihood that states will achieve their political objectives. I also discuss the strategic and operational advantages of subversion, as well as the costs and constraints that limit states from deploying this potent policy instrument more frequently in international relations. I then describe the channels through which subversion degrades state authority in target states. Thereafter I shift the focus to the target states, and argue that while they are not passive victims of foreign meddling, they are unlikely to fully recapture authority losses imposed by external adversaries. The chapter closes with a discussion of the most important hypotheses that flow from the theory.

Subversion as an Instrument of Statecraft

States are actors in the international system, and they have interests. These interests may conflict with those of other states. They compete with each other for regional hegemony, like Iran and Iraq. They dispute territory, like India and Pakistan. They clash over ideology, religion, and the nature of regimes, as Costa Rica and Nicaragua did during the Cold War. They even have preferences regarding how other states treat their populations, as evidenced in the long-standing dispute between Armenia and Azerbaijan. When these preferences conflict, they can be said to be incompatible.

States have long had a menu of policy options for pursuing their interests against states with incompatible policy preferences. Among the available options is subversion, a noncooperative strategy of political interference aimed at the territorial authority of the target state. I define subversion as the empowerment of nonstate actors as proxy groups with the intent of thwarting state administration and control over territory. For ease of exposition, let us consider three actors: the sponsor state, which seeks to disrupt the domestic authority of an adversary; a target state; and a local nonstate proxy group whose home state is the target state. Subversion can be understood as a delegation process in which a sponsor supports a proxy to degrade state authority in the target state.[1]

Subverting a target state's authority over territory is a useful and potent policy tool for advancing the sponsor's foreign policy objectives. Because subversion cripples state authority, it is a noncooperative foreign policy instrument—the kind of tool one wields against one's adversaries, not one's friends. As the gap between preferences increases, the range over which cooperative strategies are likely to produce the desired outcome shrinks. Consequently, states are more likely to utilize subversion to pursue their interests when the distance between the target's and the sponsor's policy preferences is great. Put differently, subversion is attractive when states are embroiled in irreconcilable policy disputes.

As an instrument of statecraft, subversion operates via the imposition of costs. These costs are manifested in the disruption and destabilization of the target state. When states use conventional force, they impose these costs directly on the target state. Subversion differs because by empowering proxies, states delegate the work of imposing costs to those proxy groups. To the extent that these efforts succeed, subversion makes the exercise of authority more expensive than it would be in the absence of interference. These external costs, above and beyond what target states would already face under normal circumstances, can advance the sponsoring state's policy goals in at least four ways.

First and perhaps most importantly, subversion creates bargaining leverage that sponsors exploit to prevail in their policy disputes with the target state. In this case, subversion raises the target state's costs of intransigence in the issue under dispute. Similar to the way that organized crime syndicates practice extortion, an enterprising sponsor state makes the cessation of political interference conditional on concessions from the target state.[2] As an illustration, consider the case of Syria and Turkey's dispute over the Euphrates River. Syrian agriculture depended on access to the waters of the Euphrates. As the downstream riparian state, it was especially vulnerable to Turkish efforts to dam the river. Syria began supporting the Kurdistan Workers' Party (PKK), an extremist organization in Turkey with ambitions to supplant Turkish authority in the southeastern part of the country. Damascus aided the PKK not because it felt any great love for the Turkish Kurds or sympathy for their plight, but because it needed a source of leverage over Turkey.[3] Although Syria refused to admit its culpability in supporting the PKK, it offered to eject the PKK from Syrian territory in return for water concessions from Turkey. In this way, subversion can help sponsors prevail in their policy disputes with the target.

Second, subversion can force the target to expend resources to deal with domestic political problems in its own territory that the target would not have otherwise spent. I call this phenomenon "tie-down." State resources are limited, and policymakers must prioritize how to allocate blood, treasure, time, and attention. Tie-down imposes costs by forcing targets to divert these resources from one domain to another. The disorder that results from fomenting violence, supporting alternative governing authorities, and eroding domestic sovereignty attracts the target state's attention. It also creates conditions that make it difficult for target states to ignore these problems if leaders are worried about the reputational or political consequences of weak statehood.[4] As a result, target states may reallocate resources even if the territory in question is not particularly valuable.

An example of tie-down comes from the case of India and Pakistan. Pakistan's sponsorship of separatist Sikh terrorists operating in Indian Punjab, a territory that runs along part of the Indo-Pakistani border, prompted the Indian government to spend resources to flush out and eliminate the terrorist threat. The heavy-handed Indian response amplified instability in Indian Punjab, which demanded additional resources from the state and culminated in the assassination of Prime Minister Indira Gandhi.[5] By diverting Indian attention to authority problems in its own territory and forcing India to expend resources that it would not have otherwise spent, Islamabad prevented those resources from being used to compete with, coerce, or threaten Pakistan.

Third, subversion weakens the target's ability to draw resources from the territory or denies it access to that territory altogether. By damaging state infrastructure and sowing disorder, subversion raises the costs of exercising authority and carrying out routine government activities such as revenue extraction. In turn, by making it expensive to engage in revenue extraction, the sponsor reduces the likelihood that the target state will be able to raise revenue or access economically valuable natural resources, such as timber, oil, minerals, or natural gas. For example, Ugandan-backed rebels attacked oil infrastructure in southern Sudan to deny the government resource rents, and Chevron refused to resume operations in the absence of a deal to stop the conflict.[6] Since a target's military capabilities depend in part on its fiscal resources, denying the target access to these resources negatively affects the target state's ability to compete with or threaten the sponsor, which in turn improves the sponsor's own position and security relative to the target.

Fourth, the ungoverned spaces that result from subversion may be a political end in themselves. Consider the case of territorial disputes. When two states disagree about the legal status of territory, effective control of that territory can be a crucial consideration in the resolution of the dispute. Effective control bolsters the claim to a territory by virtue of establishing an administrative status quo, particularly when no other guidance (such as colonial administrative boundaries or treaty documents) exists.[7] Thus, subversion can alter the facts on the ground in favor of the sponsor state by denying the target effective control or by putting in place an alternative authority friendly to the sponsor.

Ungoverned or partially governed spaces may also be an end when such areas serve as buffer zones. As with sovereign buffers, such as Afghanistan vis-à-vis the British and Russian Empires, subnational buffer regions dampen the likelihood of direct fighting between two countries, or between a country and a nonstate actor residing in the neighboring country.

When ungoverned spaces are occupied by friendly nonstate groups that share the ideology or political orientation of the sponsor state, such spaces also insulate populations inside the target state's territory from views that external state leaders might find internally destabilizing or domestically threatening. Buffers thus serve useful military and political functions for the sponsor state. Since direct annexation is costly, however, states must create those buffers in other ways. Subversion for the purposes of creating space governed by entities other than the target is one way to do so.

Kenya's activities against Somalia illustrate the use of subversion to create a subnational buffer. Beginning in the mid-2000s, Kenya has attempted to create a zone under Kenyan influence in the region of Somalia that borders northeastern Kenya. This buffer region is Jubaland, the unrecognized state-like entity that spans a significant portion of Somali territory along the Kenyan-Somali border. An autonomous or quasi-independent Jubaland under Kenyan influence serves Kenyan security interests by buffering against al-Shabaab militants in Somalia, thereby making it more difficult for those militants to penetrate Kenyan territory.[8]

Strategic and Operational Advantages

Subversion also has a number of strategic and operational advantages relative to other noncooperative foreign policy instruments, such as conventional force. The strategic advantages allow sponsors to pursue policy objectives against targets that they may not otherwise be able to confront due to the costs and risks of other foreign policy instruments. The operational advantages of delegation make attempts to disrupt sovereignty more efficacious. Both make subversion an attractive instrument of statecraft against foreign adversaries.

Subversion offers a number of strategic benefits. First, subversion is inexpensive compared to conventional force. Whereas a modern military requires a significant sum of money to train, equip, feed, and support, subversion shifts much of the financial and operational burden to proxy groups. At the extreme, the cheapest form of delegation involves hosting existing proxy groups on the territory of the sponsor.[9] These groups take refuge behind the shield of international borders; this costs the sponsor nothing. The inexpensive nature of subversion suggests that sponsors will favor authority-undermining strategies when they perceive such strategies to be cheaper than alternatives. For example, Apartheid-era South Africa sponsored the Mozambique National Resistance's war against the Mozambican government in part because South African leaders believed that indirect destabilization of an enemy state carried lower economic and political costs than direct military action.[10] For similar reasons, poorer states will also be more likely to favor subversion. Sponsors will thus find subversion appealing if they expect it to be economically or politically cheaper than conventional force.

Second, subversion generally does not require a high degree of military or political capability on the part of the sponsor state. This feature of subversion is distinct from cost considerations. Although military capacity can increase the effectiveness of subversion if professional soldiers train rebels and terrorists, it is by no means a requirement for successful proxy empowerment. This feature of foreign subversion means that militarily or administratively weak sponsors will prefer foreign subversion over other alternatives like the use of force. Similarly, sponsors that are militarily disadvantaged relative to their targets will also prefer subversion over outright conventional force. To be clear, subversion is not a weapon of the weak alone. Even strong states may find subversion attractive due to its low economic cost relative to more direct policy instruments like conventional force. Russian machinations against eastern Ukraine demonstrate the utility of subversion in the case of a powerful sponsor facing a weaker target.

Third, the subversion of state authority is often more difficult to observe, verify, and attribute to state actors than conventional force. This is perhaps one of the most attractive features of subversion because it provides for plausible deniability. Subversion is challenging to detect because it is secretive. Even when the target does detect subversion, the precise nature and extent of foreign involvement often remains unclear. Moreover, the delegation process creates distance between the actions of the sponsor and the actions of the proxy. This distance introduces ambiguity over culpability and intentionality, allowing the sponsor to claim innocence and ignorance.[11] In contrast, conventional military force is easy to observe and attribute to a sponsor state, and target states thus are more likely to infer hostile intent and purpose behind such actions.[12] States will thus prefer subversion if they believe they are less likely to be sanctioned for this behavior by other members of the state system.

Two examples illustrate the difficulty of detecting subversion and attributing sponsor intentionality. Consider again the case of Syrian support for the PKK. Throughout the 1980s and 1990s, Turkey accused Syria of harboring the PKK on Syrian territory. Syria denied its involvement but allowed that some PKK militants may have crossed over the border without Syrian permission. The difficulty of determining to what extent the PKK presence in Syria was a deliberate government policy partially explains why Turkey did not threaten military retaliation against Syria until 1998, years after Syria began its campaign of subversion. Similarly, ascertaining the precise nature and degree of Pakistan's support for the Afghan Taliban has bedeviled both the Afghan government in Kabul and the United States. As in the Syrian case, ambiguity surrounded the question of whether Pakistan permitted its territory to be used as a safe haven for the Taliban as a matter of state policy. Even as evidence mounted that the Inter-Services Intelligence, Pakistan's intelligence agency, had links with the Afghan Taliban, questions remained about the extent of those links and whether they included recruitment and training.

Importantly, plausible deniability does not mean that the sponsor gives up the ability to extract concessions from the target state. As I discuss in greater detail in chapter 5, Malaysia repeatedly denied training and assisting the Moro National Liberation Front (MNLF), a separatist group in the Philippines. Nevertheless, Kuala Lumpur took advantage of the MNLF's efforts, pressing Manila to abandon its territorial claim against Malaysia in exchange for a crackdown on the MNLF. Similarly, in the Syrian example, Damascus offered to eject the PKK in return for Turkish concessions on water policy—even as Damascus maintained that it was not actively supporting the PKK. In both cases, the proxy groups dealt enough damage to the target states' domestic sovereignty that the targets yielded to the demands of the sponsors, even as the sponsors continued to deny their culpability.

Fourth, when plausible deniability fails, delegation provides political cover. It allows sponsors to frame their subversive activities as consistent with international principles and norms of self-determination and humanitarianism. Even when external support is observable and attributable, the international community has been less willing to challenge sponsors when sponsors invoke these norms.[13] For example, Russia justified its support for Georgia's and Ukraine's breakaway regions as consistent with the principles of self-determination. Ugandan president Yoweri Museveni described Uganda's support for the Sudan People's Liberation Army, a secessionist group operating in what was then Sudan, as primarily humanitarian in nature.[14] As I discuss in chapter 6, Thai authorities claimed humanitarian motives when they supplied food to the Khmer Rouge, a group that sought to dislodge Vietnam and the Vietnamese-backed regime from Cambodia. Delegation makes this form of political cover possible.

The operational advantages of subversion enhance the damage dealt to target states. One important benefit that proxy groups provide is access to territory. Local nonstate actors can do things that states cannot do, and more importantly, they can go places where states cannot go. The international principles of sovereignty prohibit states from intervening in the domestic affairs of other states and demand that international borders be respected.[15] These international rules do not bind nonstate actors in the way they bind states. As a result, nonstate actors face fewer repercussions for crossing borders and accessing territory in other states. This mobility provides proxies with a crucial edge: it allows them to strike at the physical markers of state presence, construct parallel institutions, and hollow out the target state from within.

A second operational advantage is expertise. As locals, proxy groups have expert knowledge about their home countries or regions. Sponsoring states might wish to sow chaos as a means of creating bargaining leverage or inflicting costs, but these attempts will be more effective when the sponsor knows where and how to target such efforts. Local proxy groups are more likely to possess this knowledge than outside actors. Undermining state authority involves more than inflicting violence, however. It often entails dislodging the target state and its bureaucrats and replacing them with an alternative source of authority. Proto-states such as Jubaland (Somalia), South Ossetia (Georgia), and Nagorno-Karabakh (Azerbaijan) are prominent examples of institutional replacement. Whether one calls the local actors rebel rulers, warlords, or something else, the success of governance depends in part on the consent and compliance of the governed. Expertise—knowledge of local customs and interests—can help create new local institutions and practices that engender greater consent from subject populations. From a less sanguine perspective, expertise can also mean an intimate understanding of when and how to apply instruments of coercion effectively to force a population to reject the state's authority.

Costs and Constraints

Despite being attractive because of its strategic and operational advantages for confronting target states, subversion is not without costs and constraints. These costs and constraints are essential for understanding why subversion is not more widely employed as an instrument of statecraft.

The most important constraint that sponsor states face when considering the use of subversion is the availability of proxies. Proxy groups are the means of subversion, and they are integral to the effort to undermine state authority. Without proxies, even highly motivated states cannot use subversion as a foreign policy instrument. Where might foreign states find these proxies? Groups that share ascriptive or ideological ties with the potential patron are perhaps most likely to accept an external sponsor's support, but a proxy group need not share anything in common with the sponsor other than mutual hostility toward the target. Pakistan's support for Indian Sikh terrorists in the 1980s is an example of an alliance of convenience; it relied primarily on shared animosity toward the Hindu-dominated Indian state. Similarly, Iran and Iraq both sponsored Kurdish resistance groups operating on opposite sites of their shared border. This is the logic of the old adage "the enemy of my enemy is my friend." Kinship ties are useful as political cover for the hostile state's true intentions, but are not necessary for subversion so long as the preferences of the proxy and sponsor are not too misaligned.[16]

Sponsor states can also exploit existing grievances and tensions between a group and the state to increase the willingness of that group to act as a proxy. In places where the state pursues policies that marginalize and alienate some segments of the population, sponsors can work to politicize those differences, heighten the salience of identity or other ties, or empower and increase the prestige of local political entrepreneurs. Indeed, just as states construct nations, so too can external powers construct separate and distinct identities among non-core groups outside their territories that can then be politicized for foreign policy gain.[17] This does not mean that sponsors can manufacture proxy groups out of thin air, or create grievances where none exist. Russian efforts to cultivate agents of subversion in Estonia, discussed more extensively in chapter 4, show that even powerful states confront constraints in the form of proxy availability. Yet where target state policies create an opening, sponsor states can use their material, diplomatic, and political resources to enhance a group's ability to act as a proxy for subversion.

Egyptian-Ethiopian relations in the 1950s illustrate efforts by a sponsor state, Egypt, to empower a marginalized group in the target state, Ethiopia. Egypt is located in one of the world's most arid regions, and it is dependent on the waters of the Blue Nile for agriculture, industry, and basic subsistence. Because the Blue Nile originates at Lake Tana in Ethiopia, Ethiopian hydro-projects could alter the flow of the Nile in ways that threaten Egypt's water supply. After cooperative efforts to secure access to the Blue Nile failed, Egypt undertook a campaign to destabilize Ethiopia in order to stunt Nile-related development projects by diverting development funds toward security.[18] Egypt empowered the aggrieved Muslim population of Eritrea, which had recently been federated into Ethiopia and was later annexed outright. To foment ethnonationalist sentiment, Egypt provided scholarships to Muslim Eritreans to study in Egypt and invited prominent Eritrean political leaders to visit the country.[19] Radio Cairo began broadcasting propaganda to reinforce Eritrean identity, attack the Ethiopian regime, and encourage the Muslims to struggle for independence against the Christian Ethiopians in order to weaken the Ethiopian state.[20] The 30-year civil war that culminated in Eritrean independence is a testament to the success of Egypt's efforts to empower a dissident movement to further its political agenda regarding the Blue Nile.

Even when a sponsor can locate or mobilize a proxy group, subversion is subject to other costs and constraints. Although subversion may cost less than other instruments of foreign policy, it is not costless. Some modes of empowering proxies are cheap in an absolute sense—for example, when states allow their territory to be used as safe havens and training camps for proxy groups.[21] Other modes of empowerment require actual investments from the sponsor state for subversion to be effective. Arming and funding rebellions cost money; so too do projects that train and build capacity for the quasi governments that replace state authority in the areas where the target has been ejected. These investments equip proxy groups with much-needed resources and expertise they may not be able to obtain on their own.[22] In turn, this increases the likelihood that proxies will successfully degrade state authority and establish themselves as governors in place of the state. Weaker and less technically capable proxies will require greater investments to achieve effects comparable to those of stronger groups. Similarly, more consolidated targets will require more empowered proxies than less consolidated targets. Thus, even as subversion is relatively cheap compared to conventional force, the absolute costs of subversion can vary considerably from case to case.

This external support increases the likelihood that the proxy groups will prevail in the pursuit of their political objectives. As we will see in chapter 6, which discusses Thailand's use of subversion by way of the Khmer Rouge, for some groups this support means the difference between survival and obliteration. The Khmer Rouge was a defeated regime whose remaining forces consisted of severely malnourished and sickly soldiers. Thai support rejuvenated them and allowed them to return to Cambodia, where they destroyed the new regime's infrastructure and terrorized its bureaucrats. For other groups, like the Moro National Liberation Front described in chapter 5, external support proves to be a significant tactical advantage; such support allowed the MNLF to repulse the Philippine Army. For groups motivated by more mercenary impulses, material and diplomatic support can enhance their status and their material standing.

Subversion also entails some risks for the sponsor. One risk is the potential for blowback. Blowback can take the form of general instability, the spread of illicit economic activity, or other negative externalities of ungoverned space that do not remain confined within state borders. Whether blowback occurs depends on whether the proxy and foreign sponsor successfully replace the target state's administrative institutions with some stable alternative arrangement, or merely destroy state presence and move on, leaving chaos behind. In other words, blowback is more likely to occur when a territory is truly ungoverned as opposed to governed by someone other than the state.

Blowback is also more likely to occur when the sponsor loses control over the proxy. The proxy may have its own objectives that do not align with those of the sponsor, and when this occurs, the sponsor must pay more to "force" an alignment of interests. The proxy group's pursuit of its interests or its unwillingness to comply with demands from the sponsor can lead to undesirable outcomes from the sponsor's perspective. Perversely, the very thing that makes proxy groups effective at undermining state authority—the infusion of resources—also increases their independence from the sponsor.[23]

Events in eastern Ukraine since 2014 illustrate the problem of blowback. Moscow's strategy of subversion was widely successful in that its proxies ejected central authorities from the regions of Luhansk and Donetsk. Yet these proxies also seized the opportunity to traffic arms and drugs and compete among themselves for primacy. Moscow's inability to fully control Ukraine's separatists is evident in the blowback effects on its own sovereignty: after 2014, Rostov Oblast on the Russian side of the border from Luhansk saw a 25% spike in crime in just four months.[24]

These observations about costs and constraints have five implications for predicting when subversion will occur. First, as I have already argued, states will be more likely to employ subversion against state authority when confronting adversaries with which they have severe policy disputes. Only in these situations will states be willing to bear the costs and risks of dealing with proxy groups. I call this condition "motive," since states should use subversion when their foreign relations provide for sufficient motivation.

Second, subversion will occur only when proxies are available in the target state. Since subversion by definition involves delegation, willing agents, or "means" on the ground, is a necessary condition for subversion. Additionally, treating agent availability as an independent condition implies that proxies can be located by external states but not easily created by them. Without proxies, states cannot engage in subversion. Thus, proxy availability is a key constraint on the use of subversion.

Third, as the target's own level of consolidation increases, the more expensive it will be to weaken state administration and control, since these targets are less vulnerable from the outset. Subversion is less likely to succeed against fully consolidated states, which are more informed of local goings-on and will be more likely to defeat efforts to undermine their state authority. Thus, even though subversion of consolidated targets may be attractive, the costs of imposing authority losses may be quite constraining for some states. Knowing this, rational states are unlikely to invest in an expensive strategy that offers little chance of success. We should thus observe few instances of subversion being used against fully consolidated states, which reside primarily in the developed world.

Fourth, because material resources, training, and protection and safe havens are the most important means through which sponsors empower proxies, sponsors should be more willing to use subversion when they can easily deliver these investments to their proxies. A key impediment to doing so is distance, because distance increases the delivery cost. Similarly, safe havens and training camps are less valuable to proxies if those areas are difficult to reach. Just as conventional force is subject to a "loss-of-strength gradient," in which military strength declines with distance, subversion is subject to an analogous loss-of-interference gradient, in which the ability to deliver investments declines with distance.[25] As with the loss-of-strength gradient, distance should act as a constraint for all but the most capable states in the international system. This suggests that subversion will be more likely to be observed between adversaries that are contiguous and in areas bordering those adversaries. This key implication informs the statistical analyses in chapter 3.

Fifth, states should be more willing to turn to subversion as the costs of other policy instruments increase. The degree to which states will be willing to bear those costs depends in part on the costs and constraints of alternatives. Scholars of international norms have suggested that laws, rules, and norms against the use of force for some ends have made force costly, particularly when would-be violators expect rule enforcement from powerful third-party states.[26] Similarly, defensive military alliances may make conventional force undesirable against some target states.[27] If states anticipate high costs for engaging in conventional force, the primary noncooperative alternative to subversion, then those states will be more likely to favor subversion.

The first two implications, about motive and means, are the most important factors that influence the use of subversion, and as I describe later, the primary tests of these propositions appear in chapters 3 and 4. The third and fourth implications, about types of targets and the constraining role of distance, also influence the research design of chapter 3. I provide evidence for the fifth implication, about alternative foreign policy strategies, in chapters 5 and 6.

Weakening and Impeding State Consolidation

In discussing the features of subversion that make it attractive for foreign sponsors, and the constraints on its practice, it is important not to lose sight of what subversion does that makes it such a potent instrument of foreign policy. The

ultimate goal of subversion is to weaken, undermine, and degrade state authority in target states, and it is this damaging effect on state authority that makes it
appealing as a form of bargaining leverage or punishment against other states.
How, then, does subversion reduce domestic sovereignty and stunt state consolidation? There are three related channels through which subversion makes it
more difficult and more costly for targets to exercise state authority over territory.

First, proxy groups capture or destroy the physical manifestations of state
authority. Governments cannot govern without some semblance of state presence. State administration at its core involves enforcing rules and regulations.
In practice, this requires the state to interfere in and insert itself into the private
economic and social affairs of those it purports to govern; for that, states need
both infrastructure and agents. Government offices act as venues through which
the state interacts with its subjects and government bureaucrats carry out the
business of the state. To eliminate state authority, proxy groups eliminate these
embodiments of state power.

Violence is a brutally effective means to accomplish this goal. Proxy groups
that seek to wipe out state authority often target state infrastructure for destruction, attacking buildings and damaging transport links such as roads, rails, and
bridges. They also force bureaucrats to abandon their posts, and kill those who do
not flee. The psychological effects of violence on the willingness of local officials
to perform their duties should not be underestimated. Consider the challenge of
state administration in Cambodia in the 1980s. The Khmer Rouge, which had
been deposed from power by the invading Vietnamese army, transformed itself
into a guerrilla band under the protection and sponsorship of neighboring Thailand and began waging a campaign of terror against Cambodian bureaucrats.
State officials in the capital of Phnom Penh lamented the situation in Khmer
Rouge–affected areas, where high levels of insecurity and terror caused such
severe absenteeism among local officials that the state virtually ceased to exist in
any meaningful way.[28]

Violence is rarely the end in itself but rather a means to the second way
through which state authority can decline: the establishment of parallel administrative structures that replace or operate alongside the state's institutions.
Nonstate groups often seek to govern in lieu of the state.[29] To do that, they need
their own administrative institutions and infrastructure. In some cases these
parallel institutions coexist with state institutions, as in contemporary Afghanistan and parts of Turkey in the 1990s. In other cases these institutions enjoy
monopoly status, in the sense that they have completely replaced state authority, as in Georgia's breakaway provinces. By encroaching on and taking over the
state's administrative activities, proxies and their foreign sponsors degrade state
authority.

Displacing the state in favor of establishing their own authority was exactly the objective of PKK operatives in southeastern Turkey. In PKK-controlled areas of that region, the group established a parallel system of administration, prioritizing tax extraction. The PKK's commander of Erzurum Province, Ayhan Ciftci, explained the PKK's intentions to the journalist Aliza Marcus: "The idea was that whatever the state does, we do, that we should sort of share authority, they operate during the day, and we operate at night. So if the state taxes, then we have to tax too."[30] PKK bases functioned similarly to government offices in that the bases allowed the PKK to maintain a physical presence and facilitated regular tax collection from nearby small towns. According to Marcus's interviewees, most taxes were levied on businesses rather than individuals, though wealthy Kurds who had the means to pay were an exception. In the village of Mira, located between the cities of Diyarbakir and Batman, PKK operatives obtained agricultural-production information from friendly locals and used this information to assess and extract taxes from the landowners.[31] The PKK also taxed private and public companies that Ankara dispatched to the region to build infrastructure. Additionally, the PKK imposed something akin to a customs duty on cross-border smugglers, levying it on the money and goods of those seeking to travel through territory that the PKK considered to be under its administration.[32] Some would call these activities extortion, and while some true believers gladly paid up, others paid only because they dared not refuse. Yet it is not merely for the purpose of euphemism that the PKK preferred to refer to its activities as taxation, since to call extortion taxation is to give it the veneer of legitimate state authority.[33]

Proxies sometimes attempt to take over the administration of external and international affairs, which may be especially of interest to sponsors. All states jealously guard the prerogative to make foreign policy; even federalized states and states that grant autonomy to some regions reserve this right for themselves. It should thus come as no surprise that groups seeking to supplant the state engage in institution building over foreign policy. In 2006, Georgia's breakaway province of Abkhazia began issuing Abkhazian passports to the people living in territory controlled by Abkhaz separatists. Because only a handful of states recognize Abkhazia's independence, the passports are useless from a practical perspective, but they serve the valuable symbolic function of formalizing Abkhazia's status outside Georgian state authority. Similarly, at the height of its power, the PKK in Turkey arrogated to itself the right to issue visas to foreign travelers seeking to enter territory that the PKK governed—sometimes enforcing this policy with the threat of violence.[34]

The destruction of the physical manifestations of state presence and the creation of parallel or replacement institutions points to a third channel through which proxies prevent state consolidation. Citizens living in so-called "ungoverned" spaces may update their beliefs about the strength and behavior of the target state, and alter their own behavior as a result. The prestige of external support and the material resources available to the proxies increase the likelihood that this updating occurs. Confronted with new claimants to the right to rule and the material and symbolic evidence of their authority, citizens may reason that the state can no longer enforce its writ. As a result, they stop complying with the state's rules and instead comply with the pretenders' rulers. This disengagement from the state and its institutions may be subtle, but it is fundamentally damaging to state authority. The right to make and enforce rules and regulations is the very essence of authority. Citizens who switch their allegiances to nonstate governors, utilize parallel justice systems for dispute resolution, pay taxes to proxy groups, and follow regulations promulgated by entities other than the state erode and undermine the practice of state administration on the ground. Although violence and institutional replacement may be more visible, this reorientation of citizens away from the state and its reach is perhaps the most insidious way in which subversion weakens the state.

Responding to Subversion

Having explained how subversion undermines state authority, it is important to consider how target states respond. Target states are rarely passive victims in this dismantling of their domestic sovereignty. They often have strong incentives to respond to the sovereignty-undermining strategies of their adversaries, but those responses are unlikely to fully recapture authority losses. By damaging state authority, proxies alter the landscape of costs and benefits that targets face: they have increased the costs of exercising state authority, and they have reduced the benefits of doing so.

To understand why targets face an uphill battle in the recovery of their authority in the face of these altered costs and benefits, consider three types of responses. First, a target state may attempt to change the sponsoring state's behavior in an effort to shut off the source of the problem. For example, a target state might punish the sponsor state by supporting disaffected groups on the sponsor's side of the border, as Sudan did after Ugandan meddling in Sudan's southern periphery. A target state might even acquiesce to the sponsor's demands on some issue under dispute if the authority problem is sufficiently dire. Unless the target is immediately successful at altering the sponsor's behavior, however, the damage to state authority will have already been done. In the absence of other responses, there is no guarantee that state authority will simply revert to the status quo ante.

Even so, there are reasons to expect that the target state will respond by attempting to change the sponsor state's behavior. Focusing on the sponsor is politically expedient. Leaders in target states can use their foreign enemy as a political scapegoat to distract from domestic problems at home. They may claim that their problems of state authority are entirely the product of foreign machinations, and use such claims to rally the public around the flag. For example, during the height of Turkey's crisis with the Syrian-backed PKK, Ankara refused to acknowledge the domestic dimensions of Kurdish discontent that made the PKK such a threatening force to Turkish state authority in the first place.[35] Had Ankara publicly recognized the domestic elements of its Kurdish problem, it would have had to invest resources that it did not want to spend on its Kurdish population. Instead Ankara found a politically useful enemy in Syria, and focused on finding a way to cut off Syrian support for the PKK. Turkey's attempt to appease Syria with concessions largely failed to make a dent in Syrian support for the PKK and thus had no effect on restoring Turkish control over its Kurdish regions. Nor did threats to use military force convince Syria to abandon its Turkish Kurdish proxies until 1998, when Turkey massed troops on the Syrian border. By then, however, the damage to Turkish authority in the Southeast was already done.

A second type of response is to counteract the sponsor's efforts by attempting to increase state authority in the targeted regions—to do what Turkey did not want to do in its Kurdish crisis. Target states might deploy the military to restore public order, or invest in transport and administrative infrastructure to facilitate the projection of state power and authority. Yet even in this case the target state is unlikely to fully recapture authority. Foreign subversion raises the costs of statebuilding efforts above those that the state normally faces. Subversion also reduces the efficacy of those efforts. Consequently, the state would have to invest more resources to obtain the same degree of authority that it would exercise in the absence of the sponsoring state's efforts. In some cases, the required amount of resources necessary to return to the status quo ante may be prohibitively high for state leaders. For example, expending resources to improve state administration and control carries distributional consequences since those resources could be spent on other parts of the country, other political constituencies, or other policy priorities.[36] Investing too many resources to reassert authority in an area targeted by a sponsor is therefore politically risky for state leaders.

A third possibility is that the target state may simply relinquish authority in response to subversion. It is costly to reassert control, and if citizens update their beliefs about the target's capabilities and strength, the benefits of governing will be lower. A rational state may thus conclude that it is not worth contesting the territory. Georgian leaders have calculated that the costs of retaking the Russian-supported regions of Abkhazia and South Ossetia are so high that it is better to let the breakaway regions remain outside Georgian authority. But this outcome is not common. For most state leaders, the domestic risks of doing nothing and conceding authority losses are quite high. Doing nothing exposes leaders to domestic criticism and potentially removal through the ballot box or a military or palace coup. Consequently, it is more likely that target states will respond to subversion in some way, even if those responses are not fully adequate for reasserting state authority.

The only states likely to break out of this trap of incomplete state consolidation are those with a relatively high degree of state capacity in the center. In other words, the greater the degree of central state power, the less effective subversion will be at weakening state authority. If subversion operates by imposing costs on the exercise of state authority, powerful states are the most likely to have the resources and capabilities to meet and overcome those costs. For example, China can direct significant economic and military resources to govern Tibet and Xinjiang, and as a result state authority is relatively strong. Knowing this, sponsors might be less willing to meddle against strong targets, and where meddling does occur, it will be less likely to weaken the state. Relatively few states in the international system outside the developed world meet this condition, however; very few can claim China's level of central state power. For those countries, the problem of reasserting authority will be especially difficult, resulting in a lower level of state authority in the presence of sponsor states than in the absence of sponsor states.

Crippling the Leviathan

The Weberian ideal of the state is one in which the state has triumphed over its competitors and asserted its authority throughout its territory. The reality is often different. Subversion alters the facts of governance on the ground by crippling the leviathan's very ability to translate its claims of state authority into reality. The role of hostile foreign sponsors and their empowerment of proxies with the aim of destroying state authority constitutes an underappreciated yet crucial source of incomplete state consolidation. To be clear, this book's claim is not that domestic factors do not influence state authority. Nor does this book claim that international factors are the primary causes of initial state weakness. Rather, by bringing international politics back into the story of state development, this book seeks to broaden our understanding of why some states cannot overcome these initial deficits in state authority.

In this chapter I have laid out a theory of when states will use subversion and how subversion impedes state consolidation. In the remainder of the book, I focus primarily on testing the two most important hypotheses about subversion.

The overarching claim of this book is that foreign subversion weakens the state. Thus, the first hypothesis is as follows:

H1: Subversion weakens state authority.

A great deal of my theoretical discussion has focused on the conditions under which states will use subversion. Subversion is useful for pursuing one's political objectives. Yet the attractiveness of a noncooperative policy instrument like subversion is especially high in situations where states confront targets with which they have irreconcilable or intractable policy disputes on important issues. Motive alone is insufficient; subversion also requires means, or available agents. Together, these two crucial conditions produce the second hypothesis to be tested:

H2: States will be more likely to use subversion against states with which they have severe policy incompatibilities and when proxies are available.

My strategy for assessing these hypotheses about foreign subversion and its relationship to state authority in target states relies on three empirical steps spanning the next four chapters of this book. The starting point is to examine support for hypotheses 1 and 2 together. I take up this task in chapter 3, where I use statistical methods to link the conditions that favor the use of subversion to the outcome of state authority. Because I do not observe the actual use of subversion directly in that chapter due to data limitations, I assess hypothesis 2 in chapter 4 by examining whether policy incompatibility (motive) and agent availability (means) drive the use of subversion. The final two empirical chapters, chapters 5 and 6, assess hypothesis 1. These chapters offer a deep dive into two case studies to trace the process through which subversion damages state authority and prevents the consolidation of the state.

HOSTILE NEIGHBORS, WEAK PERIPHERIES

Subversion impedes state consolidation, and it is more likely to be used against states with which one has severe policy disputes and when agents are available as potential proxies. These two propositions emerged from the theoretical discussion advanced in chapter 2, and together inform the empirical approach of this chapter. The first proposition posits the harmful effects of subversion on state authority, and the second proposition suggests two factors that condition the use of subversion. If subversion is a weapon one deploys against adversaries rather than friends, then we should observe its harmful effects among states with adversarial relations—those embroiled in severe policy disagreements. Additionally, we should also observe subversion's effects in cases where proxies are available. Importantly, my theory argues that motive and means must appear together in order for subversion to occur.

Examining this overarching relationship between the factors that make subversion more likely and the outcome of state weakness offers an important inferential advantage: it is easier to observe policy incompatibilities and potential agent availability than to observe subversion itself. The features of subversion that make it an attractive instrument of statecraft are precisely those that make it hard to detect and attribute to an external sponsor. In contrast, focusing on the factors that condition the likelihood of subversion allows me to sidestep this problem, since those factors are more easily observable. To code policy incompatibility, I identify whether a state is engaged in an international rivalry. Rivalry is a type of intense and conflictual interstate relationship, one that is both competitive and adversarial. States engaged in rivalries are the ones with the incentives to use subversion. Proxying for motive this way allows me to abstract away from the particular policy issues under dispute, which vary in salience between states. As for agent availability, I code whether ethnic groups are split across national borders. The partitioning of ethnic groups has fostered grievances and support for secessionism, which make such groups potential agents for subversion. To be clear, split ethnic groups are not the only potential proxy group. Just as with rivalry, however, operationalizing agent availability as the presence of split groups offers important advantages in a large-n framework for testing my argument. I use these two indicators to capture motive and means. Then I look for their effect on state weakness, which I measure using the Myers Index, the census accuracy measure that I introduced in chapter 1.

I employ three strategies for assessing whether subversion affects state consolidation. All three approaches leverage variation between subnational units (province-years, the units of analysis) to compare the degree of state authority in particular spaces within countries, but they differ in terms of the comparisons being drawn, the rigor of the analyses, and the demands on my data. Each approach also addresses different inferential challenges. More technically inclined readers should focus on the second and third approaches, which employ regression analysis.

The first approach begins with a descriptive first look at the patterns in the data. I dichotomize the two primary independent variables of interest—policy incompatibility (rivalry) and agent availability (split ethnic groups)—as either present or absent. Then, for each of the four possible combinations of those factors, I examine the average level of state weakness. My theory predicts greater levels of state weakness when both factors favoring subversion are present. The data support this prediction, as do a series of t-tests that confirm that the average levels of state weakness across these combinations are statistically different from each other.

The second approach employs regression analysis to compare levels of state authority between regions within countries. This empirical strategy relies on a key insight from the theoretical discussion in the previous chapter. If the likelihood of subversion diminishes with distance from the adversary, then we should observe the effects of subversion among states that are contiguous. Crucially, this also suggests that regions bordering a hostile state should be more likely to have weaker state authority than regions in the same country that do not border a hostile state. This insight guides the between-province within-country comparisons in the second approach.

By using regression, I gain additional inferential leverage over the first approach. Though the descriptive analysis yields results consistent with my argument, it could be that those patterns of state weakness are the result of factors unrelated to subversion that vary across and within countries. To deal with these competing explanations for incomplete state consolidation, I control for a number of domestic factors that might have driven the patterns observed in the descriptive first cut. The within-country design also enables me to address concerns about country-level omitted variables, such as regime type or military alliances, by deploying country-year fixed effects. Together, the controls and fixed effects let me estimate the effect of subversion on state authority while also allaying concerns about confounding factors. I find that provinces that border hostile states (those with severe policy incompatibilities) and host potential proxy groups have worse levels of state authority than the provinces that do not.

The third approach to testing the effects of subversion relies on comparisons of the same region over time. While the previous empirical step compared provinces with each other and controlled for competing possible explanations for state weakness, it could still be the case that the effects I observe are due to reverse causality. The concern is that state weakness may invite foreign subversion. To be clear, this book's claim is not that the reverse pathway is not possible and does not occur. Rather, I concentrate on demonstrating the causal link between subversion and state weakness. It is therefore important to ensure that the relationships I observe are not due to reverse causality.

The analysis addresses that concern in several ways. While it is plausible that state weakness causes subversion, it is less likely that state weakness causes rivalries (my measure for policy incompatibilities) or split ethnic groups (my measure for agent availability). I also guard against reverse causality by relying on temporal variation. I compare the same unit before and after the start of rivalry; I focus on variation in policy disputes since my measure for proxies does not vary over time by construction.[1] If policy disputes drive subversion, then we should observe the effects of subversion during times when policy disputes are active and severe, and not otherwise. While some countries, such as India and Pakistan, have enduring policy incompatibilities, other states find themselves embroiled in disputes only temporarily. South Africa and Mozambique sought to undermine each other in the 1980s, but when South Africa abandoned its policy of apartheid, the central axis of dispute—and the reason for subversion—withered away. Thus, in this third analysis, I exploit the onset and termination of severe policy incompatibilities to look for the effects of subversion on state authority.

Together, the evidence paints a clear picture across all three approaches: when the factors that favor subversion are present, state authority suffers. States are more likely to have ungoverned and partially governed spaces when those spaces border adversaries and host potential proxy groups. Although the analysis does not observe subversion directly, the results suggest that its negative effects on state authority are considerable.

Data

Measuring State Authority

The central outcome of interest in this book is state authority over territory. This outcome varies spatially within countries and therefore must be measured at the subnational level. Finding suitable data is less straightforward than one might expect. While there is a large body of scholarship concerned with measuring concepts related to stateness and state authority, existing indicators like the Worldwide Governance Indicators or infant mortality are not available for a large number of countries over time or at the subnational level.

To solve this problem, I operationalize state authority using the original measure of census accuracy that I introduced in chapter 1. Although readers can consult the details in that chapter, it is helpful to briefly revisit the intuition. Recall that gathering statistical information is an important and universal function of the state, and that errors in the accuracy of that information suggest deficiencies in state authority. The measure I developed with Nan Zhang specifically examines the accuracy of age data in national population censuses. State weakness affects the quality of this data through two channels. The first is an enumerator channel, in which census interviewers avoid areas that are physically insecure or lack adequate state infrastructure. The second is a respondent channel, in which individuals do not know their precise ages because the state has not given age any meaning or social import through regulation or service provision. Both channels generate errors in age data. Enumerators introduce error by making up data to cover their shirking, and respondents introduce error by estimating their ages.

Importantly, both channels produce patterns in aggregated age data that are distinct from the patterns expected in natural populations without error. A common pattern is called age heaping or digit preference, which refers to the tendency to report some ages and not others. In the context of enumerator and respondent error in age data, individuals typically report round numbers, such as 30 or 40, rather than 32 or 39. Digit preference results in an abnormal number of ages ending in certain terminal digits. Because it is implausible that a natural population would have large numbers of individuals with ages ending in zeros or fives, digit preference indicates data-quality problems. I interpret these problems as indicative of weak state consolidation.

I quantify the degree of error using the Myers Index. Its literal interpretation is the percentage of the population expressing some form of digit preference.

Zero, the theoretical lower bound, means that 0% of the population exhibits digit preference, while 90, the theoretical upper bound, means that 90% of the population exhibits digit preference (since 10% should "correctly" report their ages with their true terminal digit). In my sample, which I describe below, I observe a maximum value of about 53. The data are highly skewed with a long right tail, so I log-transform the measure in the analyses.

Besides its conceptual validity, an important and attractive feature of the Myers Index is that it can be calculated for subnational units such as provinces whenever a census is taken. This allows me to capture the spatial variation in state consolidation within a single country at an appropriate unit of analysis—the province-year. In turn, that facilitates comparisons between provinces in the same country and over time for the same province, which is the core empirical strategy underlying this chapter. I therefore use the Myers Index as a proxy for state weakness.

Measuring the Factors That Influence Subversion

I argued in the previous chapter that states will be more likely to use subversion against targets with which they have severe policy incompatibility and where agents are available, and that subversion in turn weakens state authority. As discussed in that chapter, the specific policy incompatibilities vary widely between cases. Iran and Iraq compete for regional hegemony and prestige in the Middle East. Pakistan and India have long-standing territorial claims to Kashmir. Russian grievances against Georgia largely stem from Georgia's geopolitical gravitation to the liberal democratic West. Syria objects to Turkey's efforts to harness the waters of the Euphrates River for Turkish development purposes. Costa Rica and Nicaragua under the Sandinistas frequently clashed over territorial incursions, harassment of naval vessels, and their opposing ideological positions in the Cold War.

This heterogeneity in policy incompatibilities presents a measurement challenge for my analyses. If the particular issues under dispute between any two countries vary so greatly, it is not straightforward to measure policy incompatibilities in a systematic way. I thus eschew a focus on specific incompatibilities and instead operationalize this variable as the presence of a rival neighboring state across the border. International rivalry is an extreme form of conflictual relations among states in the international system, and thus the existence of a rivalry indicates severe policy incompatibilities between rival states. This approach allows for flexibility with respect to the substantive issues under dispute.

I code rivalry using definitions and data from a dataset developed by William Thompson and David Dreyer.[2] They define a rivalry as a pair of states that regard each other as competitors, enemies, and sources of threats (actual or latent) with the potential to be militarized. Two features of this definition are important to note. First, the authors code rivalry on the basis of leader perceptions. Rivals are the states that leaders (or their historians) say are their competitors or enemies. Second, the perceptions-based approach does not impose the condition that the relationship is actually militarized. The first component of the definition means that the bar for coding a neighbor as hostile is rather high. This threshold is appropriate for my analysis because highly antagonistic states are precisely the ones motivated to engage in subversion. These are the states where policy disagreements are severe, and that have likely exhausted other means to resolve their disputes. They are also the kinds of states more likely to run the risk that the negative externalities of poor state authority—lawlessness, smuggling, disease—may not stay confined in the target state's borders.

The second component of the definition means that it is possible to have a rivalry even if the two states never come to blows militarily. This feature in particular is crucial. It would be misleading to infer policy incompatibilities on the basis of revealed militarized behavior when the theoretical argument holds that subversion can substitute for conventional military force—that it is useful precisely because it avoids costly force. By making leader evaluations the starting point for operationalization of policy incompatibility, I allow for flexibility in the state's subsequent choice to wield a particular instrument of statecraft in the pursuit of its interests.[3]

Recall that the unit of analysis is the province-year, but that rivalry defines a conflictual relationship between states. To translate an interstate concept to the provincial level, I leverage an assumption from chapter 2, which states that the ability to subvert should decline with distance from the sponsor state. This implies that if subversion does occur, provinces near the sponsor are more likely to be affected than those that are farther away. In the context of my empirical strategy, which relies on comparisons between border provinces, this implication suggests that weak state authority will be more likely to manifest in the provinces that border a rival state than in the provinces that border a nonrival state. I therefore code whether province i in home state j borders a state engaged in a rivalry with home state j in year t. This coding approach treats all border provinces as having equal potential to be subverted by the rival state. As it is unlikely that an enemy will degrade state authority in all of the target's territory along the border, this coding decision biases against finding an effect of hostile neighbors. Of the 2,151 observations in the dataset, 610 province-years (279 unique provinces) in 114 country-years (46 unique countries) are coded as adjacent to a rival state.

An example helps to illustrate this coding scheme. In my dataset, Turkey has 10 provinces that border another country, and using the administrative divisions present in 1975, I observe these units four times: 1975, 1985, 1990, and 2000.[4] Of those 10 provinces, 4 border Syria, 1 borders Greece, and the remaining 5 border Georgia, Armenia, Iran, and Iraq.[5] According to the Thompson and Dreyer dataset, Turkey is engaged in rivalries with both Greece and Turkey during the years that Turkish provinces appear in my dataset. The rivalry with Greece is long running and concerns conflict over the Aegean Sea, competition for preeminence in the region, and the fate of ethnic kin in Cyprus. The rivalry with Syria is newer and arose due to disputes over access to the waters of the Euphrates River. Each border province-year adjacent to Greece or Turkey receives a value of 1 during the years in which the rivalry is active; the other border province-years, such as those next to Georgia and Iran, receive a value of 0.

Agent availability is the second factor that affects whether subversion occurs and damages state authority. To measure whether potential agents are available for subversion, I code the presence of a split ethnic group. A split occurs when the "homeland" of the predominant ethnic group in the province straddles an international border. Because the distribution of split ethnic groups is not coterminous with state boundaries, such groups may be less receptive to being governed by the state or may be more likely to exhibit secessionist or nationalist tendencies.[6] For its part, the state may be less inclined to provide basic governing services to split groups, which could increase grievances and foster political mobilization. Recognizing that this discontent can be exploited, external sponsors in fact have used such groups to destabilize their adversaries.[7]

Of course, while they are an important channel for subversion, split ethnic groups are not the only possible proxies. Pakistan's use of India-based terrorists and Kenya's support for breakaway Jubaland in Somalia are not cases where the agents of subversion were ethnic groups straddling a national border. However, relying on split groups provides an important advantage for large-n analysis. Because such groups are easily observable, I am able to code potential proxies in a systematic way across a wide variety of cases. Like my use of rivalry as a proxy for policy incompatibilities, this abstraction away from specific details both affords greater cross-country consistency in coding and is also a conservative measure of potential proxy groups.[8] By possibly excluding potential agents in my measure and running the risk of coding false negatives, I make it more difficult to find in favor of my theory.

I construct my measure of split ethnic groups using worldwide ethnic group data from the Georeferencing of Ethnic Groups (GREG) dataset and coding procedures from Stelios Michalopoulos and Elias Papaioannou's work on the effects of ethnic partitioning in Africa.[9] The GREG dataset is a GIS dataset based on the *Atlas Narodov Mira*, a comprehensive and carefully researched project that charted the "homelands" of territorially based ethnic groups worldwide. Soviet ethnographers produced the *Atlas Narodov Mira* in the 1960s, and it has become widely used in political science research. The GIS version allows me to identify whether ethnic homelands cross international boundaries. A split ethnic group is any group in which at least 10% of its ethnic homeland belongs to more than one country. I code this variable dichotomously to indicate the presence or absence of a split group. As with most data on ethnicity, the ethnic homelands in the GREG dataset do not change over time, and my measure is therefore time invariant. Readers should not worry about this lack of temporal variation; with the exception of rare and extreme cases of ethnic cleansing, ethnic territorial homelands tend to be stable over time.[10]

The example of Turkey again helps illustrate this coding. Of Turkey's 10 border provinces, only 3 are home to split ethnic groups. All 3 lie in southeastern Turkey, and all 3 have large populations of Kurds, who also live in Syria, Iraq, and Iran. Because my ethnicity data are time invariant, I code all 3 border provinces that host Kurds as having a split ethnic group every time they are observed. Importantly, the set of border provinces next to Turkey's rivals Syria and Greece are not identical to the set of border provinces that host Kurds. In fact, only one province—Mardin—exhibits both conditions that favor subversion. Edirne, which borders Greece, has a rival but lacks a split ethnic group that could act as a proxy group. Ağri, which borders Iran, is home to a significant population of Kurds but is not next to a rival state. Places like Mardin are precisely the places where I expect to observe greater state weakness on average compared to other border provinces.

Sample

Having defined the main variables of interest, I now turn to the issue of sample selection. Three considerations guide the construction of the sample. First, I observe data for the dependent variable only when a state conducts a census. The world's most failed states, such as Afghanistan, the Democratic Republic of the Congo, and Somalia, are unable to conduct censuses and therefore do not enter my sample. Failed states are an empirical rarity, as Thomas Risse and Eric Stollenwerk have observed.[11] Excluding failed states that do not conduct censuses limits my ability to generalize my findings to those states; however, it does not significantly reduce the size of my sample due to the infrequency of state failure.[12]

Second, I exclude developed states for theoretical and methodological reasons. As I argued in chapter 2, sponsors are unlikely to use subversion against fully consolidated states. These targets are more likely to detect and defeat subversion, which makes subversion both more expensive and more likely to fail. Most consolidated states are developed states, so these states are not the places where I would expect subversion to occur.

To be clear, excluding failed states and fully consolidated states from the sample does not equate to selection on the dependent variable. Because I use a within-country approach, I need variation in state authority within countries rather than between countries. Fully consolidated states and failed states are not the places where there is within-country variation to be explained. By definition, they have even levels of state authority throughout their territories: for the consolidated states, state authority is high everywhere, and for the failed states, state authority is absent everywhere. They are therefore unsuitable for the comparisons here that leverage variation in state authority, rivalry, and split ethnic groups between provinces.

This within-country empirical strategy greatly improves the internal validity of the analyses, and comes with little cost to external validity. Since the failed and consolidated states are empirically uncommon in the international system, few countries are excluded on the basis of these sampling rules. In contrast, states in the middle range of the sovereignty spectrum (neither fully failed nor fully consolidated) account for the majority of the world's countries. Given their prevalence in the international system, these middle-range states are an especially important set of countries to study. Here, the Myers Index is helpful in permitting the study of state authority in the middle-range countries, where it is usually hard to measure that variation. The data-generating process makes the index especially informative about variation between units in developing countries, where it is difficult to obtain valid data on state authority even at the national level. Thus, the Myers Index allows me to test my argument on a theoretically appropriate set of countries: developing states.

Third, I include only territorially contiguous states in the sample. Coding considerations rather than theoretical scope conditions drive the contiguity restriction. Because my research design compares border provinces and varies whether they are adjacent to a rival state and contain a split ethnic group, contiguity solves a vexing coding challenge. When a province shares a land border with another state, there is no ambiguity about whether those entities are neighbors. In contrast, it is unclear how to code the rivalry and split ethnic group variables for provinces in archipelago states, island states, and nonneighboring states, even though those states may very well have rivals and ethnic kin.

This coding decision has important implications for the interpretation of my results. Neighbors are not the only states that might have an incentive to subvert a target for foreign policy purposes. Great powers and regional powers will also engage in subversion if both means and motive are present. For example, the United States and the Soviet Union both utilized subversion as part of their strategies for prosecuting the Cold War. Iran, an important power in the Middle East, has provided significant support to Hamas and Hezbollah, groups that exercise state-like authority to varying degrees in parts of Israel and Lebanon, respectively. It is also possible that sponsor states could subvert state authority in the heartland of a target state or against their maritime neighbors, and the analyses in chapters 4 and 5 provide support for that claim. But proximity tends to enhance subversion, since subversion often involves providing territory for training or bases in addition to arms and equipment. Because most states in the international system lack the ability to project power over long distances, I restrict the sample to contiguous states only. Since my analysis does not account for the possible effects of great powers, regional powers, and noncontiguous adversaries, I diminish the likelihood of finding support for my theory. In other words, some units will be "treated" (targeted by great powers) but will not be coded as such. The result is that the design of my empirical test reduces the estimated effect of the interaction between rivalry and split ethnic groups.

Together, these rules determine which countries and provinces appear in my sample. Countries that enter the sample are independent developing states in 1960 and share at least one international land border with another country. Developing states are defined as those that the Minorities at Risk project codes as not members of the "Western democracies and Japan" region.[13] Additionally, because the unit of analysis is the province-year, provinces must also have at least one international land border with another country. Interior provinces and coastal provinces without land borders do not enter the sample. These rules produce a sample of 2,151 province-years, 714 unique border provinces, and 79 countries over the period 1960–2012. A full list of countries and years that appear in the sample can be found in the appendix.

A First Look at Patterns

I begin my assessment of my theory with a first cut at the patterns in the data. As I argued in chapter 2, states will be more likely to wield subversion against adversaries with severe policy disputes and when agents are available as potential proxies. If subversion weakens state authority, then we should observe greater levels of state weakness when those factors are present.

TABLE 3.1 Frequency of policy incompatibility and agent availability in the sample

	UNIQUE PROVINCES		PROVINCE-YEARS	
Variable	*N*	%	*N*	%
Incompatibility	279	39.1	610	28.4
Agent availability	312	43.7	918	42.7
Incompatibility and availability	124	17.4	238	11.1
Total observations	714	100.0	2,151	100.0

Notes: Incompatibility is operationalized as a rivalry. Agent availability is operationalized as a split ethnic group. Because policy incompatibility and agent availability are independent of each other, the percentages do not sum to 100.

Table 3.1 shows the frequency of values on the independent variables in the sample. Policy incompatibility and proxy availability are not uncommon. About 39% of border provinces lie next to a rival state at some point in time, while nearly 44% of border provinces have ethnic groups whose homelands fall across national borders. Although both factors favor subversion, they do not frequently appear together in my sample. Only 17% or 124 unique provinces and 11% or 238 province-years ever have both factors. Because I do not observe subversion directly, it is important to be clear that the claim is not that subversion occurs in all 238 province-years where the factors that make subversion more likely are jointly present.[14] Rather, these 238 cases are those where I would expect to observe lower levels of state weakness that would be consistent with the use of subversion, relative to the cases where one or both factors are missing.

Table 3.2 shows the average levels of state weakness, proxied by the Myers Index, for each combination of the two independent variables. The patterns in the table are consistent with my theoretical expectations. Recall that higher values on the Myers Index indicate greater levels of state weakness. As we see in the northwest quadrant, average raw and logged Myers scores are highest when both factors that increase the likelihood of subversion are present. This indicates that policy incompatibility and agent availability are associated with weak state authority over territory. An exemplary case that falls into this group is Iran's Kurdistan Province, which borders Iraq on the west and is home to a large Kurdish population. Baghdad has at various times attempted to exploit Kurdish discontent in Iran to undermine Iranian state authority and distract and preoccupy Tehran. Another case in this group is southeastern Turkey, which includes Mardin, a province we have already discussed. Syria sponsored the Kurdistan Workers' Party (PKK), a militant organization, in order to gain bargaining leverage over Turkey on the issue of water access. The PKK based itself on Syrian territory but sought to govern southeastern Turkey by substituting itself and its administrative institutions for those of Turkey.

TABLE 3.2   Factors favoring subversion and corresponding levels of state weakness

	INCOMPATIBILITY	NO INCOMPATIBILITY
Agents available	Raw Myers: 15.29 Logged Myers: 2.22 Observations: 238	Raw Myers: 10.92 Logged Myers: 1.93 Observations: 680
No agents available	Raw Myers: 11.30 Logged Myers: 1.93 Observations: 372	Raw Myers: 7.55 Logged Myers: 1.48 Observations: 861

Notes: The figure reports mean raw or log-transformed Myers scores. Higher values on the Myers Index indicate greater levels of state weakness. Incompatibility is operationalized as a rivalry. Agent availability is operationalized as a split ethnic group. T-tests of each comparison are statistically significant at $p < 0.05$ except the antidiagonal comparison between incompatibility/no agents available and no incompatibility/available agents. Observation total: 2,151 province-years.

The other combinations of motive and means also have average levels of state weakness consistent with my expectations. My theory predicts that states will not engage in subversion in situations in which they lack means and motive to interfere in the domestic political authority of the target. State weakness should therefore be lower in those cases than when means and motive are both available. Indeed, we see in the southeast quadrant of table 3.2 that the raw and logged Myers scores are smallest in province-years that do not border rivals and are not home to split ethnic groups.

The two intermediate cases, in which one of the two factors is present, have middling levels of state authority compared to the cases where subversion is most likely and least likely. The processes linking each factor to state weakness are probably different than when both incompatibility and agent availability are present. From the perspective of the political center, split ethnic groups might be harder or less desirable to govern, independently of whether a hostile sponsor mobilizes that group and provides material, psychological, and political support. As for rivalry in the absence of agents, these are cases in which the state is motivated to subvert but is unable to do so. That does not preclude the possibility that the hostile state will use some other policy instrument to prevail in disputes against the target. It does, however, preclude subversion, an instrument of statecraft that is particularly damaging to state authority over territory. The middling level of state authority associated with the case of incompatibility but no agents could also result from the fact that my measure captures only ethnic agents, an important type of agent but not the only possible one.

Overall, this first look at the data reveals patterns in line with my expectations about the factors that make subversion more likely and the effects of subversion on state authority. A series of t-tests confirm that the mean levels of state weakness are statistically distinguishable from each other, with the exception of the two intermediate cases where only one factor is present. Of course, it may be that the relationships I observe in table 3.2 could be driven by differences between countries or between provinces. Broadcasting authority might be harder in democratic countries, for example, or in provinces that are distant from the capital. These omitted variables threaten my ability to draw valid inferences about the effect of subversion on state authority. Fortunately, regression analysis provides a solution.

Assessing Subversion within Countries

The second empirical approach uses regression to compare levels of state authority between provinces within countries. A major advantage of moving to regression analysis is that it allows me to account for a wide variety of confounding factors that could affect state authority. By comparing provinces within countries, I am able to hold country-level factors constant and reduce the likelihood that my inferences are contaminated by differences between countries. It would be unfair, and indeed misleading, to compare Uganda's northwestern provinces with India's northwestern provinces without accounting for the fact that India is wealthier and more institutionalized at the national level than Uganda. Nor would it be appropriate to compare state authority in Uganda's northwestern border provinces in 1991 with Uganda's southeastern border provinces in 2002. I thus include in the regression country-year fixed effects.

Regression also allows me to control for the most likely subnational confounders that might affect state authority. To do so, I code a number of additional covariates. First I account for two geographic factors. A growing body of scholarship has shown that terrain ruggedness poses a significant obstacle to the exercise of state authority. Rough terrain can provide physical spaces for rebels to hide from the state.[15] Mountainous areas also directly affect state authority by increasing the transaction costs related to basic tasks of governing by virtue of being more difficult to penetrate and navigate.[16] I measure terrain ruggedness as the average "slopedness" of a province in terms of percent rise in elevation. I calculate this measure using a procedure similar to the one deployed in Nathan Nunn and Diego Puga's work on terrain ruggedness in Africa, and I use data originally produced by the U.S. Geological Survey.[17] Because the data exhibit a high degree of skew, I log-transform this variable.

Similarly, distance from the national capital should also create challenges for the extension of state authority. As Jeffrey Herbst has shown in the case of sub-Saharan Africa, places that are farther away from the center of state power are harder to govern.[18] As in the case of rough terrain, the transaction costs of exercising authority should be higher in distant areas, which should on average decrease the likelihood that the state is administratively present. I measure distance in kilometers as the geodesic distance ("as the crow flies") between the national capital and the geographic centroid of each province. In the analyses that follow, I log this variable to reduce skew.

I also control for an important demographic variable: population density. As population densities increase, the marginal cost of exercising state authority should decrease due to an economies-of-scale effect. For example, where populations cluster together over territory, a state can provide just one large hospital. In contrast, in sparsely populated rural areas, the state would have to provide many hospitals to reach the same number of people. It is often not cost effective to provide the equivalent level of services in sparsely populated areas compared to densely populated areas. State presence should therefore be lower in less dense areas. I calculate population density as the total population divided by the province's area in square kilometers. Again, I log this variable in the analyses.

I then account for two economic factors: economic development and natural resources. Measuring economic factors subnationally over time is an extremely challenging prospect. The ideal data would be government-reported data at the provincial level observed over many time periods. These data do not exist for most countries in the developing world, precisely because of weak state authority and weak administrative presence over territory. To get around this problem, I use geospatial data and GIS methods to develop an alternative indicator.

In the case of economic development, I create a proxy by measuring the suitability of land for agricultural cultivation. Agriculture is a large and important component of economic output for many developing countries around the world. For example, in Ethiopia in 2008, agriculture accounted for 43% of the country's GDP and about 80% of its exports.[19] In India, the agricultural sector employed about 70% of all Indian workers in 1961 and 55% of all of Indian workers in 2011.[20] As with GDP, no data exist to measure agricultural productivity for subnational units over time. I can, however, estimate the level of agricultural output by looking at its inputs, where data do exist. Land suitability is one such input. Where the land is more suitable for agricultural activity, there should be greater levels of agriculture, which should correlate with economic development. In Ethiopia, for example, the arid Somali and Afar regions have the highest poverty rates in the country, while Gambella, a region with high land suitability, enjoys a significantly lower poverty rate.[21] I measure land suitability using geospatial data drawn from an index that is the product of two components reflecting the climatic and soil suitability for cultivation.[22] While soil suitability might be affected by technological advances like the Green Revolution, climatic suitability would not. The land-suitability index ranges from 0 (unsuitable for agriculture) to 1 (highly suitable for agriculture). Although it is not possible to construct a time-series version of this measure, it importantly allows me to control for subnational variation in economic development.

One might worry about the validity of measuring an inherently time-varying characteristic with a time-invariant approach. The lack of time-series data on economic development is not ideal, but it is not devastating. A large literature on the political economy of development has shown that historical or otherwise static characteristics, such as factor endowments and early institutions, can have profound and surprisingly persistent effects on economic development over time.[23] This literature suggests that a time-invariant measure such as land suitability should correlate with economic development. Even though the measure is imperfect, it improves on the alternative of omitting economic development completely from my regressions.

I also code another economic variable, natural resources, as a proxy for the material value of a territory. It is not immediately clear what relationship one might expect to observe between valuable territory and state authority. On the one hand, states should derive greater benefits from exercising authority over more valuable territories, and should therefore be more likely to govern such territory. On the other hand, enemy states may be more likely to target valuable territory either to gain those benefits for themselves or to gain greater bargaining leverage in their dealings with the target state. Either way, to ignore this variable would be to risk omitted variable bias. Because natural resource endowments can yield rents to the state, I proxy for value using the percentage of territory containing known oil and gas deposits.

The aforementioned variables are measured at the subnational level. There may be additional country-level factors that also affect the state's exercise of authority, such as regime type or alliance relationships. The country-year fixed effects that I use to ensure that my comparisons are between provinces in the same country and year do double duty here, as they also control for these national-level factors. Table 3.3 shows descriptive statistics for the dependent variable, independent variable, and covariates.

Combining propositions from my theory, I expect to observe that border provinces next to rival states that also have split ethnic groups should have greater levels of state weakness as measured by the Myers Index. Because these two conditions must appear together, in the regression I interact the rivalry and split ethnic group variables. As discussed, I include country-year fixed effects to address potential concerns about omitted variable bias but also ensure that proper within-country comparisons are being drawn. In addition, I cluster the standard errors by country-year.

TABLE 3.3 Descriptive statistics for main variables

VARIABLE	MEAN	STD. DEV.	MIN.	MAX.
State weakness	1.78	1.07	−1.08	3.97
Rivalry	0.28	0.45	0	1
Split ethnic group	0.43	0.50	0	1
Terrain ruggedness	−0.11	1.24	−5.33	2.13
Distance from capital	5.97	1.06	1.33	8.24
Population density	3.55	2.24	−6.80	11.91
Economic development	0.48	0.29	0	1
Natural resources	0.069	0.17	0	0.07

Notes: State weakness, terrain ruggedness, distance from the capital, and population density are log-transformed. Total observations: 2,151 province-years.

To assist with the interpretation of the effect sizes, I standardize the Myers variable and the continuous covariates to have mean 0 and standard deviation 1. This transformation means that the results can be understood as shifts in standard deviations. In other words, the coefficients on the predictors represent the fraction of a standard deviation shift in the outcome variable that results from a one standard deviation shift in the predictor (or moving from 0 to 1 on a dichotomous predictor such as rivalry).

The main regression results appear in the plot given in figure 3.1.[24] The plot shows the point estimates and the 95% confidence intervals. Since higher values on the Myers Index indicate greater levels of state weakness, I expect to observe a positive coefficient on the interaction term. Interactive effects are difficult to interpret, however, so figure 3.2 presents the marginal effects holding the covariates at their means. Importantly, this graphical depiction also allows us to visualize three important comparisons. First, the dashed line shows the effect of having a rival holding constant the absence of a split ethnic group. Since one of the two factors that influence subversion is missing, I do not expect that having a rivalry will affect state weakness. Indeed, rivalry has no statistically significant effect on state weakness compared to the case without a rival ($p = 0.58$). Second, the solid line shows the effect of having a rival holding constant the presence of a split ethnic group. This comparison examines what happens when I move from having only one factor present to having both factors present. In this case, I do observe a statistically significant effect of means in combination with motive, compared to the case of means without motive ($p = 0.004$). Third, I can now compare the change represented by the solid line with the change represented by the dashed line. My analysis shows that having a rival versus not having a rival has a significantly different effect on state weakness for split groups versus non-split groups ($p = 0.04$).

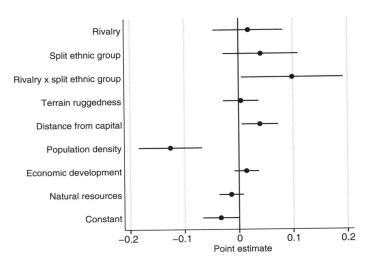

FIGURE 3.1. Effect of factors favoring subversion on state weakness. OLS model with country-year fixed effects and standard errors clustered by country-year. The dependent variable is state weakness, operationalized as the logged Myers Index. Higher values indicate greater state weakness. All continuous variables are standardized to have mean 0 and standard deviation 1. Rivalry and split ethnic group are dichotomous. Bars refer to 95% confidence intervals. Total observations: 2,151 province-years.

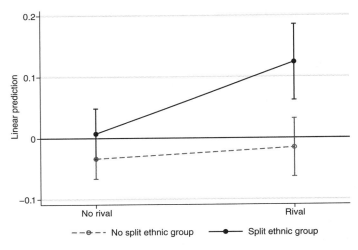

FIGURE 3.2. Marginal effects on state weakness. Marginal effects holding covariates at their means. The dependent variable is state weakness, operationalized as the logged Myers Index. Higher values indicate greater state weakness. Bars refer to 95% confidence intervals. Total observations: 2,151 province-years.

What these results mean is that when both motive and means appear together, as operationalized by rivalry and the presence of a split ethnic group, state weakness is greater. On their own, the main effects for rivalry and split ethnic group are not statistically distinguishable from zero. In other words, having only an adversary or only a partitioned ethnic group does not on its own produce ungoverned spaces. It is only when both appear together that we see a powerful deleterious effect on state consolidation. The effect size of their interaction is considerable: when both factors are present, we observe an 11% standard deviation increase in state weakness. This suggests a more complicated relationship between domestic and international factors and their consequences for state authority than was previously appreciated.

How large and important is the effect of subversion on state authority? Because the Myers Index is a proxy measure for state weakness, the scores are not directly interpretable. It is thus more useful to interpret the substantive significance of an 11% standard deviation shift in terms of equivalent shifts in national-level Myers scores. This move abstracts away from the specifics of which spaces within countries are ungoverned, a key advantage of the Myers Index for statistical analysis. However, it permits tractable comparisons using places familiar to readers, and allows me to utilize a breadth of data to concretize the effect of subversion on state authority. To do this, I return to the example of the Philippines, a country we have already encountered in chapter 1 and will see again in chapter 5. Translating the effect to the national level, an 11% standard deviation increase in state weakness is the equivalent of shifting from the level of state authority in the Philippines in 2010 to the level of state authority in the Philippines in 2000, when the state was weaker and its reach more tenuous. Put differently, while still exercising due caution against overclaiming, we can think of the national-level improvement from 2000 and 2010 as the increase in state consolidation that would have happened in the absence of subversion.

Several indicators of state authority and state performance suggest that the subversion penalty is substantively meaningful.[25] According to the Worldwide Governance Indicators, a prominent rating and ranking series of the World Bank Group, the Philippines improved its government effectiveness from a score of -0.14 in 2000 to -0.02 in 2010, or from 46th best to 42nd best in terms of its percentile ranking.[26] In terms of human welfare outcomes, infants were more likely to survive to their first birthday in 2010 than in 2000, as infant mortality rates improved from 30 deaths to 24.9 deaths per 1,000 live births. As I discussed in chapter 1, infant mortality is a common proxy for state authority due to its close relationship to the state.[27]

Measures that are more directly sensitive to contact with the state also point toward the interpretation that an 11% shift represents a meaningful change in state authority. Consider taxation. Scholars have recognized that certain forms of taxation require greater administrative capacity, denser interactions between state and society, and heavier surveillance of private economic activity.[28] Effective taxation on income and property depends on state presence to a greater degree than flat head taxes or customs duties at the border; this is one reason why income taxes developed relatively late in history and why they are more likely to be found in strong states than in weak states. In my own work with Nan Zhang, we demonstrate that access to information is in fact foundational for the exercise of state authority, including in the domain of income taxation.[29] Tax data from the Philippines corroborate the improvements in state authority suggested by the Myers Index: the Philippine state collected more taxes from income, profits, and capital gains as a share of overall tax revenue in 2010 than in 2000 (44.1% vs. 44.7%).

Similarly, birth registration data also indicate greater contact between state and society, a cornerstone of state authority. Whereas income taxation depends on access to information, birth registration is a direct measure of that access. Indeed, in the Philippines, birth registration improved from 83% in 2000 to 90.2% in 2010. As we see across a variety of indicators, the subversion penalty of 11% of a standard deviation is thus highly consequential for the exercise of state authority.

Turning now to the covariates, it appears that the effect of terrain ruggedness on state authority is not statistically distinguishable from zero. At first blush, this lack of explanatory power is somewhat surprising; I expected to observe a harmful effect of mountainous terrain. Although it is possible that this result is due to lack of precision, the fact that the estimated coefficient is close to zero suggests a potential substantive explanation. Mountains are places where rebels can be based, and they provide refuge for populations fleeing the reach of the state. In Southeast Asia, for example, ethnic and cultural minorities historically took up residence in the highlands to evade the coercive reach of valley kingdoms.[30] This would suggest that mountains might be detrimental to the exercise of state authority. Yet many centers of political power can be found among mountainous regions. Santiago, Chile, and Thimphu, Bhutan, are both high-altitude capitals.[31] Other capitals sit in valleys or lowland areas but are located in administrative regions that are mountainous relative to other provinces in the same country: Kathmandu, Nepal; Bujumbura, Burundi; and Asunción, Paraguay, are examples. All three sit in regions with levels of terrain ruggedness above their country means. When all of these possibilities are taken together, the overall effect appears to be a wash.

In the case of the other geographic covariate, distance from the capital, the results bear out as expected. As distance from the national capital increases, the likelihood that the state exercises authority decreases. The deleterious effect of distance is also somewhat large relative to other predictors: for each standard deviation shift in logged distance, the model predicts a corresponding shift of about 4% of a standard deviation shift in logged Myers scores. Besides helping to provide a more precise estimate of the effect of hostile neighbors, the result for distance also provides evidence to support the existence of a more general effect of distance on state authority beyond sub-Saharan Africa, the region where Herbst had originally theorized about the challenges posed by distance.[32]

Neither of the two economic covariates reaches statistical significance. In the case of the development variable, this lack of statistical significance is almost certainly an artifact of the way that the variable was constructed. While level of development changes over time, the variable itself is time invariant because it is operationalized as the suitability of land for agriculture. It could be that because the measure is static, over-time changes in economic development vary enough that initial physical inputs are not predictive with precision.

Finally, turning to natural resources, territory that is more valuable in terms of its natural resource endowments is more likely to be governed by the state. The coefficient, however, is estimated quite imprecisely and does not reach conventional levels of statistical significance. As previously discussed, it is not ex ante obvious what to expect, since the fact that an external sponsor can gain significant bargaining leverage by successfully disrupting authority over valuable territory should offset the target state's desire to control territory rich in natural resources. These opposing effects could explain why I detect no clear relationship either way.

What does this second empirical test tell us about the sources of incomplete state consolidation and the deficiencies of state authority over territory? Through a comparison of border provinces within the same country-year, I uncovered evidence of a contemporaneous effect of subversion on state consolidation in target states. The results show that the interactive relationship between rivalry, my proxy for policy incompatibilities, and split ethnic groups, my proxy for agent availability, affects state authority over territory. It is the combination of motive and means that makes subversion more likely to weaken state authority. The effect is large and substantively important, and as I show in the appendix, it withstands a number of sensitivity and robustness checks.

The regression results improve on the previous analysis by allowing me to control for national and subnational confounders. Skeptical readers may still worry about the possibility of reverse causality. It might be that state weakness invites rival states or precipitates the onset of policy incompatibilities. Left unaddressed, this endogeneity problem threatens my ability to draw valid causal inferences about the effect of subversion on state authority. The next section therefore confronts this challenge head-on.

Tracking Subversion's Effects over Time

In this third statistical test of my argument, I investigate how the onset or termination of policy incompatibilities between two contiguous states affects state authority in border regions. Whereas the previous analysis drew comparisons between regions, this analysis draws comparisons over time within the same region. If policy incompatibilities drive subversion, then we should observe the deleterious effects of subversion during times when states are actually engaged in disputes, and not otherwise. The focus in this section is on over-time variation in motive rather than means. Though it is in principle possible for incomplete state consolidation to cause the emergence of proxies, it is less plausible that state weakness causes ethnic groups to become split across international lines. Thus I focus on rivalry as the likely source of reverse causality in these empirics.

Before proceeding to the analysis, three caveats are worth mentioning. One is that there is less over-time variation in rivalry to exploit in my sample than I would prefer, a difficulty that will not surprise scholars of international rivalry. What this means is that there are fewer observations with which to draw inferences about how the onset of hostile relations affects state authority over territory, which in turn will pose challenges for obtaining precise estimates of that effect.

A second caveat is that I have observations only when census data are available to construct the dependent variable. Of course, this data limitation was present in the previous analyses, but because the comparisons were between provinces within countries, a single census provided enough data to conduct those comparisons. Since the present analysis relies on intertemporal variation, I require at least two rounds of censuses to be able to draw comparisons. Moreover, there must be a change in rivalry between those sets of observations. Some countries, like Mozambique, enter my sample only after they have experienced a change in the independent variable of rivalry. Because there is no temporal variation in Mozambique's relationship with its neighbor South Africa for the years Mozambique appears in my sample, it cannot contribute to the estimation of the effect of rivalry over time.

A third caveat is that the dependent variable is not observed at regular intervals. Many countries conduct censuses once per decade, but those censuses may not occur at regular 10-year intervals. For example, Mali conducted censuses in 1976, 1987, 1997, and 2007. This irregular spacing in the dependent variable poses an obstacle to first-differences regression, the technique I employ for analysis. To mitigate this problem, I transform the data into province-decades, where each observation is the province-decade average. The advantage of this approach is that it allows me to use first-differences regression analysis (as opposed to an analysis in levels). The trade-off is that there is a possibility that changes in the dependent variable actually precede changes in the predictors and that this information is obscured in the conversion of the unit of analysis to the province-decade. For this reason, I also report an alternate specification in the appendix.

Still, it is valuable to conduct a within-country analysis even in spite of these limitations. Figure 3.3 reports the results of a first-difference regression, which estimates the effect of changes in rivalry on changes in state authority.[33] All time-invariant covariates drop out, including my measure for proxy groups, which is time invariant by construction. Population density remains in the regression since data are available for that measure over time. The first-differences estimator also addresses the secular downward trend in Myers scores over time. As before, I standardize my continuous variables to have mean 0 and standard deviation 1 and present the results in a coefficient plot showing the point estimates and 95% confidence intervals.

As figure 3.3 indicates, the estimated effect of rivals is somewhat similar to the estimates from previous cross-sectional regressions: rivals are associated with a 16% standard deviation increase in state weakness when province fixed effects

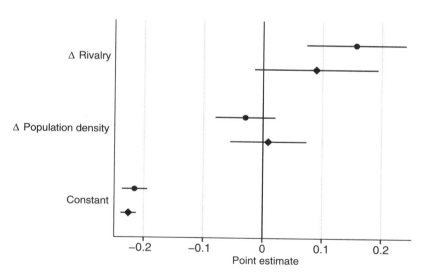

FIGURE 3.3.   Effect of rivalry on state weakness over time. First-difference model with and without province fixed effects; standard errors clustered by province. The dependent variable is state weakness, operationalized as the logged Myers Index. Higher values indicate greater state weakness. State weakness and population density are standardized to have mean 0 and standard deviation 1. Rivalry is dichotomous. All time-invariant measures, such as split ethnic group, drop out. Total observations: 1,208 province-decades.

are excluded, and a 9% increase when fixed effects are included. In the latter case, the effect of rivalry is estimated somewhat imprecisely. The 95% confidence intervals just barely cross the 0 line, indicating that the estimate is no longer statistically significant at the usual thresholds, though it remains significant at the $p < 0.10$ level. Still, both results support my theoretical expectations. The analysis indicates that countries that experience the onset of rivalry see a loss of state authority in the provinces bordering the enemy state, relative to border provinces not next to enemy states.[34]

In many ways, this over-time analysis is the most demanding of my data. Yet the evidence helps reassure us that reverse causality, the most likely threat to inference, is not driving these results. In later chapters, I further address the problem of reverse causality with a series of case studies that use process tracing to explore the effects of subversion on state authority.

Getting the Big Picture

What should we make of this evidence? This chapter offered three different tests of implications from my theory. I predicted a relationship between two key conditions—policy incompatibility and the availability of proxy groups—that make subversion likely, and the effects of subversion on state authority. To examine whether the evidence supported that prediction, I drew on an original measure of state weakness that varies subnationally, which I previously introduced in chapter 1. This measure itself is a contribution, as it permits an analysis of the state's reach over territory within countries, across time, for a large number of states. Indeed, the measure resolves a key barrier to the study of state consolidation by allowing for analysis at a level below that of the state.

This chapter used that measure of state weakness in three ways. The first analysis offered a simple examination of average levels of state weakness for different combinations of policy incompatibility and agent availability. As expected, state weakness was greatest in places where both the motive and means for engaging in subversion were present. The between-province regression improved on that analysis by adding in control variables at the national and subnational levels, reducing the likelihood that omitted variables might be driving the observed patterns in the data and allowing for a more precise estimation of subversion's effects. The within-province regression went one step further. By exploiting the over-time variation in policy incompatibilities, this third test addressed concerns that reverse causality could be driving my results.

Taken together, the analyses in this chapter point to an important finding: rival neighboring states weaken state authority over territory in target countries when proxies are available. These rivals are states with severe policy incompatibilities with the target, and they are especially likely to pursue their policy interests using foreign subversion as an instrument of statecraft. The effect of subversion on state authority is large and important, and the consequences of these state authority deficits are considerable in human welfare terms.

In fact, my results likely underestimate the true effect of motive and means. My empirical strategy could not account for the possible involvement of non-contiguous great powers and regional powers like the United States and Iran. Moreover, ethnic groups are only one possible type of proxy, though a very important one. These analytical decisions diminished the likelihood of finding in favor of my argument. Were I to properly account for these states that have the capabilities to subvert over large distances, as well as the diversity of potential proxies, the estimated effect of subversion on state authority would be larger and more statistically significant—and more deleterious for human well-being.

Of course, it was already known that incomplete state consolidation has pernicious effects on human welfare. What is new in this book is the rigorous statistical evidence pointing to a previously underappreciated yet important international dimension of state weakness. The comparative politics literature has largely understood the problem of incomplete state consolidation as a function of domestic factors that influence the costs and benefits of exercising state authority. My analysis shows that weak state authority over territory is also a function of a previously overlooked international factor: subversion. This is not to say that the comparative politics literature is wrong. Rather, the results show that subversion has an important and sizeable influence on state weakness. Subversion alters the costs and benefits of exercising authority above and beyond the explanatory power of domestic factors alone. Even after accounting for these domestic determinants, this chapter shows that foreign adversaries undermine the state. Thus, to more fully understand why state authority over territory is deficient in some countries, and why ungoverned spaces tend to persist once they emerge, we must account for both international and domestic factors.

The large-n statistical analyses tested an important implication from the theory, and showed that rival neighbors weaken the state when proxies are available. This quantitative evidence shows support for the theorized relationship between state authority and the factors that favor subversion, and demonstrates that this relationship holds for a large sample of developing countries across world regions and time periods. The advantages of this high-flying quantitative cut at the evidence come at the expense of being able to observe the underlying policy incompatibilities or the actual use of subversion as a foreign policy instrument. The next chapter turns to this task through a medium-n investigation of Russian relations with the Soviet successor states.

THE ROOTS OF SUBVERSION

Subversion is a powerful tool of foreign policy. It imposes costs on the exercise of state authority, increases state weakness, and impedes state consolidation. It is an important missing explanation for the prevalence and persistence of ungoverned and undergoverned space in the developing world. Subversion is not, however, the only factor that contributes to state weakness. Numerous domestic factors, such as distance and geography, also affect the extent to which states govern their territories. Nor do all states use subversion against all targets. An empirical investigation into the conditions under which subversion is likely to be employed is therefore necessary for understanding when subversion is a part of the story of state weakness and when other explanations dominate.

This chapter turns to the task of evaluating the two most important propositions about when states engage in subversion, a critical step for understanding when subversion contributes to weak state authority. Two conditions influence the use of subversion: (1) the divergence in policy preferences between the target state and the state sponsoring subversion, and (2) the presence of local nonstate agents in the target state. Only when both are present do I expect to observe subversion against target states. I evaluate the influence of these factors through a comparison of Russia's relations with the fourteen other Soviet successor states.

This focused medium-n design is ideal for examining the political decision to engage in subversion for three reasons. By restricting attention to a region of the world that was formerly a single country, I hold constant a number of historical and cultural factors common to the domestic politics and international relations of that region. Russian geopolitical preeminence in the region also lets me hold constant the identity of the potential sponsor state, Russia, while also leveraging rich variation across my independent and dependent variables between dyads and over time. This approach allows me to gauge how the sponsor's strategy varies across target state characteristics, which yields important insights into the conditions under which states employ subversion. Again, the goal is to understand the boundary conditions for subversion as an explanation for state weakness.

Second, the analysis allows me to improve on the measurement of policy preferences from chapter 3. Policy preferences are hard to observe and code in a systematic way, since the kinds of policies that matter for any given pair of states can vary considerably. In the case of Russia, a single issue dominates Russian foreign policy with respect to the post-Soviet states: orientation toward the U.S.-led international order.[1] For nearly the entirety of its independence, Russia has strongly preferred that the post-Soviet states orient their foreign policies toward Moscow and avoid integration with the West. The primacy of this issue area is a constant in Russia's relations with each of the successor states. What varies are the positions of each state in that issue area, which give rise to convergence with or divergence from Moscow's preferences. For example, Kazakhstan's desire for close geopolitical relations with Russia over the West is congruent with Moscow's preferences, while the three Baltic states diverge from Russia, instead seeking institutional integration with the West. The degree of policy incompatibility also varies within dyads over time. Georgia in the 1990s oriented its foreign policy toward Moscow, but it reversed course in the 2000s by orienting its foreign policy toward the West. When the gap in foreign policy preferences is large, I expect that Russia will be more likely to utilize subversion.

Third, the analysis offers an important advantage in terms of observing agent availability. Proxy availability is a function of state policies in the target country. While the large-n analysis had to use a blunt measure of proxy availability in order to cover a large number of countries, similarities across the post-Soviet states allow for greater nuance in measuring agent availability. The post-Soviet states were named for their dominant ethnic groups, but were by no means homogenous entities. Ethnic mixing and Russian emigration resulted in large populations of nontitular minorities and "stranded" Russians residing "abroad" at the time of the Soviet Union's dissolution. The successor states varied considerably in their treatment of these nontitular groups, particularly in terms of policies that respected or threatened nontitular cultural identities. Those policies in turn affected the willingness of the nontitulars to mobilize and seek or accept Russian influence in their affairs. When target state policies alienate a nontitular group, that group is a more likely potential agent for subversion, and I expect that Russia will be more likely to employ subversion against the target state.

Much like the analysis in chapter 3, this chapter's approach examines the variables of policy incompatibility and agent availability and investigates how these factors condition Russia's choice of foreign policy strategy. Because this chapter's purpose is to assess the conditions under which these factors influence the use of subversion, the outcome of interest in the present analysis is the use of subversion; it thus represents an intermediate step in the theory of territorial subversion and its consequences for state authority. My approach to testing this intermediate step exploits the advantages of a medium-n design that straddles two methodological approaches and benefits from both. The number of cases is large enough to permit informative cross-case comparisons. Yet the commonalities between them allow me to explore an exemplar case from each of the combinations of policy incompatibility and agent availability and increase confidence in my ability to generalize the overarching causal processes from the examined case to the others that share the same values on motive and means.

I examine three cases in depth, varying whether one or both of the factors are present. These three cases are Georgia from 1999 to the present, Estonia from 1994 to the present, and Ukraine from 1992 to 1995. As table 4.1 shows, each case represents a unique combination of motive and means for that period of observation. Georgia exemplifies the case of motive and means together (the northwest cell of table 4.1), and I expect to observe Russian subversion. Estonia exemplifies the case of motive without means (the southwest cell), and I expect to observe no subversion. Ukraine exemplifies the case of means without motive (the northeast cell), and I again expect to observe no subversion here. I follow each case forward in time until they change values on either policy incompatibility or agent availability. For example, I begin my discussion of Georgia in 1999 when it is a case of policy incompatibility and agent availability, values it maintains to the present period. In contrast, I begin my study of Ukraine in 1992 as a case of policy compatibility without agent availability. I end in 1996, when Ukraine shifts to a case of policy compatibility and agent unavailability. In 2014, it shifts again to a case where both factors are present, resulting in Russian subversion against eastern Ukraine—a discussion I take up in the region-wide survey at the end of this chapter. Because my purpose here is to illuminate the causal role of motive and means in subversion, and because I argue that both factors are necessary for states to engage in subversion, I do not include an in-depth case discussion in which both factors are absent (the southeast cell of table 4.1).

I select these cases for several reasons. All three are important and well-known countries in the post-Soviet space, and in all three, closer ties with the West were theoretically possible. They also exhibit some variation over time on either policy incompatibility or agent availability, which allows me to examine the timing of Russian decision-making and link those decisions with changes in the motive or

TABLE 4.1 Classification of Georgia, Estonia, and Ukraine

	INCOMPATIBILITY	NO INCOMPATIBILITY
Agents available	Georgia 1999–present Subversion observed	Ukraine 1992–95 No subversion observed
No agents available	Estonia 1994–present No subversion observed	No in-depth case discussed

Note: I argue that policy incompatibility and agent availability are necessary conditions for subversion to occur. Because this chapter demonstrates the necessity of those conditions, I do not consider a case in which they are jointly absent.

means. As we will see, the cases are in some sense "least likely" cases, in that they stack the deck against finding support for my argument that both incompatibility and proxies are required for subversion. Put differently, if only one factor were sufficient, then we should observe subversion in both Estonia and Ukraine. Estonia is strategically important and Russia was highly motivated to prevent it from integrating with the West, but Moscow did not subvert Estonia. Ukraine has a special place in the narrative of Russian history and close kinship links that were highly salient in Russian domestic politics at the time, but it was not a target of subversion until 2014. In contrast, if kinship ties drive foreign support, as some literature suggests, then we should not observe subversion in Georgia, where the Abkhaz and the Ossetians share no ties with Russia. Together, these cases demonstrate that both motive and means must be present for subversion to occur, and that ethnic or linguistic ties need not be a precondition for subversion. If the evidence supports my argument in these cases, then it is likely that similar causal processes unfold in the cases that take on the same values for means and motive.

My focus in this chapter is to examine the conditions that influence when states use subversion by drawing comparisons between cases. This task and considerations of space necessarily require that I skip over many historical details and nuances familiar to scholars of the post-Soviet world. For the details that I am not able to provide, readers can consult a rich literature in political science, foreign policy, and area studies.[2] This task also informs the organization of this chapter. My aim is not to offer a comprehensive case history or chronological narrative of each case in turn. Rather, I structure the discussion around the causal variables of motive and means and the outcome variable of subversion. This approach allows me to highlight the factors that I argue condition subversion. It also allows me to exploit in a more direct way the variation between the cases, one of the key inferential advantages of studying the post-Soviet space in a medium-*n* design. After the in-depth analyses, I briefly survey the remaining countries in the post-Soviet space, grouped by their combinations of motives and means, and show that their outcomes follow my predictions. Before turning to that analysis, the next section introduces my coding of policy incompatibility and agent availability in the post-1991 Russian context.

The Russian Context

In the first part of this section, I introduce orientation toward the West and the liberal international order as the main issue in Russia's foreign policy, and describe my strategy for observing differences in preferences regarding that issue. In the second part, I discuss how the nontitular minorities are potential proxies for Russian subversion. Variation in proxy availability comes not from the size or presence of nontitular minorities, but from their dissatisfaction with the status quo in the target state and their consequent political mobilization. Both geopolitical orientation and nontitular dissatisfaction vary over time and between countries.

Russia, the West, and the Liberal International Order

My theoretical argument holds that severe policy disputes drive the use of subversion. For Russia after the Cold War, the dominant foreign policy issue in its relations with the post-Soviet states has been orientation toward the liberal international order.

The West has long served as a reference point in Russian foreign policy. The question of the degree to which Western values and institutions should influence Russia stems from several factors, including politics, economics, geography, culture, history, and economics. In the early 1990s, the experience of the Cold War also loomed large. Four decades of geopolitical rivalry were not easily forgotten overnight, nor could the West's ideological victory over the Soviet Union be dismissed so easily during Russia's identity crisis. The West was therefore a model, its values and institutions to be emulated or rejected.[3] If the West won the Cold War because of what it was, it was only natural that the choice before Russia's leaders in early 1992 was about whether Russia would transform itself to become like the West. Yet the West's role as a reference point was hardly a function of its Cold War success alone; it reflected a much longer history of competition. The analyst Janusz Bugajski, for example, sees anti-Westernism's dominance in Russian political thinking as the continuation of five centuries of civilizational and geopolitical rivalry.[4]

While the one constant in Russia's post–Cold War foreign policy was the West as a reference point, Russia's view on the U.S.-led order evolved over time. In the early years of the Yeltsin administration, Russia sought to join the West. Like other members of the liberal foreign policy elite, President Boris Yeltsin and Foreign Minister Andrei Kozyrev believed that the Bolsheviks had perverted and hijacked Russia's true Western identity and that it was time to return Russia to the Western fold.[5] Only by taking its place in the West could Russia transform itself and restore its status as a great power. However, fractious domestic politics and increasing disillusionment with liberal reforms resulted in a change in course for foreign policy beginning in late 1993 and maturing in 1996 during the tenure of Foreign Minister Yevgeny Primakov. Rather than emulate the West, Russia cast itself in opposition and as an alternative to the West. Opposition toward the West escalated further after the ascension of Vladimir Putin to the presidency in 2000. The language of geopolitics pervaded official foreign policy statements.[6] Zero-sum logic, where a loss for Russia was a gain for the West, dominated Russia's foreign policy thinking.

The question of relations with the West and the liberal international order profoundly influences Russia's relations with the other fourteen Soviet successor states. The post-Soviet space holds pride of place in Russia's foreign policy consciousness, and consequently Moscow took a keen interest in those states' foreign affairs. In part this interest stemmed from Moscow's belief that Russia requires a sphere of influence to be a credible great power; insistence on a sphere was both a call for attention and a demand for acknowledgment.[7] The post-Soviet space's geographic proximity and historical position within the Russian empire made it a natural choice for a sphere. So too did its economic opportunities, in the form of markets and sources of raw materials and energy supplies, but also its liabilities, in the form of instability and the potential for encirclement.

Because Russia treated the post-Soviet space as its own sphere of influence, it sought to preclude outside influences in that region. Given Russia's growing opposition to the U.S.-led order, Western influence was particularly objectionable. On this issue Russia's foreign policy elite were in agreement: involvement by Western actors constituted a threat and could not be abided.[8] Russia's rejection of the U.S.-led international order profoundly influenced Moscow's views on the successor states' foreign policies. The Kremlinologist Lilia Shevtsova has noted that Russia's political class "sees the world through the prism of Russian-U.S. relations," a view that is especially true with respect to the post-Soviet space.[9] Jeffrey Mankoff agrees, observing that "Moscow's relations with the other former Soviet republics . . . have largely been a function of its position with respect to Europe and, more fundamentally, the United States."[10]

As a result, the primary foreign policy issue between Moscow and the fourteen other successor states was orientation toward the U.S.-led international order. Would those states pursue a Russia-centric foreign policy, compatible with Russia's preferences and opposition to the West, or would they chart a more Western-centric course, widening the gulf between their preferences and Moscow's? In practical terms, excluding Western influence meant excluding so-called Western ideas, values, and domestic institutions from the region, and preventing the successor states from forming strong political, economic, and institutional links with the West at Russia's expense.

I thus look for evidence of foreign policy orientation and incompatibility in the integrationist behavior of the post-Soviet states. Membership in regional organizations is a clear indicator of this behavior, since institutions formalize political, military, and economic relationships and provide for integration. Moreover, Russia treats institutions in the post-Soviet space as symbols of Russian dominance and vehicles for keeping member states in the Russian orbit.[11] These institutions include the Commonwealth of Independent States (CIS), the Collective Security Treaty and its successor the Collective Security Treaty Organization, and the Eurasian Economic Community and its successor the Eurasian Economic Union.

I also look for evidence of foreign policy orientation in the bilateral political, military, and economic ties between each country and Moscow or the West. Of particular interest is whether these ties exclude one pole or balance between the poles. For example, Kazakhstan enhanced its economic links with Moscow by giving preferential treatment to Russia as it privatized its economy, suggesting a Russia-centric orientation. To be clear, these bilateral ties alone are not the same as foreign policy orientation, but they can be treated as qualitative indicators of or proxies for foreign policy orientation.

I expect that when the preferences of Russia and any given successor country with respect to foreign policy orientation are similar, Russia will have little motivation to subvert state authority in that successor country. When the gap in preferences is wide, then the likelihood that Russia will be motivated to pursue subversion is high. Put differently, the convergence or divergence in preferences provides the motivation for subversion. This is the first factor that conditions the use of subversion.

Nationalist Policies and the Nontitular Minorities

I also argued in chapter 2 that states need proxies—agents—in order to engage in subversion. Disagreements about orientation toward the West provide the motive for subversion; proxies provide the means. Where might one find these agents in the post-Soviet space? I exploit features common to the successor states to look for variation in proxy availability by examining state policies toward minority groups. When state policies are hostile toward minorities, those minorities should be more willing to act as agents of subversion for Russia.

During the Soviet period, the successor states were constituent republics organized on the basis of ethnicity, and at independence, the republics became the homelands of their titular ethnic group (now national group). These states were not ethnically homogeneous even when they had been republics. In addition to the titular groups, a number of other ethnic groups called the union republics home. As of the 1989 census, ethnic Russians accounted for a considerable fraction of the nontitular groups.[12] As migrants, they settled throughout the Soviet Union, from Central Asia to the Baltics to Transcaucasia, with many having arrived decades prior to the collapse of the union. These Russian settlers were primarily defined in sociocultural and economic terms rather than by ethnicity per se, but remained a nontitular "other" in the republics.[13] Ethnic mixing of other groups also occurred. For example, the 1989 census recorded 13 ethnicities of a population of at least 5,000 or larger residing in Georgia, including Georgians, Armenians, Russians, Azerbaijanis, Ossetians, Greeks, and Abkhazians.[14] Considerable numbers of Uzbeks called Turkmenistan and Tajikistan home. Armenians constituted a small but important share of Azerbaijan's population, as did Poles in Lithuania.

Upon independence, this demographic situation posed a number of challenges for the new states that fostered the potential for grievances among the nontitulars. The primary issue concerned the process of state- and nationbuilding. The end of the Cold War eliminated the old organizing principle of statehood, international socialism, in favor of self-determination for the titular nationalities.[15] As a result, the nation was to be the basis of the state. National identity mattered all the more because Russians and Russian identity had claimed a privileged place during the Soviet period and carried significant advantages to "Russified" populations conversant with Russo-Soviet culture.[16] Freed from the domination of Russian culture, and operating under different organizing principles of statehood, the leaders of the new states saw nation- and statebuilding as intimately fused.

While the nation was to be the basis of the state, the policies that the post-Soviet states pursued in their quest to create or recover a national identity determined whether nationbuilding proved problematic for intergroup relations. That is, it is not identity or group differences themselves that drive the availability of proxies for subversion, but rather the state's policies toward nontitular groups. For example, automatic citizenship (called the "zero option") sidestepped questions of who belonged by granting citizenship to those residing in the country prior to independence. Most states chose the zero option. Estonia and Latvia did not, initially excluding permanent residents—mostly ethnic Russians—from citizenship. Similarly, policies that governed the language of education and administration also affected whether the nontitulars felt threatened. In Uzbekistan and Kyrgyzstan, provisions in the laws that elevated Uzbek and Kyrgyz to state languages took effect only gradually, and Kyrgyzstan added a clause to its law declaring that no one could be discriminated against for not speaking the state language.[17] In Moldova, the parliament passed several laws in 1989 that established Moldovan as the state language, switched the script from Cyrillic characters to Latin characters, and effectively required Russians to learn Moldovan if they did not already know it.[18] The exclusivist elements of the language policy threatened Moldova's ethnic minorities and provoked countermobilization among the nontitulars.[19] This countermobilization, which occurred in places like Georgia, Ukraine, and Moldova, provided agents that Russia could exploit.

These policies were especially momentous because of the uncertainty and vulnerability in the immediate postindependence period. The Russian minorities in particular experienced a profound sense of crisis, loss, and insults of "everyday nationalism."[20] As the scholars Charles King and Neil Melvin note, "Russians went from being the privileged bearers of modernity in a backward periphery to often unwelcome *colons* caught in the center of movements of national resistance and national renaissance."[21] The suddenness and incompleteness of the national transformations also exacerbated the vulnerability of the non-Russian minorities, particularly those without a homeland elsewhere. The conversion from Soviet republic to independent state meant that ethnic groups that lacked a republic in the Soviet days were suddenly outside their nation-state, or without a nation-state at all.

The political-demographic situation in the post-Soviet states provides an excellent opportunity to code agent availability. Because the incomplete national transformation was common to all post-Soviet states, each state had to decide whether it would pursue policies to construct national identity, and what kind of policies. Each state also had to choose whether those policies and their implementation would be exclusionary and discriminatory. The variation in those decisions and the political mobilization that those decisions did or did not provoke allow me to identify whether agents were available in each post-Soviet state. Importantly, my focus on state policies, rather than on the identities of the nontitulars, offers useful analytic leverage because policies vary over time within countries. For example, Latvia and Estonia liberalized their initially harsh citizenship laws and eliminated language-proficiency requirements for individuals running for elected office, moves that helped mitigate the tensions.[22] Thus, in the sections that follow, to code agent availability I examine the policies that states pursued that affected the legal status, political protections, and privileges of the nontitular minorities.

Motives

My analysis of the factors that condition the use of subversion begins by examining the role of motive. When Moscow finds itself with divergent and incompatible policy preferences with the other post-Soviet states, it will be highly motivated to engage in subversion. Two of the three cases examined here exhibit this condition: Georgia since 1999 and Estonia since 1994. In contrast, Ukraine of the early 1990s features little policy incompatibility with respect to orientation toward the liberal West.

Georgia

Georgia from 1999 to the present is a case of policy incompatibility with Russia. Although Tbilisi initially pursued a fence-sitting foreign policy that balanced between Russia and the West, it ultimately chose to embrace the West. This choice placed the country directly in Moscow's crosshairs. A Georgia unabashedly courting the West and seeking entry into NATO was the antithesis of Moscow's foreign policy preferences.

Russian-Georgian relations were not always so disharmonious. After a brief period of tensions between Moscow and Tbilisi in the early 1990s, the two countries reached an implicit bargain that stabilized their relations: Russia would diplomatically isolate Georgia's separatist region of Abkhazia in return for Georgia's entry into the Commonwealth of Independent States (CIS) and its collective security structures.[23] From late 1993 until 1999, relations were generally amicable. However, in 1999 Tbilisi took its first meaningful steps to rid Georgia of Russian influence by announcing its intention to close Russian military bases on its territory. It also withdrew from the Collective Security Treaty, the security arm of the CIS and the legal predecessor of the more robust Collective Security Treaty Organization. These moves represented qualitative shifts in Georgia's relations with Russia. Previously, Moscow had tolerated Georgia's earlier efforts to diversify its external relations and institutional membership beyond Russian-led organizations. For example, Georgia had cofounded GU(U)AM, a regional organization that took its name from the five states that formed it as an alternative to the CIS.[24] Georgia also formed strategic partnerships with Ukraine and Azerbaijan. These actions did not directly challenge Russian influence because they did not come at the expense of Russia itself. Refusing to renew the Russia-dominated Collective Security Treaty and closing the military bases was different. These were the opening salvos in Georgia's battle to move from the Russian orbit to the West.

The 2003 Rose Revolution further fractured Tbilisi's relationship with Moscow by decisively altering Georgia's foreign policy orientation. The Rose Revolution saw the peaceful transfer of presidential power from Eduard Shavardnadze to Mikheil Saakashvili. This shift in leadership marked a generational change in Georgian politics from the old Soviet elite to a younger English-speaking crop of leaders and signaled an ideological break with the past and with Russia itself.[25] Under the Saakashvili administration, Georgia pursued an ambitious agenda of reform that included economic liberalization, institution building, anticorruption, and the reestablishment of Georgia's territorial integrity.[26]

These internal domestic reforms were part of Saakashvili's vision for a Caucasus that would act as a democratic pro-Western corridor with Georgia as its leader.[27] Although Georgia had floated its ambitions to integrate into the West prior to the Rose Revolution, Saakashvili's overtly pro-Western government made fast-track admission into Western institutions a central foreign policy objective. Whereas Shevardnadze's Georgia had walked a fine line between the geopolitical orbits of Russia and the West, Saakashvili's Georgia made no secret of its intention to break free of the Russian shadow. In fact, the 2005 National Security Concept strongly linked Georgia's reform process and Western integration.[28] Indeed, after the Baltic states, Georgia held the distinction of being the most open and unambiguous of the post-Soviet states in terms of its courtship of NATO.[29]

For Russia, Georgia's pivot to the West was anathema. A pro-Western Georgia undermined the credibility of the CIS as a regional security organization, which underpinned Russia's effort to maintain a sphere of influence.[30] Worse, Moscow fretted, if Georgia joined the West, then Azerbaijan and even Armenia would follow, putting all of the Caucasus in Western hands.[31] This fear of a domino effect stemmed from Russia's conviction that the Rose Revolution was a U.S.-backed scheme to thwart Russian influence in the Caucasus. U.S. actions did little to dispel Moscow's paranoia. U.S. president George W. Bush feted Saakashvili in Washington when the latter visited in 2004. When Bush traveled to Georgia in 2005, he famously but hyperbolically referred to the country as a beacon of democracy, even though Saakashvili was hardly a democrat.[32] U.S. economic assistance further stoked Russian fears, as Moscow interpreted the aid as evidence of the West's geopolitical machinations in the post-Soviet space.[33]

Because of these incompatible preferences regarding Georgia's foreign policy orientation, Russia and Georgia exhibited an extreme degree of policy dispute that started in 1999 and reached its apex during Saakashvili's 2004–13 presidency. These incompatible preferences fed into Moscow's motivation to use whatever foreign policy instruments it had available to alter Georgia's preferences and prevent it from integrating with the West. Subversion was an attractive instrument of statecraft for these purposes. However, my theory holds that motive alone is not sufficient for subversion to occur; we should observe it only when both motive and means are present. We will shortly see that in the case of Georgia, both ingredients would prove to be in place.

Estonia

Like Georgia, Estonia since 1994 exemplifies extreme policy incompatibility. Unlike Georgia, upon independence Estonia had no qualms about where its future lay: in the arms of Europe. Tallinn's Western ambitions put it on a collision course with Russia's preferences regarding Estonia's foreign policy orientation. Because of its history of forcible incorporation into the Soviet Union, postindependence Estonia had little interest in joining the Russian-led sphere, worrying that it would fall under Moscow's subjugation again. Tallinn could not immediately pursue this objective because it first had to secure the withdrawal of former Soviet troops based on its territory. Now under Russian command, these troops posed such a latent threat to Estonian security that Tallinn could not make foreign policy freely until they were withdrawn.[34] In any case, the West was not particularly enthusiastic about welcoming Estonia and the Baltics into the fold, preferring instead to concentrate its efforts on integrating the Czech Republic, Hungary, and Poland, the former satellite states. For the first few years after independence, Estonia expressed the foreign policy aim of geopolitical neutrality—a politically expedient position that was also effectively its only reasonable course of action.

After settling the troop withdrawal issue in 1994, and removing this check on its foreign policy, Estonia made its intention to break with Russia clear. Institutional integration with the West would complete Estonia's "return" to Europe; NATO membership and the alliance's security guarantees would free Tallinn from a future Russian threat. In 1994 Tallinn applied for NATO membership, and in the fall of 1995 it applied for EU membership. To persuade Western Europe that it was serious about integration, Estonia and its two Baltic neighbors undertook the painful and difficult transformations necessary to secure their admission to the Western club. Tallinn modernized its military, privatized large parts of its economy, and reformed its political institutions.

This decisive turn to the West precipitated a period of intense policy incompatibility with Moscow. Russia was willing to tolerate Estonia's EU ambitions, recognizing that it could profit from its economic interdependence with Estonia if the latter eventually joined the EU.[35] Tallinn's NATO ambitions were a different matter entirely. Unlike the former satellite states, which were already moving toward NATO membership, the accession of Estonia and the other Baltics would bring the alliance into the post-Soviet space proper. Russia's sensitivity toward that psychological barrier cannot be overstated.[36] Worse, NATO would bring the West to Russia's very doorstep. Behind the immediate security issues loomed the larger problem of geopolitical competition. By 1995, Russia had abandoned its embrace of the West in favor of maintaining a sphere of influence in the post-Soviet space as a counter to the West. The accession of three former Soviet republics would constitute a severe blow to Russia's attempt to maintain that sphere of influence.

Moscow spoke ominously about the prospect of NATO expansion to Estonia and the Baltics. In 1995, a study reportedly commissioned by the Russian defense minister called for stationing troops in the Baltics if they tried to join NATO.[37] In 1997 Moscow warned that admission would create "serious barriers" between the Baltic states and Russia.[38] The Russian military openly rehearsed war games against the Baltic states, and denigrated them as little more than giant criminal enterprises.[39]

From 1994 to the present, Russian and Estonian preferences regarding the latter's foreign policy orientation have been irreconcilable. Consequently, Moscow was clearly motivated to stymie Tallinn's efforts to join the West. Impeding state consolidation in Estonia and fracturing its sovereignty could influence Estonian calculations; it would also make the country an unappealing candidate for either NATO membership or EU accession. Estonia ultimately prevailed in its objectives, joining both NATO and the EU in 2004. Even after accession, Moscow's overarching policy objectives remained the same: blocking further integration with the West. Just as in the Georgian case, Russia had ample motivation to engage in subversion. Again, however, motivation on its own is not enough to predict subversion. Only when motivation combines with agent availability (a condition that we will see is lacking in Estonia) does my theory expect subversion as an outcome.

Ukraine

For the period 1992–95, Ukraine is a case of little to no policy incompatibility with Russia. Whereas Estonia broke for the West as soon as it was free of Russian troops on its territory, and Georgia altered course in 1999 in the final years of the Shevardnadze administration, Ukraine in the early 1990s did not attempt to flee the Russian orbit. This situation suited Russian interests. In fact, though Moscow cared considerably about the foreign policy orientations of all the successor states, Ukraine's geopolitical alignment was especially important. Throughout its history, Russia treated Ukraine as a little brother, a metaphor that evokes fraternal closeness but also an unequal relationship. During the imperial period, Russians considered Ukrainians to be a subdivision of the greater Russian nation, and they thus denied the existence of a distinct Ukrainian nation.[40] The breakup between Russia and Ukraine provoked and compounded Russia's post-Soviet crisis of identity. After the dissolution of the Soviet Union, the chief editor of the daily *Moskovskiye Novosti* captured the mood by lamenting, "Millions of Russians are convinced that without Ukraine not only can there be no great Russia, but there cannot be any kind of Russia at all."[41] One scholar of Ukraine, Tor Bukkvoll, has even gone as far as to attribute Russia's foreign policy behavior toward Ukraine to Russians' cognitive inability to cope with an independent and sovereign Ukrainian state.[42] The question of whether Ukraine would tilt toward the West or remain in the Russian orbit thus weighed heavily on Moscow.

In the early and mid-1990s, Ukraine charted a middle course. Until 1994, Kiev's choices were not Russia versus the West, but Russia versus something closer to geopolitical nonalignment. Ukraine's relations with the Commonwealth of Independent States illustrate Kiev's delicate balancing act. On the one hand, Ukraine, Russia, and Belarus together founded the CIS in December 1991 despite disagreements about the organization's purpose. On the other hand, Ukraine was reluctant to take part in CIS initiatives aimed at greater integration among CIS members, preferring that its participation remain largely symbolic. In late 1992, however, Ukraine's dire economic situation ultimately forced it to move closer to Russia and the CIS economically. Kiev did so only begrudgingly, and in protocol meetings continued to oppose Russian ideas for greater integration.[43]

Closer ties with the West were not an option until after 1994. Preoccupied with Ukraine's Soviet-era nuclear arsenal, the United States was in no mood to welcome Kiev to the Western fold without disarmament. With progress on denuclearization, which culminated in Ukraine's accession to the Nuclear Non-Proliferation Treaty, the West became more open to ties with Ukraine. Even so, Kiev continued to balance between Russia and the West. In 1994, Ukraine joined NATO's Partnership for Peace, an individualized program of bilateral cooperation with the alliance. That same year, it also signed a Partnership and Cooperation Agreement with the European Union. However, Kiev also took care to attend to its eastern neighbor. In October 1994, Ukraine signed a CIS agreement that established the Interstate Economic Committee, the CIS's first supranational organ. The creation of this organ was a significant development for the CIS and relations between Ukraine and Russia because it was the first effort to endow the CIS with more than just symbolic functions. Thus, Ukraine matched its outreach to the West with additional ties to Russia. In doing so, Kiev managed its high-wire tightrope act of keeping Russia at arm's length without totally alienating Moscow.

Ukraine's willingness to pay lip service to ties with Russia and its circumspection about the West indicates a surprising degree of foreign policy convergence with Moscow, which would last until about 1996.[44] To be sure, Russia preferred closer relations, and it insisted that Ukraine's obligations as a strategic partner included the coordination of foreign and security policy with Moscow.[45] However, so long as Ukraine did not turn its back on Russia, Moscow had little motivation to undermine its neighbor's governance and state authority.

Ukraine thus represents the case of no policy incompatibility. This coding does not mean that Russia and Ukraine saw eye to eye on all other issues. However, because of Russia's unusually extreme views about Ukraine's foreign policy orientation, Kiev's willingness to balance between Russia and the West indicates convergence on the dominant issue in their relations. Because my theory argues that both policy incompatibility and agent availability must be in place for subversion to occur, the absence of incompatibility suggests that we should observe an absence of subversion during this time period, whether or not agents are available.

Means

Because subversion requires cooperation with agents on the ground, the second factor that influences whether states engage in subversion is the availability of proxies in the territory of the target state. Two of the three cases exhibit agent availability. As a result of state policies in Georgia and Ukraine, agents are available during the time periods of study. In contrast, despite some initially discriminatory state policies in Estonia, Estonia's Russian minority has generally lacked an interest in cooperating with Moscow, rendering agents unavailable in that country.

Georgia

Georgia was born a multiethnic state, but its problems of interethnic relations began long before the country achieved formal independence. Mounting tensions and waves of national mobilizations and countermobilizations—what Mark Beissinger has termed the "tidal influences" of nationalisms on each other—polarized Georgia's population along identity lines.[46] As a result of pre- and postindependence politics, two groups emerged in Georgia as agents available for Russian subversion: the Abkhaz and the South Ossetians. The two groups are distinct and the situations of their respective ethnic "homelands" were markedly different in the Soviet period, but for analytic convenience, I follow other scholars in treating these groups together.

At the time of the 1989 census, Georgians constituted 70% of the population of the Georgian Soviet Socialist Republic (SSR).[47] The remaining 30% of the population was ethnically diverse and included Abkhaz (1.8%) and Ossetians (3.0%). While most Abkhaz in the Soviet Union lived in the Abkhazian Autonomous Soviet Socialist Republic (ASSR), they were a minority even within that territory, making up only about 17.8% of the population of 525,061.[48] The

Ossetians in the South Ossetia Autonomous Oblast (AO) fared a little better, constitutirg about 67% of the oblast's population of less than 100,000.[49]

Although intergroup relations had been stable for much of the Soviet period, tensions rapidly escalated in the late 1980s. This escalation proceeded in three phases: a war of words, a war of laws, and a war of guns.[50] The war of words began with the emergence of a Georgian liberation movement opposed to the Soviet regime. This movement embraced nationalism as the only anti-Communist force that would promote the interests of Georgians.[51] As such, it was both ethnocentric and "remedial," in that it sought to redress the injustices inflicted on ethnic Georgians under Soviet rule and Moscow's Russification policies.[52] The Georgian nationalist mobilization provoked countermobilizations among the Abkhaz and the Ossetians. All three groups promoted discourses on past injustices at the hands of out-groups, which further divided and alienated the groups from each other.

The war of laws involved maneuvers by each group to improve their respective administrative unit's legal status. The Georgian national movement pushed for the independence of Georgia from the Soviet Union. The Abkhaz and Ossetians interpreted this effort as detrimental to their own political situation. They also reasoned that nothing prevented them from using Georgia's own playbook against it. Just as Georgia was a subordinate unit with a particular set of privileges as an SSR within the Soviet Union, South Ossetia and Abkhazia were subordinate units with autonomous status in Georgia, and they too could use their special administrative position to assert themselves against their dominant political entity. In 1989, South Ossetia sought to raise its status from an AO to an ASSR; it also demanded unification with North Ossetia, a territory inside the Russian SSR. The Georgian Supreme Soviet responded by abolishing South Ossetia's autonomy. Not long after, the Abkhazian ASSR declared its own sovereignty and demanded that it be incorporated into the Soviet Union as an SSR. Tbilisi flatly rejected this decision as invalid. Although each group articulated essentially the same set of demands for self-governance, the charged political atmosphere encouraged the least generous interpretation of events. The Georgians viewed the Abkhaz and Ossetians as traitors. The Abkhaz and Ossetians saw the Georgians as oppressive cultural assimilators.[53]

The war of guns began on the eve of Georgian independence when Tbilisi deployed armed force to assert itself over South Ossetia. In spring 1991, Tbilisi sent the National Guard, a poorly paid and barely trained precursor to the national army, to retake control of Tskhinvali, South Ossetia's main city. After being repulsed, Tbilisi tried again in September 1991, and again in June 1992 after Georgia received its independence. Georgian troops attacked the civilian population and looted what they could; they also leveled nearly 80% of the dwellings in Tskhinvali during the June 1992 incursion.[54] As for Abkhazia, Georgian troops entered in August 1992, precipitating the civil war in that territory. As the wealthier of the two regions, Abkhazia had more lootable resources, to which the underpaid Georgian troops gladly helped themselves. The cities of Sukhumi and Gagra, famous as holiday resorts during the Soviet period, were devastated. Georgian troops also systematically destroyed Abkhaz cultural monuments and symbols and carried out a campaign of assault and murder along ethnic lines.[55]

The policies that Georgia undertook on the eve of the Soviet Union's collapse set the stage for the emergence of agents willing to cooperate with external powers. Georgian elites espoused a radical and exclusionary vision of political nationalism that denigrated the country's minorities as "ungrateful guests" whose concerns were illegitimate.[56] Moreover, Tbilisi's policies, including the heavy-handed attempts to bring South Ossetia and Abkhazia to heel, served only to drive the Abkhaz and Ossetians further away. Ironically, by depicting and treating the Abkhaz and Ossetians as traitors, Georgia inadvertently encouraged them to look to foreign powers for help. As we will see in the next section, both groups eventually found that help in Moscow after 1999. Thus, in Georgia both ingredients for subversion were in place: the country's embrace of the West provided the motive, and the Abkhaz and the Ossetians provided the means.

Estonia

Estonia differs from Georgia on the crucial factor of agent availability: from 1994 onward, it completely lacked proxies. Yet at the time of Estonia's independence, observers inside and outside Estonia worried that the country's large Russian population could be a fifth column for Moscow. Nearly a third of Estonia's population was culturally or ethnically Russian. Many were concentrated in the northeast towns of Kohlta-Järve, Sillamäe, and Narva, which were 77%, 97%, and 96% Russophone, respectively.[57] The receptiveness of this group to Russian overtures depended not on their identity, but on the policies of their new home state. To be sure, at the outset of independence, Tallinn did not treat its Russian minority gently. It passed discriminatory citizenship, language, and land reform policies as a means to exclude Russians from political and economic life.[58] The citizenship law, for example, did not grant automatic citizenship. Anyone who arrived after 1940 had to go through a naturalization process that required knowledge of the Estonian language. Because many ethnic Russians immigrated to Estonia after World War II, they were not considered citizens in 1992 despite having resided in the country for decades. The citizenship law effectively disenfranchised Russians and barred them from political participation. Had such policies remained in place and continued to marginalize Estonia's nontitular population, the cultural

Russians could have become available as agents of subversion. Indeed, elites in Narva and Sillamäe briefly threatened secession when they held referenda on the political status of their towns.[59]

Despite an inauspicious start to independence, Estonia adopted a more pragmatic approach and gradually liberalized some of its policies. In 1993, it relaxed some of the provisions of the citizenship regulations, though the law remained controversial. Gradual Estonianization in education and publishing helped smooth the transition from the Soviet period in spheres related to everyday life.[60] Privatization proceeded with few complaints of ethnic discrimination.[61] Even in the realm of public office, where Estonianization did occur relatively quickly, the government was pragmatic on the matter of language requirements.[62] After 1996, the government began providing more Russian-language materials and sought to make Estonian-language instruction more affordable.[63] By 2000, Estonia's elites were resigned to an integration program that charted a middle course between assimilation and cultural preservation.[64]

Less hostile treatment from Tallinn helped neuter the potential for antistate collective action, which already faced significant obstacles even in the absence of discriminatory state policies. Russia did not inspire much envy or longing that could have been exploited to mobilize the population. In a 1994 poll, only 20% of Russian-speaking respondents rated the Russian economic system favorably, while more than twice that percentage rated Estonia's present economic system favorably.[65] The Russian town of Ivangorod, located across the river from Narva, offered a visceral symbol of Russian economic decline. It was not only Russia that felt distant and foreign: Estonia's Russians considered themselves distinct from Russians in Russia. Interviews conducted by the sociologist Lisa Fein suggest that by 2000, the gulf between Estonian Russians and Russians in Russia was so wide that it could not be bridged.[66] One interviewee's response to Fein's question about the distinction between Russians in Estonia and Russia is especially illuminating: "In Russia, we are called Estonians."[67]

Another barrier for agent availability was the lack of ethnic entrepreneurs. Estonia's Russians had no leaders with the credibility, stature, or institutional resources to organize local support. Local Russian elites had such poor standing that even non-Estonians preferred Estonian politicians in opinion polls.[68] Just as the image of Russia did little to engender collective action, so too did the image of Russian elites in Estonia. After 1993, many elites chose to make their fortunes in the private sector rather than in local administration or politics, creating a new business elite at the expense of ethnic leadership.[69]

After 1993, the result of these two factors—moderate treatment from Tallinn and Russia's total lack of appeal to Estonian Russians—meant that no agents for subversion were available in Estonia. We saw in the previous discussion that

Estonia's decisive break for the West provided ample fodder for incompatible policy preference with Russia. Yet motive alone is insufficient; means and motive must both be present. Because this case features an absence of agents, I expect to observe no subversion even in the face of a highly motivated Russian state.

Ukraine

At least in the early and mid-1990s, and so long as Ukraine avoided an enthusiastic embrace of the West, Russia had little motivation for undermining state authority in Ukraine. Had it wanted to do so, however, it would have found ample opportunity and willing proxies among some segments of the population in Ukraine's region of Crimea. At independence, ethnic Russians constituted 67% of Crimea's population, while ethnic Ukrainians made up 25.7%.[70] Identity lines cut across ethnicity and language: 47% of the population considered Russian to be its native language, and 90.5% had fluency in Russian.[71] Unlike in other parts of the post-Soviet space, in Crimea 75% of the population at independence arrived after 1945, and were therefore likely to regard Russia as their homeland.[72]

Agent availability is a function of state policy rather than one of identity on its own. A majority of voters in Crimea supported Ukraine's independence from the USSR, even though the Ukrainian national idea was weaker and support for independence was less vigorous there than elsewhere in Ukraine. Leonid Kravchuk, who became Ukraine's first postindependence president, directly appealed to Crimea's Russians during the independence campaign, emphasizing their indigenous links to the territory of Ukraine.[73] Widespread belief in Ukraine's economic potential also influenced the vote.[74] Thus, it was not destined that Crimea would later come to oppose Kiev's rule and produce proxies for subversion.

Two factors played an important role in shaping the availability of proxies in postindependence Ukraine. First, center-periphery relations emerged as the key issue in Crimean politics, and quickly took on an ethnic character. Kiev pushed policies to enhance its administrative control over Crimea and "Ukrainize" the population in Crimea.[75] As in other post-Soviet states, issues of language and education were especially thorny. For example, the state sought to reverse linguistic Russification and promote the Ukrainian language instead. The central questions animating the debate among Ukraine's Russians, according to Paul Kolstoe, were about "the means, the speed, and the ultimate goals of this policy, and not the policy itself."[76] These policies produced considerable anxiety and tensions among Crimea's Russian population.

Second, Crimea's special institutional status allowed elites to capitalize on these tensions. On the eve of the Soviet Union's dissolution, Crimea was granted the status of an Autonomous Soviet Socialist Republic, a status it had once held when it was a part of the Russian SSR. In early 1992, Crimea received the status of autonomous republic within the state of Ukraine. This institutional status provided valuable resources that elites used to mobilize Crimea's Russian population.[77] But because Crimea's autonomy was only vaguely defined, elites were able to exploit fears of Ukrainization to cast debates over center-periphery relations in ethnic terms.[78] In this atmosphere of radical nationalism, Crimea's Russian movement was born.

Regional politicians in Crimea precipitated the first major crisis of the postindependence period. On May 5, 1992, the Crimean parliament adopted the Act on State Independence, a declaration that would provide for Crimea's quasi independence conditional on the results of a referendum. The next day, the parliament passed the Constitution for Crimea with the support of Crimea's leadership under Nikolai Bagrov and the emerging radical pro-Russian faction under Yuriy Meshkov. Ukraine's parliament rejected both the constitution and the Act on State Independence. Kiev and Simferopol eventually defused tensions through a series of negotiations. Yet the controversy of the summer of 1992 widened a split in the Russian movement and led to the formation of the separatist Republican Party of Crimea–Party of the Republican Movement of Crimea (RPK-RDK) under Meshkov.[79] In the face of Kiev's efforts to control Crimea and promote Ukrainization, the RPK-RDK and the idea of Crimean separatism became a defense against domination from the center.[80]

The second crisis occurred at the end of 1993 and came to a head in early 1994. The Crimean parliament voted to create a presidency of Crimea and set elections for the presidency for January 1994, moves that further radicalized Crimean politics.[81] In the initial round of voting, six candidates stood for office, though only one—Nikolai Bagrov—supported Crimea's continued status as a part of Ukraine.[82] Bagrov's political transformation was remarkable. As David Marples and David Duke observe, "The fact that the formerly troublesome Bagrov had now become a moderate in Crimean politics illustrates the polarization that had occurred in Crimean politics."[83] The second round featured a runoff election between Meshkov, representing the Russian nationalists and an ill-defined notion of separatism, and Bagrov, representing the old Soviet elite and the status quo. Meshkov defeated Bagrov handily, winning about 73% of the vote to Bagrov's paltry 23%.[84]

Fresh off his electoral victory, Meshkov used Crimea's institutional resources to distance Crimea further from Kiev. He announced a new referendum on the status of Crimea, installed a Russian citizen in the post of deputy prime minister, and put Crimea on Moscow's time zone.[85] In April of that year, parliamentary elections resulted in victory for Meshkov's party. The elections coincided with a "consultative opinion poll"—the referendum downgraded to a poll—that showed that overwhelming majorities supported further institutional moves toward separatism. In May, Simferopol reinstated the controversial 1992 constitution, further exacerbating tensions with Kiev.

The 1992 and 1994 crises were the outward signs of the profound degree of pro-Russian sentiment in Crimea. Whereas Crimea had once supported Ukraine's independence, ethnic mobilization and polarization in the face of Kiev's heavy-handed policies in Crimea helped turn the population in favor of nationalists like Meshkov. Thus, large segments of Crimea's population, represented by Meshkov and his party, could have acted as agents for foreign subversion against Ukraine during the pivotal years of 1992–95. This window of opportunity was not large: Crimea's separatist movement collapsed almost as quickly as it emerged. Meshkov's inability to deliver policies or even articulate a clear and precise solution for Crimea's social and economic woes led to the Russian movement's downfall. Yet while the movement existed, proxies in Crimea were available for foreign meddling. Recall, however, that my theory requires both policy incompatibility and agent availability. Though proxies were available in 1992–95, I have already shown that Russia lacked the motive to use them. I thus expect to observe no subversion during this time period.

Subversion

Subversion requires motive and means. Without motive, there is no reason to engage in this form of statecraft, and the foreign state will not subvert the target's state authority. Without means, the foreign state will lack the ability to undermine state authority. The cases bear out this prediction. As I show in this section, Russia subverted Georgia after 1999, but not Estonia from 1994 to the present or Ukraine from 1992 to 1995. Moscow's inability to undermine state authority in Estonia despite being highly motivated to do so points to the constraining power of agent availability in the target state. Meanwhile, the fact that Moscow declined to aid Crimean separatists attests to the importance of policy divergence as a precondition for subversion.

Georgia

In Georgia, we find the two essential ingredients for subversion: a highly motivated sponsor, bent on blocking Georgia's integration with Western institutions, and proxies on the ground willing to accept foreign support. Beginning with Putin's presidency in Russia and accelerating with Saakashvili's presidency in Georgia, the availability of both key ingredients for subversion resulted in Russia employing that instrument of statecraft against Tblisi.

Russian involvement in Georgia's breakaway provinces predated Mikheil Saa-kashvili's pro-Western presidency, but this involvement did not take the form of subversion before 1999. When the civil wars in Abkhazia and South Ossetia broke out in the early 1990s, Moscow sought to contain the conflicts, fearing spillover to the northern Caucasus.[86] This policy of containment rather than exploita-tion for subversion remained in place during the period of stable relations from 1993 to 1999. Russia imposed sanctions on Abkhazia in late 1993, encouraged the Abkhaz to compromise with the government, and tended to side with Georgian proposals for conflict resolution, such as Tbilisi's 1995 proposal for "asymmetri-cal federalism."[87] In 1996, Russia and the CIS presidents imposed a near-total blockade on Abkhazia in an attempt to coerce it into negotiations. While it is important not to overstate Russian interest in genuine conflict resolution, the 1990s were generally a period in which Russia did not seek to exacerbate Geor-gia's state authority problems. My theory attributes Russian restraint during that time to the relative foreign policy congruence between Moscow and Tbilisi.

All of that would change starting in 1999 when that congruence evaporated. After Georgia began signaling its desire to free itself from Moscow, Russia altered its policy toward the separatist republics from containment to active subversion. Russian activities to undermine Georgian state authority can be roughly sorted into two categories of proxy empowerment: efforts that treated the breakaway provinces as political entities distinct from Georgia proper, and efforts to build administrative structures in Abkhazia and South Ossetia. The former are exam-ples of political, diplomatic, and symbolic support, while the latter are examples of material support and capacity building. Both categories of activity under-mined Georgian state authority and prevented Tbilisi from consolidating control over its territory.

Russia's first acts of subversion followed Tbilisi's decision to leave the Collec-tive Security Treaty, the CIS's security arm, and close the Russian military bases on Georgian territory in 1999. Moscow announced a new visa regime for Georgians working in Russia, but in a move clearly designed to undermine Georgia's state authority, exempted residents of Abkhazia and South Ossetia.[88] In 2002, Rus-sia began handing out Russian passports in Abkhazia and South Ossetia.[89] After the 2003 Rose Revolution that brought Saakashvili to power, Moscow dramati-cally expanded the passport program. As with the visa program, the timing of Russian activities is illuminating. Ousted leader Eduard Shevardnadze resigned the presidency on November 23, 2003. Six days later, on November 29, Russian's minister of foreign affairs, Igor Ivanov, met with the leaders of Abkhazia and South Ossetia in Moscow and jointly agreed to accelerate passport distribution in their regions.[90] Perhaps more than any other form of subversion, the passport policy demonstrates the instrumental nature of subversion and the importance of agents on the ground regardless of kinship links. Neither the Abkhaz nor the South Ossetians were Slavs, much less Russians, and neither group spoke Russian. The passports thus played an important role by giving Russia political cover and pretext to cloak its subversion in the claims of intervention on behalf of its own citizens.[91]

Subversion also took the form of quasi-diplomatic recognition. In April 2005, for example, Foreign Minister Sergei Lavrov received the foreign ministers of Abkhazia and South Ossetia (as well as the foreign minister from Moldova's own separatist proto-state Transnistria) in Moscow as if they were the representatives of fully sovereign states. Shortly thereafter, Putin received President Sergey Bagapsh of Abkhazia and President Eduard Kokoity of South Ossetia at his Sochi residence.[92] In official speeches and communications, the Russian Foreign Ministry began to refer to Abkhazia and South Ossetia as "republics" and Bagapsh and Kokoity as "presidents."[93] By treating Abkhazia and South Ossetia as if they were recognized states, Moscow rhetorically and diplomatically reinforced their status as outside the authority of Tbilisi.

Russia also sought to pressure Georgia into abandoning Western integration by altering the facts of governance on the ground. In a dramatic shift from the 1990s-era policy of conflict containment, Moscow thwarted a possible peace deal between South Ossetia and Georgia by supporting Kokoity in South Ossetia's 2001 presidential elections. Kokoity was a professional wrestler and businessman as well as the proto-state's former trade representative to Moscow. Importantly, unlike previous leaders in South Ossetia, Kokoity opposed autonomy within Georgia in favor of legal independence, putting to rest any possibility that Georgia would peacefully reassert authority over South Ossetia.[94] Moscow similarly attempted to install its favored candidate, Raul Khadjimba, into Abkhazia's presidency in the 2004 elections. It ultimately notched a half victory, settling for a power-sharing agreement between Sergey Bagapsh, the actual victor at the polls, and Khadjimba.[95]

In addition to supporting pro-Russian leadership, Moscow also assisted its proxies in building and running state-like institutions. Abkhazia and South Ossetia would be ungoverned only in the sense that Tbilisi did not govern them. Moscow paid for a significant portion of the administrative budgets of both regions.[96] It provided expertise by installing former Russian officials in key administrative posts. It also helped the breakaway provinces obtain one of the most potent symbols of a sovereign state: well-armed militaries. Moscow offered extremely generous subsidies that paid for Abkhazia's and South Ossetia's militaries, with subsidies reaching half of Abkhazia's GDP and one and a half times South Ossetia's GDP.[97] As Russian-Georgian relations continued to deteriorate over Saakashvili's courtship of the West, Moscow also sent military equipment, arms, and ammunition at no cost to the republics. By 2008, Abkhazia and South Ossetia received more than twice the total amount of equipment held by all of Georgia.[98]

These combined efforts, which began in 1999 and expanded both qualitatively and quantitatively after the Rose Revolution, were clearly aimed at subverting Georgian state authority in an effort to alter Tbilisi's foreign policy trajectory. According to witnesses and Georgian officials, Putin and Saakashvili had candid if strained conversations in which Putin directly linked Russian involvement in the breakaway regions with the larger issue of Georgia's geopolitical orientation.[99] If Tbilisi expected Russian help in resolving issues, it needed to accommodate Russia's preference that Georgia stay out of the West. If it chose another course, it should not expect assistance. In early 2007, the Russian ambassador to Georgia, Vyacheslav Kovalenko, reiterated Russia's offer one last time: declare permanent neutrality and promise not to seek NATO membership in return for Russia's assistance in resolving Georgia's problems with Abkhazia and South Ossetia.[100] Tbilisi regarded these offers as little better than extortion and repeatedly rebuffed Moscow.

In subversion, Moscow wielded a powerful weapon that cemented Georgia's de facto division into governed and ungoverned spaces. As of 2018, Tbilisi administered only 80% of Georgian territory; the rest remained outside the state's authority. Georgian state officials have no access to territory that is juridically part of their own country. The 2014 census excluded Abkhazia and South Ossetia, and government statistics for both regions have disappeared from the reports of the National Statistics Office. Tbilisi cannot levy taxes from either region. Though ungoverned from the perspective of Tbilisi, Abkhazia and South Ossetia are not without government. Both act as de facto states. With cooperation from Moscow, they operate checkpoints and exercise passport and custom controls between their territory and Georgian-administered territory, as if the internal boundary were an international border. They conduct economic transactions using the Russian ruble rather than the Georgian lari, though Abkhazia produces its own currency, the apsar. Education, health, and policing are under the authority of the unrecognized governments in Sukhumi and Tskhinvali, not Tbilisi.

Russian subversion took a powerful toll on Georgian state authority. Though Moscow's actions have not been costless—it continues to provide financial support for Abkhazia and South Ossetia—the price Russia paid in the international arena for its actions against Georgia in the 2000s was quite low. Compared to the widespread condemnation and the onslaught of economic sanctions that it provoked in 2014 for utilizing a more conventional tool of statecraft in its annexation of Crimea, subversion was a bargain, one of the instrument's key advantages over the use of force. While subversion in fact strengthened Tbilisi's preferences for Western integration, it also frustrated Georgia's prospects for realizing those preferences.[101] Crippling the Georgian leviathan effectively stalled NATO and EU membership for the foreseeable future. Moreover, undermining Georgia's state authority forced Tbilisi to expend significant amounts of political energy and capital that it could have devoted to other activities.[102] In this sense, subversion was a resounding success.

Despite the potency of this instrument of statecraft, Russia chose to employ it against Georgia only when it became apparent that the two states had irreconcilable and diametrically opposed policy preferences regarding the latter's geopolitical orientation. As long as Tbilisi behaved deferentially toward Moscow, Russia did not actively work to inflame Georgia's separatist problems, even if it could have been more helpful in promoting their resolution. Once Tbilisi decided on a full-fledged embrace of the West, however, Moscow reversed course and sought to undermine state authority, and it expanded and accelerated its subversive activities after the Rose Revolution. That Moscow could engage in subversion at all was a function of the availability of willing proxies on the ground. The Abkhaz and the South Ossetians had already defied Tbilisi's authority, but Russian subversion significantly worsened the situation and further weakened the Georgian state. By empowering and cooperating with both groups, Moscow effectively impeded state consolidation in Georgia. This case thus supports my argument about the conditions that influence the use of subversion: states must have both the motivation to undermine state authority and the means on the ground in the target to do so.

Estonia

Estonia's move toward European integration was incompatible with Russia's preference that it and the Baltic states remain out of the Western orbit. My theory predicts that Russia would therefore seek to empower local agents, if available, to undermine Estonia's state authority as a means to alter Estonia's behavior. Because subversion relies on delegation to proxies, subversion should occur only when both motive and means are present. While the Estonian case features no shortage of motive, the absence of agents meant that the means were unavailable. As expected, I observe no instance of territorial subversion against Estonia.

Russia's failure to degrade Estonia's state authority is not for lack of interest. As previously discussed, the northeastern region of Estonia was home to a large population of ethnic Russians that constituted a minority within the new state. Unlike Georgia and Ukraine, Estonia moderated its state- and nationbuilding policies so as to balance between the state's desire that the ethnic Russians assimilate and the ethnic Russians' desire to preserve their culture and identity. Finding no willing proxies in Estonia's Northeast, Moscow attempted to create them by politicizing Estonia's minority issue. If Estonian Russians did not feel marginalized, Russian policy would help them "realize" their ill treatment at the hands of the titular majority.

To achieve this objective, Moscow hijacked the rhetoric of human rights and humanitarianism to criticize Tallinn for its treatment of the Russian minority. The Russian government denounced abuses perpetrated on ethnic kin in Estonia and the Baltics in public addresses, in parliament debates, and in international forums like the Organization for Security and Cooperation in Europe.[103] Russian state television, available to viewers in northeastern Estonia, regularly depicted the region as a victim of Estonian nationalism.[104] Many ethnic Estonians apparently shared Russia's faith that this strategy would work, claiming that the ethnic Russians were susceptible to propaganda and would be fifth columnists in the event of a military crisis.[105]

Why was Moscow so intent on creating proxies? Its overarching foreign policy goal was to stop Estonia's integration with the West. It could achieve this by altering Tallinn's preferences or by rendering the country unattractive as a candidate for NATO and the EU. Subversion would provide the means to either outcome. By crippling the state authority of a target country, subversion imposes costs on governance in the target country that provides the sponsor with bargaining leverage and punishes the target state. The disorder and ungoverned spaces that result are also an end in themselves. Short of invading Estonia or employing conventional force to change Tallinn's mind about integration, Moscow had to resort to more indirect policy instruments like subversion. For that, it needed proxies.

The policy incompatibility between Russia and Estonia widened even more after the three Baltic states acceded to NATO, and even after conditions for Estonia's Russian population improved further. Now the political objective was to drive a wedge between the Baltics and the West, and to punish the Baltics for joining NATO. Estonia's lack of proxies remained an obstacle for Moscow, and it continued to wage a propaganda campaign to mobilize Estonia's Russian population. In its 2005 annual report, the Estonian Internal Security Service described efforts by Russia's Department for Interregional and Cultural Ties with Foreign Countries to manipulate Estonia's Russians into revolting against the state.[106] In 2008, in an attempt to stoke domestic tensions, Russian news agencies falsely reported stories about Russian villages in Estonia seeking independence.[107]

Although Moscow tried to gain political cover for its activities by draping them in the language of rights and the protection of minorities, it was less interested in helping Russians "stranded abroad" and more interested in exploiting them as proxies for subversion. Two pieces of evidence point toward this interpretation. First, there has been little concrete evidence to support Russian accusations of repression and mistreatment. It is true that Estonia's new laws sought to exclude the nontitular minority from political participation, but the international community did not substantiate Moscow's wilder claims of discrimination.[108] Second, Moscow was quite selective about whose cause it took up. The Yeltsin administration ignored entreaties from Crimea's Russians and also turned a blind eye to anti-Russian discrimination in Kazakhstan. We also saw in the previous section that Russia came to the aid of Georgia's Abkhaz and Ossetian populations, even though they are neither ethnic Russians nor Russian speaking—more evidence of Russia's instrumental approach to minority issues.[109] As Charles King and Neil Melvin have observed, "In no case did the Russian government act on behalf of its diaspora unless its broader interests were served, a fact that militant nationalists . . . severely criticized."[110] Certainly some Russian politicians felt genuine concern for coethnics in Estonia. However, the government behaved much more strategically and followed the logic of "the enemy of my enemy is my friend."

Moscow's campaign to create proxies for subversion where none existed has yet to bear fruit in Estonia. Even after years of misinformation and propaganda, Russians in Estonia's Northeast do not oppose the Estonian state, and have not mobilized against it. A 2013 study of Narva's Russian population found that they were "politically fractured, disengaged, and unincorporated" but nonetheless identified Estonia or Narva as their homeland rather than Russia.[111] They recognize that Estonia's membership in the European Union affords them numerous privileges that would be lost if they supported a campaign to thwart state authority or detach the region from the country. Despite the fears of Estonia's more nationalistic politicians, the country's ethnic minority has not been a fifth column, and has little desire to act as one.

This failure to cultivate agents and the resulting absence of Russian subversion against Estonia illustrate the importance of agent availability as a condition for subversion. Moscow had ample motive to undermine Estonian state authority in its quest to block Tallinn's integration with the West. But political will is not enough. It needs to be coupled to means, and means cannot be conjured out of thin air. Without proxies on Estonian territory, subversion was a tool absent from Russia's foreign policy toolkit. The Estonian case thus illuminates why such a potent instrument of statecraft is not deployed more frequently in international relations: subversion depends crucially on agents that cannot easily be manufactured when they do not exist.

Ukraine

Whereas Estonia from 1994 to the present exemplifies the case of motive without means, Ukraine from 1992 to 1995 exemplifies the case of means without motive.

In both cases, one crucial condition is absent, leading me to predict an absence of subversion. Like Estonia, Ukraine bears out this prediction.

In the early 1990s, Moscow had ample opportunity to cultivate proxies in Ukraine to deploy in the service of pursuing its foreign policy aims. Center-periphery issues and Kiev's attempt to Ukrainize Crimea's population stoked tensions that Crimean nationalists exploited in a bid for independence. Yet Moscow refrained from capitalizing on those tensions. Recall that the Yeltsin administration generally supported Kiev's position that Crimea should remain within Ukraine, and it did not encourage the nationalists to statebuild in defiance of Kiev's authority.[112] In fact, when Crimean president Yuriy Meshkov arrived in Moscow in 1994 seeking Russian guarantees for Crimea should it break from Ukraine, Yeltsin and Prime Minister Viktor Chernomyrdin refused to meet with him. Official Moscow's cold reception and unwillingness to entertain Meshkov's requests for support caused Meshkov to moderate his demands.[113] Even when faced with a direct request for assistance from a would-be proxy in a region with historic ties to Russia, Moscow chose not to undermine Ukrainian state authority over Crimea.

Why do we observe no subversion against Ukraine during the 1992–95 period? The means of subversion were available, so proxy absence cannot explain it. Instead my theory suggests that we should examine Moscow's motives—or lack thereof. However, establishing that a condition (policy incompatibility) is necessary for shaping an outcome (subversion) is challenging when the outcome does not occur. To do so, I show the absence of motive, and I also consider and rule out alternative explanations for the absence of subversion.

First, as a baseline condition, I expect to observe a lack of motive. As I argued in chapter 2, states reserve subversion as an instrument of statecraft for only the most important foreign policy issues. Until 1996, there is little evidence that Kiev and Moscow seriously diverged on the matter of Ukraine's geostrategic orientation, the issue most central in Russian foreign policy. Several developments that would later strain the Ukrainian-Russian relationship, such as Ukraine's participation in NATO's Membership Action Plan in 1999 and the Orange Revolution in 2004, did not occur during the window in which proxies were available.

Second, I examine alternative explanations for the absence of subversion against Ukraine as a way to assess the importance of motive in the subversion calculation. Two explanations are worth considering. On the domestic political front, Yeltsin faced a political challenge from nationalists who objected to his liberalizing policies. Nationalists in the Russian Duma were almost certainly motivated by genuine concern for the plight of their coethnics in Crimea, which was exacerbated by Russian angst over the loss of Crimea and the city of Sevastopol. Yeltsin's domestic opposition politicized the issue as a weapon against him. Had he acquiesced to their pressure, it would have handed the opposition a significant political victory that very well could have obviated any short-term political benefits to Yeltsin himself.

However, Russian domestic politics on its own does not explain why Russia did not wield subversion in pursuit of its foreign policy objectives with Ukraine. After Russia's own constitutional crisis of 1993, Yeltsin defeated his nationalist opposition. The new parliament established after the constitutional crisis was more moderate and cautious toward Crimea than its virulently nationalist predecessor.[114] The Yeltsin administration did adjust its foreign policy objectives, putting greater emphasis on the post-Soviet space as a concession to the nationalists. Even though Yeltsin had a freer hand and a more moderate parliament, and could have supported Crimea's pro-Russian groups without fears of strengthening his domestic opposition, his administration refused to subvert Ukraine's state authority. Although it is possible that the political environment constrained Yeltsin's ability to intervene in Crimean affairs prior to 1994, the more permissive conditions thereafter cannot explain the failure to subvert Ukraine at that time.

Another alternative explanation concerns the potential for spillover, particularly with respect to the North Caucasus. Like other post-Soviet states, Russia was a multiethnic country. Russia's Chechens, denied their own nation-state, mobilized to demand national self-determination in the late 1980s. Thus, Russia faced its own secessionist threat. It could be that Russia avoided subversion in Ukraine not because of the absence of foreign policy incompatibility with Kiev, but because it feared that its interference in Crimea could stir up similar troubles in Chechnya and elsewhere in the North Caucasus. While concerns about Chechnya certainly influenced Russian thinking once the war began in late 1994, it is unlikely that these concerns fully account for Russia's unwillingness to subvert Ukraine when the window to do so remained open.[115] Indeed, as we saw in the previous section, Moscow showed no compunction when it came to the defense of Estonia's Russian minority. Its accusations of Estonian mistreatment of the Russian population there, which coincided with the Chechen wars of the 1990s, bordered on the hyperbolic. But they also coincided with motive, which was lacking in the Ukrainian case. Indeed, James Hughes and Gwendolyn Sasse attribute Russia's limited involvement in Crimea to Russia's preference at that time for accommodation with the West—or, in the language of my theory, a lack of policy incompatibility.[116]

My theory suggests that Russia did not engage in subversion against Ukraine because it lacked the motivation to do so. Put differently, one of the two crucial conditions for subversion was missing. Indeed, this case illustrates that even when proxies were available in the form of Meshkov and the pro-Russian movement in Crimea, Russia did not move to cripple the Ukrainian state. This failure to act points to the importance of motivation in conditioning the use of subversion.

Motive, Means, and Subversion from the Baltics to the Steppe

This chapter has thus far focused on Georgia, Estonia, and Ukraine as lenses into the factors that condition the use of subversion as a foreign policy instrument. Georgia from 1999 onward featured both motive and means. Estonia from 1994 to the present featured motive without means. Ukraine from 1992 to 1995 featured means without motive. Only in the Georgian case did we observe Russia deploying subversion. These cases also act as lenses into the remaining Russia/post-Soviet-state dyads. I expect that the dyads that take on the same combination of values on these conditions as the equivalent cases studied in depth in this chapter will follow the same logic and process as those cases. While it is not possible to consider all the post-Soviet states in detail, this section briefly surveys the remaining dyads. Table 4.2 summarizes each grouping of cases.

TABLE 4.2   Classification of post-Soviet cases

	INCOMPATIBILITY	NO INCOMPATIBILITY
Agents available	***Georgia 1999–present***	**Ukraine 1992–95**
	Moldova 2004–present	Azerbaijan 1992–present[a]
	Ukraine 2014–present	Estonia 1992–94
	Subversion expected	Georgia 1992–98
		Kazakhstan 1992–late 1990s
		Latvia 1992–94
		Moldova 1992–2003
		Tajikistan 1992–97
		No subversion expected
No agents available	**Estonia 1994–present**	Armenia 1992–present
	Latvia 1994–present	Belarus 1992–present
	Lithuania 1994–present	Kazakhstan late 1990s–present
	No subversion expected	Kyrgyzstan 1992–present
		Lithuania 1992–94
		Tajikistan 1998–present
		Turkmenistan 1992–present
		Ukraine 1996–2014
		Uzbekistan 1992–present
		No subversion expected

Notes: Bold indicates a case studied in depth in this chapter. Italics indicates Russian subversion observed.

[a] Subversion occurred in this case, but the sponsor state was Armenia, a state with a policy incompatibility with Azerbaijan.

Policy Incompatibility, Agents Available

The only countries in the post-Soviet space where Russia was motivated to undermine state authority and where it found willing proxies to assist in those efforts are precisely the countries where subversion occurred. These countries appear in the northwest cell of table 4.2, and include Moldova from 2004 to the present and Ukraine since 2014. Like Georgia, Moldova also sought to escape the Russian orbit. Although it joined the CIS under duress, it refused to participate in initiatives that sought to bind member states closer to Russia, and it resisted Russian efforts to force it into other regional institutions. In contrast to its cautious behavior toward the Russian sphere, Moldova has been indiscriminate in its zeal for acquiring membership in Western-led organizations, from the Council of Europe to the Balkan Security Pact to La Francophonie.[117] EU membership has been elusive, though not for lack of trying. After President Vladimir Voronin reoriented the country's foreign policy toward the West in 2004, Moldova began forming closer ties with Brussels. As preliminary as these steps have been, Russia recognized the warning signs and sought to block Chișinău's drift toward the West.

Moscow's primary instrument of leverage was its proxies in Transnistria, Moldova's breakaway republic. Transnistria won de facto statehood after a brief civil war around the time of Moldova's independence that saw the intervention of Russia's Fourteenth Army on behalf of Transnistria. Prior to Moldova's reorientation toward Europe, Russia acted as an "older brother" to Moldova in its efforts to resolve the conflict in Transnistria.[118] This tendency toward conflict containment parallels Russia's role in containing and constraining Georgia's breakaway republics before 1999. After the 2004 realignment, the foreign policy gulf that emerged between Russia and Moldova was wide enough to motivate Russia into "switching sides" on Transnistria. Whereas it had once worked to reintegrate Transnistria into Moldova—and, in turn, secure terms friendly to Russia's geopolitical interests—it now sided with Transnistria against Moldova and its new Western backers. As with Georgia, Moscow's support for Transnistria allowed the region to survive outside Chișinău's control. By no means was this outcome inevitable. Until Moscow was sufficiently motivated to engage in subversion, it did not actively undermine Moldovan state authority, despite the presence of proxies in Transnistria. Only when Chișinău rejected the Russian geopolitical embrace did Moscow turn Transnistria into a weapon. This case thus illustrates the importance of motive in combination with available means for subversion.

Ukraine since 2014 also bears similarities to Georgia. Like Georgia, Ukraine underwent a "color" revolution in 2004, but unlike Georgia's, Ukraine's revolution did not immediately produce or accelerate a turn to the West. Ukraine's fractious domestic politics did serve up a three-way internal rivalry that left Ukraine suspended between Russia and the West. As Dmitri Trenin has observed, the issue was that "most Ukrainians do not want to be a part of Russia, but they do not want to part with Russia, either."[119] This state of affairs suited Moscow just fine. Until the Euromaidan Revolution in 2014 that ousted pro-Russian president Viktor Yanukovych, Moscow had little need to impair Ukrainian state authority. Ambiguity about its future kept Ukraine neither in the West nor with Russia. The Euromaidan protests, however, set the stage for Ukraine to bolt for the West by eliminating this ambiguity. The Donbas and Crimean regions of Ukraine rejected the Euromaidan movement's call for closer political and economic ties to Europe in favor of stronger ties with Russia. They also resented the actions of the Ukrainian parliament; immediately after the revolution, the parliament voted to repeal a law that granted the Russian language the privileged status of a regional language. Thus, agents once again emerged in Ukrainian society, this time in the Russian-speaking East. With both motive and means in place in 2014, Russia annexed Crimea and subverted Ukrainian authority in Donbas.[120] The state that had seemed to escape the chaos and conflict of the early 1990s found itself engulfed in war and denied authority over its own territory.

Moldova since 2004 and Ukraine since 2014 both follow the same patterns as Georgia. When these states pursued foreign policies that prioritized integration with the West and disassociation from the Russian sphere, the resulting gulf in policy preferences provided Russia with the motivation to subvert. Similarly, both states had proxies available for that subversion. The agents in South Ossetia, Abkhazia, and Transnistria had fought a civil war against the governments in Georgia and Moldova, but Ukraine demonstrates that agents can appear even without the precondition of civil war. Together, Moldova and Ukraine and the in-depth discussion of Georgia support my claim that both motive and means condition the use of subversion.

Policy Incompatibility, No Agents Available

The cases of policy incompatibility where agents were unavailable are few in the post-Soviet space. They include Latvia and Lithuania from 1994 to the present; their similarities to Estonia are considerable enough that many analysts treat them as a group (the southwest cell of table 4.2). Like Estonia, Latvia and Lithuania made Western integration their foreign policy priority after 1994, putting them at odds with Moscow. As with Estonia, the lack of subversion against Latvia and Lithuania can be attributed to the absence of willing proxy groups on the ground. Lithuania had fewer Russians as a proportion of its population, and its policies toward its minorities were more liberal than those of its Baltic neighbors to the north. Vilnius avoided provoking nationalistic grievances by opting for the zero option of automatic citizenship for all residents. Though it did adopt a law privileging the Lithuanian language, the country's Russians recognized the inevitability of transitioning from Russian to Lithuanian and began making preparations for integration.[121] Latvia's Russians were territorially concentrated in the region of Latgale, and Latvia followed Estonia's example by first failing to grant automatic citizenship to its Russians and later liberalizing its policies. Although its Russians were deprived of some political rights due to their lack of citizenship, Latvia's extension of nonpolitical human rights and opportunities for economic advancement in the Latvian private sector functioned as a safety valve for the Russian community's frustrations.[122]

In none of the Baltic states could Moscow identify agents for subversion. Even though Estonia and Latvia had considerable numbers of Russians while Lithuania did not, moderate state- and nationbuilding policies from 1994 onward avoided stoking the kinds of grievances that mobilized agents in other cases. Even though all three countries antagonized Moscow with their determination to embrace the U.S.-led liberal order, Russia was unable to employ subversion against them. Together, these three cases support my argument that both motive and means are necessary for subversion to occur.

No Policy Incompatibility, Agents Available

The third set of cases are those with foreign policy alignment with Moscow and available agents (the northeast cell of table 4.2). These cases are Estonia from 1992 to 1994, Latvia from 1992 to 1994, Tajikistan from 1992 to 1997, Kazakhstan from 1992 to 1995, and Azerbaijan since independence. This set also includes Georgia and Moldova, which we have already encountered, but for the periods before 1999 and 2004, respectively.

I begin with Estonia and Latvia. We have already seen in our previous discussion of Estonia that the country's early foreign policy congruence with Russia was an artifact of the constraints it faced due to the presence of Russian troops on its territory. Latvia was in a similar bind. Until both countries could secure a troop-withdrawal agreement with Moscow, neither could risk provoking Russia with a full-fledged attempt to integrate with the West. Similarly, though both countries had territorially concentrated and marginalized Russian minorities, the window during which they were mobilized and politically organized was open only briefly in the early 1990s—and did not coincide with the period of policy incompatibility that would later characterize both states.

Unlike the two Baltic states, Kazakhstan and Tajikistan have freely pursued foreign policies that aligned them closely with Moscow. They joined Russian-led regional organizations like the Collective Security Treaty Organization, the Eurasian Economic Community, and the Eurasian Economic Union. Kazakhstan has been an especially enterprising partner in regional institution building, and has pushed for greater integration not only between itself and Russia, but in the post-Soviet space more generally.[123] Tajikistan too dutifully signed up for new institutional memberships whenever the opportunity arose. Both have forged important links with Russia in matters of economic and security cooperation, and neither state has shown much interest in integration with the West at Russia's expense.

Both countries also experienced moments in which their nontitular groups could have acted as the agents of Russian subversion. Kazakhstan gained its independence with the distinction of being the only post-Soviet country in which the titular group was a minority in its new state. Russians outnumbered Kazakhs, and they formed political associations that worked to defend the cultural distinctiveness and rights of ethnic Russians. Their activism was short lived, however. Mass emigration to Russia, the movement of Kazakhstan's capital from Almaty to Astana in 1997, and the failure of the associations to cooperate with each other led to their virtual disappearance from political life.[124]

Unlike Kazakhstan, potential proxies in Tajikistan were well organized under the banner of the United Tajik Opposition (UTO), an alliance of antiregime forces that formed to wage a civil war against the government in Dushanbe. Though agents were available during the course of the war, Russia had little interest in engaging in subversion, instead intervening on behalf of the incumbent government in Dushanbe. In 1997, the UTO and the Tajik state struck a peace deal that provided for their incorporation into government, politics, and the military. This settlement eliminated the UTO as a potential proxy for subversion.

Compared to Tajikistan and Kazakhstan, Azerbaijan has tried to strike a balance between Russia and the West. For the most part, it has succeeded. Although it is a member of the CIS, it withdrew from the Collective Security Treaty Organization and cofounded GU(U)AM, the regional organization meant to offer an alternative to the CIS. It actively diversified its external relations beyond Russia, seen most clearly in its support for the Baku-Tbilisi-Ceyhan (BTC) pipeline project that opened in 2006. The BTC is a massive crude-oil pipeline that carries Azerbaijani oil through Georgia to Turkey's Mediterranean coast; a gas pipeline that runs parallel to the BTC but terminates in Erzerum later followed. By bypassing Russian territory entirely, the pipelines provide for considerable geopolitical independence from Russia. Without Baku's own support, it is unlikely that the U.S.-backed BTC project would have gotten off the ground at all.[125] The project thus symbolized a triumph for U.S. diplomacy and an apex of U.S. relations with Baku.

Yet Azerbaijan has deftly kept its balance between Russia and the West despite carving out an independent foreign policy. Even as it formed diplomatic and energy links with the West, Baku understood the geopolitical realities of its Caucasus neighborhood. It publicly denied any ambitions of joining NATO, and it continued to offer concessions and assurances to Russia.[126] For example, Azerbaijan became an important partner in the proposed North–South Transport Corridor, which would link Russia to India and improve trade connectivity for the economies on the route. Baku also increased bilateral trade and investment ties with Russia. As the Eurasian expert Svante Cornell has observed, personal politics also played an important role in smoothing relations between Russia and Azerbaijan.[127] Azerbaijan's former president, Heydar Aliyev, struck up a close relationship with Vladimir Putin that built at least in part on their shared background in the KGB, the Soviet Union's security service.

The availability of agents in Azerbaijan means that Russia has the opportunity to stir up trouble if it should so desire. Azerbaijan does not exercise authority over the region of Nagorno-Karabakh, a breakaway republic whose unrecognized government could be the agent of subversion. As with South Ossetia and Abkhazia in Georgia, Russian involvement cannot explain the emergence of the conflict in Karabakh. Yet the parallels between Georgia and Azerbaijan, at least with respect to Russian relations with the separatist republics, end there. As a member of the Organization for Security and Cooperation in Europe's Minsk Group, a multilateral conflict-resolution effort, Moscow has certainly been in a position to obstruct or facilitate the peace process. While it has not been particularly helpful with Karabakh, Russia has not embarked on a program of building state structures of administration and coercion—the bread and butter of subversion. Rather, on Karabakh Russia has taken a back seat to another player in the region: Armenia. Yerevan is so heavily invested in the fate of Armenian-populated Karabakh that Armenia's elite equates Armenia's national interest with the interests of Karabakh.[128] Armenian subversion rather than Russian subversion permits Karabakh's survival as a space outside Baku's administration.[129] The lack of Russian involvement in subversion is a consequence of Baku's geopolitical balancing act between Russia and the West.

In none of these cases do we observe subversion. Whereas the previous set of cases featured an absence of means and an absence of subversion, the present set feature an absence of motive and an absence of subversion. Thus, these cases again support my theoretical claims that both policy incompatibility and agent availability condition the use of subversion.

No Policy Incompatibility, No Agents Available

The fourth group of cases, representing the southeast cell in table 4.2, are those exhibiting foreign policy convergence and a lack of available agents. This group includes Armenia, Belarus, Kyrgyzstan, Turkmenistan, and Uzbekistan since independence. It also includes countries we have already encountered but observed in different periods: Kazakhstan since the late 1990s (following the gradual depoliticization of the Russian associations), Tajikistan since 1998 (following the conclusion of the civil war), and Ukraine from 1996 to 2014 (following the collapse of the Crimean separatist movement). Lithuania before 1994 falls into this group as well, having enjoyed relatively warm relations with Moscow on account of farsighted decisions to settle the troop-withdrawal issue quickly and to grant Russia access to its military bases in the exclave of Kaliningrad.

Like Kazakhstan and Tajikistan, Armenia, Belarus, and Kyrgyzstan pursued foreign policies that aligned them closely with Moscow. They joined the rapidly proliferating set of Russian-led regional clubs and they struck close security and economic ties with Russia. These relationships have not been without their difficulties, but Moscow has generally tolerated frictions so long as its partners demonstrated fealty on the issue of foreign policy orientation. For example, Tajikistan successfully exploited Moscow's fears about a recidivist slide back into instability in order to extract more military assistance. Belarus's attempts to extort Moscow for concessions have been even more nakedly transparent.[130] Kyrgyzstan allowed the United States to open an air base at Manas International Airport with Russia's blessing, but failed to close it down per its commitment to do so. These are irritants, but small ones. They are the price Moscow pays in return for solidarity in the post-Soviet space against the liberal international order. Armenia, Belarus, Kazakhstan, Kyrgyzstan, and Tajikistan, like Ukraine until 2014, have given Moscow little motivation to engage in foreign subversion.

Uzbekistan and Turkmenistan have had more complicated relations with Moscow than their Central Asian neighbors. Uzbekistan has never quite decided whether it will allow itself to be a part of the Russian sphere. It is a member of the CIS, but in 1997 joined with Azerbaijan, Georgia, Ukraine, and Moldova to form GU(U)AM. By 2005, Tashkent had a change of heart and withdrew its membership. It joined the Eurasian Economic Community but later left. It founded the Collective Security Treaty with Russia, Armenia, and the four Central Asian states, but suspended its membership twice. Turkmenistan has opted for a somewhat different strategy of managing relations with Moscow by declaring its doctrine of "positive neutrality." In practice, Ashgabat has eschewed most multilateral cooperation, particularly with the CIS, and its bilateral political and economic cooperation with Moscow has fluctuated in intensity.[131] Both countries treat Russia with some ambivalence, but this ambivalence has not translated into a desire to join the West.[132] While Uzbekistan and Turkmenistan have proved more prickly than the other post-Soviet states, Moscow has been willing to overlook or ignore rhetoric from both countries so long as they did not directly challenge Russia's geopolitical dominance.

In none of these cases during these time periods were agents available for subversion. To be clear, a lack of agents does not mean that minorities enjoyed cultural rights and a climate free of discrimination. Rather, to the extent that these populations did experience discrimination and oppression, these grievances did not morph into the kind of political mobilization that we witnessed in Georgia, Moldova, or even Ukraine in the early 1990s and again in 2014. In Uzbekistan, a militant group called the Islamic Movement of Uzbekistan formed in the late 1990s with the stated goal of overthrowing the autocratic government of President Islam Karimov, but quickly decamped abroad to attack more appealing targets elsewhere in Central Asia. As we have already seen, in Kazakhstan Russian associations virtually vanished from political life, instead confining themselves to cultural activities.[133] In Turkmenistan, the regime abused and oppressed its ethnic Russian and Uzbek populations to such a degree that tens of thousands of Russians emigrated while many Uzbeks attempted to change their official nationality to become Turkmen.[134] Though ethnic tensions between Uzbeks and Kyrgyz sometimes flare in Kyrgyzstan, agents have not appeared there that could be directed against state authority. Nor have potential proxies reappeared in Tajikistan. Homogeneous Armenia escaped the problem of nationbuilding in a diverse state. In Belarus, which had no territories with strong non-Russian national identity and where Russian remains the dominant language, identity politics have not been salient.[135]

Because my theory holds that both motive and means condition subversion, it is not surprising that we observe no subversion in the cases where both factors are absent. Still, these cases are useful for providing additional evidence that subversion occurs only when states have both the will to undermine state authority and the capability in the form of proxies to do so.

The Politics of Subversion

Although this survey of the remaining countries in the post-Soviet space has been necessarily brief, it is still valuable for learning about the politics of subversion. The commonalities between the cases allow me to examine one case from each cell of table 4.2, excluding the southwest cell where motive and means are both absent, and assume that the remaining cases that take on similar values follow the same logic as the exemplar case. Indeed, in cases like Kazakhstan and Uzbekistan, where the policy distance with Moscow was small and Moscow therefore lacked motivation to subvert, I observe a situation like that of Ukraine in the 1990s: no political interference in territorial state authority. In cases such as Latvia and Lithuania, where foreign policy divergence provided motivation but where the means of subversion were unavailable, subversion did not occur, just as we saw in Estonia after 1994. Finally, in cases where the policy distance was large and where agents were available, such as Moldova after 2004, the outcome mirrors that of Georgia after 1999, where Russia wielded subversion to considerable harmful effect. The evidence across the post-Soviet space thus supports my arguments about the importance of motive and means for the use of subversion.

Lessons from the Post-Soviet Experience

The medium-n analysis in this chapter, which built on an in-depth examination of Ukraine, Estonia, and Georgia and a briefer survey of the remaining countries in the post-Soviet space, has borne out my expectation that states engage in subversion when both motive and means are present. My focus on the former Soviet Union allowed me to hold constant the policy space over which state preferences converge or diverge while exploiting variation in the conditions of motives and means. I have also built on the large-n quantitative analysis in chapter 3 by directly showing the link between the conditions that facilitate subversion and the deployment of subversion as a policy instrument. From an evidentiary standpoint, then, this chapter has tested propositions from the theoretical discussion in chapter 2 while also filling in an unobserved component from the statistical analysis in chapter 3.

The evidence reveals several important takeaways. First, the cases show that motive and means must coincide together. Though it was highly motivated, Russia did not subvert Estonia because it could not find agents on the ground. If motive were the entirety of the subversion story, then Estonia would have been a most likely case for subversion. Tallinn unabashedly courted the West. Its ambitions to integrate and its strategic objective of escaping Russian influence were nakedly apparent. Furthermore, the prospect of Estonia and the other Baltic states joining NATO was psychologically and geopolitically toxic to Moscow. Accession would have brought the military alliance to Russia's western doorstep. Despite Moscow's efforts to find proxies, none were available in Estonia. Russia thus could not and did not employ subversion against Estonia.

Nor did Russia act in the early 1990s to undermine Ukraine's state consolidation efforts over Crimea. If means were the entirety of the subversion story, and states opportunistically sowed chaos, then Ukraine from 1992 to 1995 would have been a most likely case. Ukrainians and Russians are closely linked. Given their shared history and kinship ties, Russian intervention was more likely in Ukraine than in any other part of the post-Soviet space. Crimean president Yuriy

Meshkov certainly thought so when he directly appealed to Moscow for assistance. However, because of Kiev's geopolitical congruence with Moscow, Moscow had little motivation to subvert, and declined to intervene until both motive and means were present in 2014.

Only when Moscow had both motive and means did it actually employ subversion as an instrument of foreign policy. This was the case with Georgia. By helping the Abkhaz and Ossetians build administrative and coercive institutions, Moscow undermined Georgian state authority and impeded state consolidation efforts. Neither the Abkhaz nor the Ossetians have ethnic ties to Russia, nor are they colinguists. Russian subversion against Georgia thus demonstrates that the identity of proxies matters less than their availability and willingness to cooperate with a foreign sponsor.

The evidence from across the post-Soviet space points to a second important lesson that supports the arguments advanced in chapter 2's theoretical discussion. Like the conventional use of force, subversion is an instrument of statecraft that one deploys against adversaries—states with which the policy disagreements are considerable and difficult to reconcile. As we see in the cases discussed in this chapter, Moscow's relationships with the post-Soviet states are not frictionless. Uzbekistan and Azerbaijan follow independent foreign policies. Belarus and Tajikistan extract concessions from Russia. Yet at least with respect to foreign policy orientation, ambiguity suits Moscow well enough. Where Moscow encountered states whose commitments to Western integration were firm, and whose preferences were unlikely to be reconciled with Russia's, it chose to employ one of the most potent and punitive instruments in its policy toolkit.

A third lesson that emerges from the evidence in this chapter is the difficulty of creating agents. Proxies are crucial to the operation of subversion. They offer plausible deniability and political cover, and they carry out the dirty work of weakening state authority. However, the Estonia case demonstrates that proxies cannot be easily manufactured out of thin air. Russian attempts to mobilize Estonia's Russian population against Tallinn as an agent of subversion have failed completely. It is no small irony that the very minorities that Estonian elites once feared were fifth columnists for Russia refused to be mobilized by a hostile foreign power.

These last two lessons thus point to the limits of subversion. The evidence in this chapter shows when states are likely to wield subversion as an instrument of statecraft, and which states are likely to do so. The evidence also shows why subversion is not more frequently deployed in international relations. The coincidence of motives and means, where the threshold for motive is high and where the means already exist, places a high bar on subversion's use. We should not, however, confuse the frequency of subversion with its pernicious effects on state authority. The next two chapters examine the impact of subversion on governance and state administration through case studies of the Philippines in the 1970s and Vietnamese-occupied Cambodia in the 1980s. Together, these chapters show that subversion considerably weakens state authority and impedes state consolidation over territory.

UNDERMINING STATE AUTHORITY IN THE PHILIPPINES

Foreign subversion weakens the state and prevents state consolidation. Chapter 2 laid out an argument about the effects of subversion on state authority and theorized about the conditions that affect its use in international relations. The empirical strategy thus far has sought to test this theory in two ways. First, because subversion is hard to observe directly, the statistical analysis in chapter 3 established a relationship between the factors that influence the use of subversion—policy incompatibility and proxy availability—and state weakness, the predicted outcome of subversion. The large-n statistical analysis allowed me to control for a number of potential confounders and address the issue of reverse causality, while also improving generalizability through cross-case analysis. The benefits of this approach came with some trade-offs. I was not able to capture subversion in the statistical analysis, nor could I probe causal mechanisms. For that reason, the second component of my empirical strategy linked policy incompatibility and proxy availability to the use of subversion by examining Russian interference in the post-Soviet space. This task formed an important step in the evidentiary chain and tested propositions from my theory about when states engage in subversion.

This chapter and the following chapter together constitute the third part of my empirical strategy. Using case-study evidence from two Southeast Asian countries during the Cold War, I link subversion to state weakness, thereby completing the evidentiary chain begun in chapter 3. I also take advantage of qualitative approaches to illustrate causal mechanisms in a way that was not possible in the large-n statistical analysis. This evidence builds on and complements the evidence in chapters 3 and 4 while compensating for the limitations of those analytic approaches.

In this chapter, I investigate Malaysia's role in undermining state authority in the southern Philippines in the 1970s. My theory holds that subversion degrades state authority and impedes state consolidation efforts. There are two ways we can detect the insidious effects of subversion on state authority: by examining state authority in a region before and after subversion, and by comparing state authority in that region to state authority in other regions in the same country. These two approaches mirror the between-province and within-province analyses from chapter 3, and I follow both approaches here using qualitative methods.

I show that Malaysia and the Philippines were embroiled in an intractable territorial dispute over the status of a part of Sabah, a territory in eastern Malaysia. These fundamentally incompatible policy preferences regarding the territorial claim and its resolution led Malaysia to subvert state authority in the Philippine region of Mindanao. As a tool of Malaysian statecraft, subversion provided the means to extract bargaining leverage over the dispute and impose costs on Manila that would distract it from pursuing the claim. This external support had significant and far-reaching effects on state consolidation in the southern Philippines.

This case offers a number of important features for analysis. From a theoretical standpoint, it illustrates several facets of the theory. The case shows how subversion can be used to achieve bargaining leverage and promote tie-down. It also illuminates the importance of external involvement in the degradation of state authority above and beyond the influence of domestic factors alone. Additionally, by focusing on two weak states, this chapter supports my claim that subversion is a policy tool available to both the strong and the weak. The sponsor state, Malaysia, is not a great power. At the time of its involvement in the Philippines, it was not even a minor power in the region. Malaysia's lack of significant or sophisticated military capability is precisely what makes the case particularly valuable for theory, and for thinking about the set of states involved in perpetrating persistent state weakness.

The case also offers useful methodological advantages that complement and improve on the evidence already presented. Because it examines two maritime states, the Malaysia-Philippines case is out of sample with respect to the quantitative analysis in chapter 3, which included only territorially contiguous states.[1] The temporal variation allows me to trace the causal mechanisms and show the direction of causality in a more robust way. The analysis, which draws primarily on U.S. diplomatic records and secondary literature from scholars inside and outside the region, also offers a window into Malaysian decision-making and intentionality. Assessing intentionality is an admittedly challenging task. Subversion is useful because it provides for plausible deniability and political cover; states are therefore unwilling and unlikely to acknowledge their sovereignty-undermining efforts in public statements. Relying on the private assessments and communications of the U.S. diplomatic community as well as the analysis of regional experts can help mitigate this problem. Finally, the qualitative approach permits a much deeper dive into the details and nuances of how subversion promotes weak state authority—the central claim of this book. Dislodging the state and blocking it from asserting control can be an incredibly violent process. As we will see, even when the sponsor ends its use of subversion, the effects on state authority tend to persist.

The Dispute over Sabah

Malaysia became an independent state in 1963, and the circumstances of its birth immediately precipitated an intractable dispute with the Philippines, Malaysia's maritime neighbor to the east. Independent Malaysia consisted of the former British colonies of Malaya and Singapore on the Asian mainland and Sabah (North Borneo) and Sarawak on the island of Borneo. The Philippines, however, objected to the inclusion of Sabah in the new Malaysian state on historical and legal grounds. Sabah had once been a part of the Sultanate of Sulu, which at its height in the late 17th and early 18th centuries controlled territory around the Sulu Sea spanning from the northern part of Borneo to portions of the eastern and southern Philippines. The arrival of the Spanish, British, and Americans to the region gradually eroded the sultanate's authority and its territorial holdings. In 1878, the sultan of Sulu transferred authority over Sabah to two Westerners who later formed the British North Borneo Company to administer Sabah. Sabah became a protectorate of the British Empire, and after World War II, a Crown colony. The sultanate also concluded agreements with the Philippines in 1903 and 1962 that ceded the sultanate's holdings to the Philippines.[2] These agreements made the Philippines the successor state to the Sultanate of Sulu.

In 1961, the Federation of Malaya and the British government began contemplating whether to unify the British colonies in Southeast Asia as the new country of Malaysia.[3] This prompted the Philippines to articulate its claim to Sabah. Manila argued that as the sultanate's legal successor, it was entitled to the territories under the control of the sultanate at the time at which sovereignty was transferred to Manila. The British rejected this argument.

Meanwhile, preparations to create Malaysia continued. Two inquiries were formed to ascertain whether the populations in Sabah and Sarawak supported the Malaysia project. The first commission was led by Lord Cameron Cobbold, the former governor of the Bank of England, in 1962. The second commission was led by the United Nations under the auspices of the UN secretary-general in 1963. Instead of holding a plebiscite, the Cobbold Commission and the UN Malaysia Mission arranged for consultations with the local populations. Both inquiries concluded that the people of Sabah and Sarawak supported the formation of Malaysia.[4] The Philippines rejected the findings on self-determination grounds and cited the absence of a plebiscite. Nevertheless, in September 1963, the governments of the United Kingdom, Malaya, North Borneo, Sarawak, and Singapore enacted the Malaysia Agreement, bringing about the creation of Malaysia, of which the entire territory of Sabah became a constituent part.

Even after Malaysia emerged as an independent state, Manila continued to object to the inclusion of the eastern part of Sabah in the new state. Malaysia regarded the Philippine claim as completely without merit. To use the language of my theory, Kuala Lumpur and Manila found themselves articulating opposing and irreconcilable positions over the status of Sabah. First, the two states disagreed on the interpretation of the Malay word *pajak* in the 1878 agreement that provided for Sabah's transfer. The Philippine government insisted that the intended meaning of the word was "lease." As evidence, Manila pointed to the annual transfers of $5,300 in Malayan dollars (the equivalent of about $1,600 in U.S. dollars) by the British government, and later the Malaysian government, to the heirs of the sultan of Sulu as payment of rent.[5] If the 1878 agreement was in fact a lease, then the sultanate retained sovereignty over Sabah, which would have then been passed to the Philippines in 1962. From this perspective, the British acquisition of sovereignty over Sabah was illegal and unwarranted.

But Malaysia understood the word *pajak* to mean "cession." Britain acquired sovereignty over eastern Sabah as the successor to the British North Borneo Company, and through occupation and administration of the territory for a period of 86 years.[6] Sovereignty then passed to Malaysia via the 1963 Malaysia Agreement. Because the 1878 agreement provided for annual payments to the sultanate in perpetuity, Malaysia continued these transfers, but considered them cession payments, not rental payments. Moreover, Malaysia also disputed the legality of subsequent agreements that favored the Philippines. R. Ramani, the legal adviser to the Malaysian Ministry of Foreign Affairs (MFA), argued that the sultan of Sulu had no international standing to cede the sultanate's remaining territory to the Philippines in 1962.[7] To support this argument, Kuala Lumpur cited a public declaration by former Philippine president Manuel Quezon. Quezon refused to recognize any legal successors to Sultan Mawallil Wasit Kiram, who died in 1936. Malaysia reasoned that the 1962 cession therefore had no standing.

The two states also expressed different opinions about the nature of self-determination in the territory. Malaysia pointed to four opportunities that the people of Sabah had to express their desire to join with the Philippines or object to the merger that formed Malaysia: the Cobbold Commission, the December 1962 elections in what was then North Borneo, the UN Mission, and the 1967 Sabah state elections. The Cobbold Commission and the UN Mission were direct attempts to ascertain the view of the population on the question of Malaysia. The electoral results, which delivered wins to parties supportive of the federation, provided indirect evidence of local support. In each instance the people of Sabah affirmed their intent on remaining with Malaysia. In Kuala Lumpur's view, the matter was settled.

Manila disagreed. Because it regarded the findings of the Cobbold Commission and the UN Mission as illegitimate and flawed, the conclusions of those panels could not be accepted as the final legal expression of self-determination. When Malaysia argued that the people of Sabah had expressed support for the idea of Malaysia in the 1962 and 1967 elections, the Philippines retorted that no election could substitute for a true plebiscite or referendum that directly addressed the question of Sabah's status. Manila therefore demanded that, after a legal determination of the status of Sabah, the Sabahans be given an opportunity to decide whether to join with the Philippines or join with some other state. Throughout the years in which the dispute remained on Manila's foreign policy agenda, the Philippines insisted on a new plebiscite as the ultimate deciding factor of the fate of Sabah.[8]

Neither state could reach a compromise on the dispute—or even on how to address the dispute. In its public statements, Malaysia initially treated the claim as a nonissue; to acknowledge it would legitimize it. For the Philippines, the matter directly engaged questions of its history and identity as a state. Although Kuala Lumpur preferred to minimize the issue, Manila repeatedly raised the claim in its public and private diplomatic relations. It demanded that the matter be brought before the International Court of Justice and that Malaysia hold another plebiscite on the status of Sabah. In 1967, Malaysian deputy prime minister Tun Abdul Razak stated that he saw no reason to submit the claim to the court since the Philippines had no case.[9] Kuala Lumpur also reiterated its assertion that no further plebiscite should be held.

Manila escalated the dispute further. Although Manila repeatedly professed that it was only interested in a peaceful resolution of the dispute, its actions suggested more nefarious intentions. In 1967, the Armed Forces of the Philippines (AFP) established a training camp on Simunul, a Philippine island in the Sulu Archipelago located near the coast of Sabah. Major Eduardo Martelino of the AFP was in charge of training a special forces group called Jabidah for an Operation Merdeka, *merdeka* being a Malay word for freedom. In January 1968, U.S. intelligence indicated that several hundred Filipinos were receiving military training and instruction in the Malay language.[10] A few months later, one of the recruits, Jibin Arula, independently corroborated these earlier reports. According to Arula, the recruits were trained in jungle warfare, sabotage, and infiltration in order to induce revolt in a "certain country."[11] He later revealed the country to be Malaysia and reported that the objective was to claim Sabah.[12]

The Malaysian government became aware of the training activities on Simunul as early as January 1968 and conveyed this knowledge to the Philippine government. President Marcos subsequently ordered its termination, but the U.S. embassy in Manila determined that training was ongoing as of February 1968 on the basis of reports from well-informed American and foreign priests conducting missionary work in Sulu.[13] The sources told U.S. embassy officials that trainees arrived in batches of 35 to 70, some hailing from the Sulu Archipelago, others coming from the Visayas region of the central Philippines, and that those from the Visayas were being taught the Malay language. Local residents reported spotting Major Martelino along with a Philippine intelligence officer. The mayor of Jolo, an important city on Jolo Island in the Sulu Archipelago, told the priests that he suspected that some infiltration of Sabah had already taken place.

Operation Merdeka failed before it could be launched. However, the mission became a public scandal when news broke about a massacre in 1968 at Corregidor Island, a new training site closer to Manila, where the AFP slaughtered the Filipino Muslim recruits preparing for Operation Merdeka. The mission itself, as well as the public fallout over the "Corregidor Affair," plunged Malaysian relations with the Philippines into crisis. Manila's refusal to drop the Sabah claim and its clandestine activities convinced Kuala Lumpur that Manila would not be reasoned with. Moreover, the Sabah issue and the Corregidor Affair also threatened to kill the newly founded Association of Southeast Asian Nations (ASEAN), a regional organization created in 1967 by Indonesia, Malaysia, the Philippines, Singapore, and Thailand.[14] ASEAN's purpose was to promote regional economic cooperation and, to a lesser extent, the peaceful resolution of disputes. Manila's behavior thus represented an especially egregious instance of bad faith. Confronted with incompatible policy preferences and a recalcitrant Philippines, Malaysia looked for ways to gain leverage over Manila in the hope of forcing Manila to back down. Subversion provided one such means to gain that leverage.

Malaysian Subversion

Divergent and incompatible preferences regarding Sabah thus provided the motivation to subvert. Malaysia's next task was to find proxies to assist in that subversion. It found them in the large, multiethnic Muslim population called

Moros (the Spanish word for Muslim) in the regions of western and central Mindanao, the second-largest island in the Philippines. Although the Moros are a Muslim minority in a Christian-majority state, their grievances against Manila's rule had less to do with religious identity and more to do with state policies that promoted the settlement of Mindanao's territory by Christian settlers from elsewhere in the Philippine archipelago.[15] Over time, the state's failure to address questions of economic development and poverty, cultural and religious autonomy, and property rights and ancestral domain—issues that tended to fall along north-south, Christian-Muslim dimensions—marginalized and alienated Mindanao's Muslim population. These grievances helped make proxies available for Malaysian subversion.

Though both means and motive were in place, Kuala Lumpur tried to exhaust other policy options before turning to subversion. These options included threats to Manila that alluded to Malaysia's readiness to subvert. In April 1968 at the height of the Corregidor scandal, Muhammed Ghazali bin Shafie, permanent secretary of the Malaysian Ministry of Foreign Affairs, erupted at a U.S. embassy officer about what Malaysia would do to the Philippines if Manila did not back off. He identified anti-Manila sentiments among the Sulu Muslims and said that Malaysia could foment disturbances by arming and training those Muslims, using Sabah as a launch point into Sulu.[16] He also mentioned that Sabah's security forces had experienced confrontation (*konfrontasi*) with Indonesia, and this experience of undeclared war rendered them knowledgeable and competent in mounting unconventional operations in an aggressor's own territory.[17] Around the same time, MFA assistant secretary for Southeast Asian affairs Zainal Abidin bin Sulong told a member of the Australian High Commission that Malaysia could easily exploit Muslim dissatisfaction in the South if the Philippines went too far in pressing its claim to Sabah.[18] Two months later, MFA deputy secretary Hussein bin Osman echoed these sentiments when he indicated to the U.S. embassy in Kuala Lumpur that it would be a simple matter for Malaysia to stir up problems among the Muslims of the southern Philippines if the Philippines tried to "play rough" after the Bangkok talks over Sabah.[19]

These statements were clearly coercive and designed to influence Manila's position on the Sabah issue. The April statements followed the Corregidor Affair and Philippine attempts to elevate the Sabah claim at the United Nations, while the June statement by Hussein preceded talks at Bangkok on Sabah between the Philippines and Malaysia. U.S. diplomatic communications suggest that Kuala Lumpur wanted to compel Manila to either alter its approach to the Sabah claim or drop the claim altogether. It is noteworthy that three separate members of the MFA—including two of its three most senior officials—communicated to external powers Malaysia's willingness to undermine Philippine state authority in the South. The Malaysian officials likely did so for two reasons. First, Kuala Lumpur could reasonably expect that its threats would be passed on to Manila via third-party channels while minimizing the risk of escalation. Second, as U.S. and Australian diplomatic staff noted in their communications, the statements by Ghazali, Zainal, and Hussein were likely designed to elicit U.S. and Commonwealth pressure on Manila to moderate its behavior regarding Sabah. As an ally of the Philippines and its former colonizer, the United States maintained a special interest in Philippine affairs. Several diplomatic cables make reference to Kuala Lumpur's belief that the United States also exercised influence over Manila, despite repeated American denials of such influence. Still, external pressure from powerful members of the international system could increase the probability that coercion would succeed, freeing Malaysia from having to follow through on its threat to subvert.

The Philippines did not moderate its behavior. In fact, the situation escalated and further inflamed tensions between the two countries. The June 1968 Bangkok talks over the status of Sabah collapsed in acrimony. In September 1968, President Marcos signed a bill from the legislature that redefined the boundaries of the territorial sea of the Philippines to include Sabah, and made reference to the Philippines' acquisition of "dominion and sovereignty" over Sabah.[20] For Malaysia, the logical conclusion of the legislation would be an attempt to physically establish sovereignty over Sabah, which Kuala Lumpur expected to take the form of armed infiltration.[21] The fact that Marcos signed the legislation into law only reinforced Malaysia's conviction that the Philippines would not let the Sabah issue disappear quietly.

Malaysia's threats had failed, and its remaining options were limited. Kuala Lumpur was unwilling to lend the claim any air of credibility by agreeing to adjudication at the International Court of Justice. Such a move could result in Sabah's exit from the Malaysian federation.[22] With Singapore's own exit just a few years prior, Sabah's departure could endanger the federation or lead to its collapse. Nor would Malaysia entertain a plebiscite or referendum, which could have had adverse domestic consequences in Sabah for turning back the plebiscite.[23] Milder punitive measures, such as abrogating cooperative agreements or withdrawing the Malaysian ambassador following the passage of the bellicose Philippine legislation, had little effect on Manila's position on Sabah. Malaysia was also constrained with respect to the use of force as a means to compel the Philippines to change its behavior. According to a diplomatic cable, Prime Minister Tunku Abdul Rahman told the U.S. ambassador that Malaysia had the logistic base but not the military capacity to conduct a conventional militarized operation against the Philippines.[24] Malaysia's membership in ASEAN further constrained its options, since overt conventional force could destroy the new-born organization.

Having exhausted other options and finding threats alone to be insufficient, Malaysia decided to subvert state authority in Manila's southern periphery. At the very least, domestic disturbances in Mindanao could force Manila to divert resources to the South that could otherwise be spent on the Sabah issue—an example of tie-down. Kuala Lumpur could also take advantage of internal disorder to gain leverage over the Sabah issue if it positioned itself as helpful for the resolution of that disorder. Subversion also carried an important political advantage for Kuala Lumpur. Because it was more discreet than conventional force, subversion would achieve Malaysian objectives while avoiding creating complications for ASEAN.

Malaysia subversion began in 1968 or 1969. Its empowerment of proxies took the form of training, harboring, and arming Moro dissident groups that organized in Mindanao in the late 1960s following the Corregidor Affair. Among these groups were the Muslim Independence Movement (also known as the Mindanao Independence Movement), led by former Cotabato governor Datu Udtog Matalam; Ansar el-Islam, led by former Lanao del Sur senator Ahmad Domocao Alonto; the Bangsa Moro Liberation Organization, led by former congressman Sultan Rashid Lucman; and eventually the Moro National Liberation Front (MNLF), led by Nur Misuari, a former professor of political science at the University of the Philippines who had once been a part of the Muslim Independence Movement. The dissident groups represented three different major ethnic groups (Maguindanao, Maranao, and Tausug) and three different regions of Mindanao, and at the time did not constitute a unified force.

Lucman, a prominent Muslim leader in the South, was among the first to form links with Malaysia. In his history of the Moro struggle, Lucman's son recounted a secret meeting between the elder Lucman and Malaysian prime minister Rahman in early 1968. During the meeting, they discussed "the planned military training of 10,000 Moros in sabotage, counter-insurgency, and guerrilla tactics," who would be "armed and provided for by the Malaysian Special Forces."[25] The purpose of the training was to fight for the independence of Mindanao as a means to erase the Sabah claim.[26] Lucman helped recruit and organize the first batch of soldiers, known as the First 90 or Top 90. Among them was Nur Misuari, the future leader of the MNLF. He and the other recruits traveled to Pulau Pangkor, an island off the coast of peninsular Malaysia, to train and prepare for a guerrilla war against the Philippine state. According to Misuari's authorized biographer, officers from the Malaysian military administered the camp. General Jaqui, the personal representative to then prime minister Abdul Razak Hussein and former attaché to Saudi Arabia, managed the camp, while Major Saifi and

Captain Affendi were responsible for overseeing the training.[27] There, Misuari organized the MNLF, which launched its war for independence in the early 1970s.

U.S. diplomatic communications corroborate the Malaysian central government's active role in undermining Philippine authority. In 1969, the U.S. government had acquired intelligence that the Malaysian External Intelligence Organization, the Malaysian equivalent of the U.S. Central Intelligence Agency, was involved in clandestine activities directed against the southern Philippines.[28] These activities continued throughout the early 1970s, despite official denials. At the height of the MNLF war against the Philippines in 1975, for example, the U.S. embassy in Manila reported that the Armed Forces of the Philippines captured some French-manufactured ammunition rounds fired against AFP headquarters in Cotabato City in Mindanao. The AFP showed the rounds to the visiting French military attaché, Colonel Loussouarn, who checked the serial numbers on the rounds and determined that the rounds originated from a lot of ammunition recently sold to the government of Malaysia. Loussouarn concluded that the Malaysian government was officially supplying the "expensive ammunition to secessionist forces in Mindanao, since [the] quantities involved could hardly have 'leaked' out of Malaysian arsenals."[29]

Local Malaysian politicians in Sabah also fomented unrest in the southern Philippines. Paramount among them was Sabah's chief minister, Tun Mustapha, a powerful politician whose United Sabah National Organization party dominated local politics. After Operation Merdeka became public knowledge, he began pressuring Kuala Lumpur to take a hawkish line on the Philippines. Concurrently he began his own program to undermine the Philippines. In May 1968, the Philippines claimed to be in possession of a letter purportedly written by Mustapha to the Filipino Muslims that encouraged them to join Malaysia.[30] He also supplied guns and money to the militants in the southern Philippines.

Although Mustapha's activities were self-aggrandizing, his involvement in the southern Philippines proved to be politically useful to Kuala Lumpur even as it genuinely exasperated central authorities who preferred a tighter leash on affairs in Sabah. Mustapha's personal activities advanced Kuala Lumpur's strategy of undermining Philippine administration and control as a means of gaining leverage on the Sabah claim and as a diversion from future foreign adventurism against Sabah. When the unrest in the South erupted into open conflict against the Philippine state in 1972, Malaysia made the linkage between the Sabah claim and Mustapha's activities quite explicit, but in a way that allowed it to shift all culpability to Mustapha. For example, in early 1973, MFA secretary-general Zaiton Ibrahim bin Ahmad said that the central government could not effectively control Mustapha as long as the Philippines maintained a claim on Sabah.[31] Malaysian officials also told their Philippine counterparts that if Marcos really wanted to end the problems in the southern Philippines, he would use his power to put the Sabah claim to rest once and for all.[32] At first the Philippines was unwilling to acquiesce to Malaysian demands, which Manila regarded as blackmail for Sabah.[33] But as the problems in Sulu and Mindanao increasingly jeopardized Philippine domestic authority, Marcos indicated that dropping the Sabah claim could be arranged as long as the Sulu Archipelago remained juridically within the Philippines.[34]

The fact that Mustapha was somewhat of a loose cannon and an irritant to central authorities also provided political cover useful for Malaysian subversion. Mustapha's involvement in the southern Philippines allowed Kuala Lumpur to deny its own culpability and to claim it lacked full control over a powerful local politician who exploited the Sabah situation for his own political gain. Kuala Lumpur characterized the Philippine claim as an emotional issue for Sabah, which did not wish to join the Philippines and remained suspicious of Philippine intentions—sentiments that could be easily exploited by an opportunistic Mustapha. Kuala Lumpur also pointed to the religious and familial ties between the residents of Sabah and Sulu, which engendered popular sympathy for the plight of the Sulu Muslims. Mustapha himself had connections to the region: he was a Muslim and an ethnic Tausug, one of the same ethnic groups from the Sulu Archipelago, and he was a distant relative of the sultan of Sulu. He also profited politically from bellicose rhetoric and clandestine support for the struggle of the Philippine Muslims.[35]

Throughout this period, Kuala Lumpur sought to characterize the MNLF conflict as an internal problem for the Philippines while also seeking to profit politically from the chaos. This required a delicate balancing act. While it is true that Malaysia's second prime minister, Tun Abdul Razak, regarded Mustapha as a domestic political threat and attempted to neutralize him in 1974, it is also undeniable that Malaysia carefully exploited Mustapha's activities for the purpose of foreign policy gain on the Sabah issue.[36] Given the central government's own involvement in training, arming, and sheltering the MNLF on Malaysian territory, Kuala Lumpur's protestations of its innocence exemplify one of the most useful features of subversion as an instrument of foreign policy: plausible deniability. Mustapha and the MNLF provided the bargaining leverage that Malaysia sought. While it claimed that it was not responsible for the collapse of the state in Mindanao, Kuala Lumpur could help Manila with its Mustapha problem if Manila would help Malaysia on the Sabah issue.

Effects on Philippine State Authority in Muslim Mindanao

To what degree did foreign subversion from Malaysia undermine governance in Mindanao? There are two ways to answer this question. One way emphasizes the dependent variable of state authority and looks for evidence of state weakness.

The other emphasizes the causal effect of Malaysia's role in contributing to that weakness. Together, both help me not only assess what state authority looked like on the ground, but also trace Malaysia's role in degrading that state authority and impeding state consolidation.

I begin with the task of investigating state weakness. First, I compare the degree of state authority and control in central and western Mindanao—the areas where agents were available—before and after the onset of subversion and the MNLF war. Malaysian efforts to undermine state authority began in 1968 or 1969, but the MNLF, Malaysia's proxies, did not openly challenge Philippine state authority until 1972. I therefore do not expect to detect evidence of subversion's harmful influence on state authority before 1972. Second, I compare state authority in those parts of Mindanao with the non-Muslim parts of Mindanao, which were not the targets of Malaysian subversion and where agents were not available. I expect to observe evidence of increasing state weakness only in the Moro-populated parts of Mindanao, particularly since the MNLF's objective was the independence of Muslim Mindanao. State weakness in other parts of Mindanao would indicate some other factor at work. Both comparisons are important, as the first approach holds constant agent availability and examines the timing of onset, and the second approach holds constant Malaysian motivation while varying agent availability.

As a first cut, I examine the locations and timing of major episodes of antistate violence. Maintaining order and security is the foremost responsibility of the state. The absence of order indicates both that the state lacks authority and that it is actively fighting a competitor for the right to exercise authority.[37] Table 5.1 lists violent clashes or battles between the state and the MNLF on the island of Mindanao. The table covers the period 1963–79. As the table indicates, violence did not begin until 1972, a few years after Malaysian training began. Only when the MNLF was sufficiently organized and armed did violence break out. This indicates a significant shift from the status quo ante and a weakening of state control.

I also compare violence between the regions of Mindanao. All of Mindanao's Moro-majority provinces saw fighting between the state and the MNLF during this time period. The Christian-majority areas generally escaped violence in the 1970s. In 1971, an unrelated attack took place in Surigao del Sur between the state and the New People's Army, then a fledgling rebel organization that was mainly based in the northern island of Luzon.[38] The other exception occurred in Bukidnon, a Christian-majority province bordering Cotabato and the Lanao regions. In 1975 it was the site of a clash in which the MNLF massacred 33 civilians.[39] In general, however, the state maintained order in the Christian-dominated areas of Mindanao. The absence of violence in those regions is not surprising since the Malaysian-backed MNLF articulated secessionist objectives. Still, the

TABLE 5.1   Sites of antistate violence in Mindanao, 1963–79

MAJORITY GROUP	PROVINCE	MAJOR VIOLENT ATTACKS
Moro	Cotabato	1973, 1974, 1975
Moro	Lanao del Norte	1975, 1977
Moro	Lanao del Sur	1972, 1975
Moro	Sulu	1974, 1975, 1976, 1977
Moro	Zamboanga del Norte	1973
Moro	Zamboanga del Sur	1973, 1974, 1975, 1976, 1977, 1978
Christian	Agusan	None
Christian	Bukidnon	1975
Christian	Davao	None
Christian	Misamis Occidental	None
Christian	Misamis Oriental	None
Christian	Surigao	1971 (New People's Army)

Sources: Antistate violence data come from Dixon and Sarkees 2016, 541–42, 551–52; Keesing's Worldwide 2018; Mullenbach and Nurullayev 2018.

Notes: Table lists the provincial divisions of the island of Mindanao at the time of the 1960 census. Violent incidents that occurred on Mindanao but lack specific provincial location data are omitted. MNLF attacks without more precise location information occurred in 1976 and 1977. The New People's Army was the armed wing of the Communist Party of the Philippines, which operated elsewhere in the 1970s.

comparison is illuminating because it provides a useful counterfactual: despite Mindanao's distance from the political center, state authorities could maintain political order in other parts of Mindanao even as they struggled to impose that order in the Moro areas.

Other indicators of state activity show how the state continued to consolidate control over the parts of Mindanao not affected by the MNLF conflict. Consider the example of public health. In the late 1960s and 1970s, state hospitals constituted an important part of Mindanao's health infrastructure. While private hospitals outnumbered public hospitals in the region, public hospitals often had greater bed capacity and could serve a larger population. Government statistics indicate that in some provinces, such as Cotabato, the state supplied half of the region's hospitals, while in other provinces, such as Zamboanga del Sur, the only hospitals available were state hospitals. The state's uneven reach after the start of Malaysian subversion and the MNLF conflict is evident in the public health sector. As shown in figure 5.1, from the late 1960s to the 1970s the state increased the number of hospitals in the Christian parts of Mindanao. This indicates that the state was able to improve its presence in those provinces. In the Moro-dominated parts of Mindanao, including the areas affected by fighting, the state could not or did not improve state presence in that way. Despite having a larger population and continued population growth (figure 5.2), the Moro provinces saw only a slow increase in state hospitals during that same period. The improvement in state presence in the Christian areas relative to the areas affected by Malaysian

A

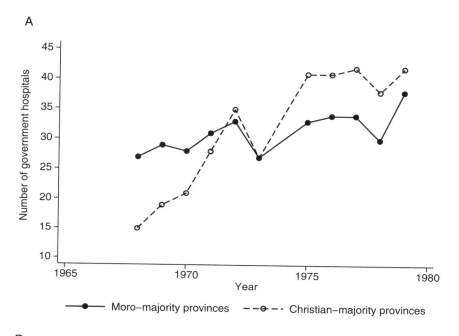

Moro–majority provinces ——•——   Christian–majority provinces --o--

B

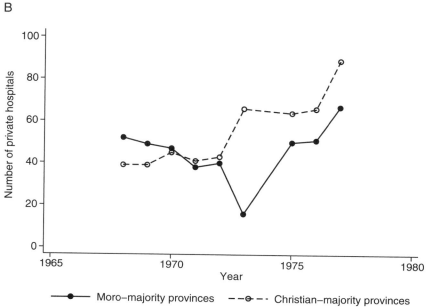

Moro–majority provinces ——•——   Christian–majority provinces --o--

FIGURE 5.1. Hospitals in Mindanao, 1968–79: (A) Public hospitals; (B) Private hospitals. Y-axis scales differ for presentational purposes. Hospital data collected from Bureau of the Census and Statistics, *Journal of Philippine Statistics*. Private hospital data are available only from 1968 to 1977.

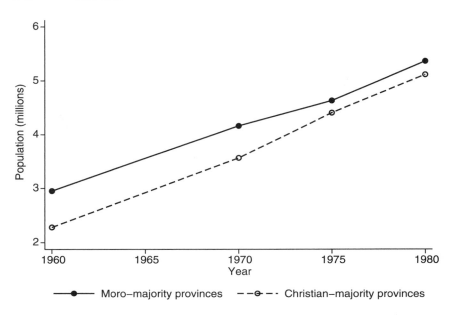

FIGURE 5.2. Population of Mindanao. Population data collected from Bureau of the Census and Statistics, *Census of the Philippines*. The Philippines conducted censuses in 1960, 1970, 1975, and 1980. Population figures are counts of population aged 1–75, inclusive, rather than total population.

subversion and the MNLF war cannot be attributed to private sector substitution. As the lower panel of figure 5.1 shows, the number of private hospitals increased more rapidly in the Christian areas than in the Moro areas—again, despite the Christian areas' smaller population.

I also look at data on government employment for evidence of the MNLF conflict's role in impeding state consolidation in Mindanao. Just as the exercise of state authority requires the physical manifestations of state presence, bureaucrats and civil servants are the actors that carry out the everyday business of state administration. Government statistics on public sector employment at the provincial level shed light on the unevenness of state presence between the Moro-majority and Christian-majority provinces of Mindanao. Figure 5.3 depicts the number of permanent and temporary provincial government employees for the years 1967–79.[40] Two features of the data stand out. First, there is some volatility in the data, including a temporary but steep rise in provincial government employment for 1969–71. Second, and more interesting, the data series for the Moro-majority provinces and the Christian-majority provinces are nearly overlapping except during the most violent years of the MNLF war in the 1970s. A gap

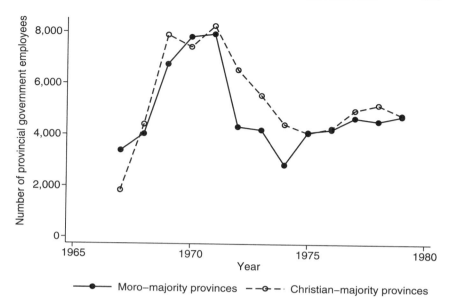

FIGURE 5.3. Provincial government employment, 1967–79. Provincial employment data collected from Bureau of the Census and Statistics, *Journal of Philippine Statistics*. Figures include permanent and temporary employees of the provincial government and exclude casual employees.

in employment emerges in 1972, the first year of fighting in the MNLF conflict, and does not close until 1975. The timing of the gap and the fact that the Moro-majority provinces lost more employees than the Christian-majority provinces point toward a state authority deficit in precisely the places where the MNLF contested Manila's rule.

The previous data point to the interpretation that levels of state authority did indeed change in Mindanao. State weakness increased, as major episodes of armed conflict broke out in areas that had lacked violence before. Manila also faced challenges in consolidating its authority. State presence increased in the places unaffected by the MNLF conflict but not in the places where the Moros sought to dislodge the state. Thus, temporal and spatial comparisons lead to the same conclusion about state weakness on the ground.

But can the state's problems can be attributed to Malaysian subversion as opposed to competing factors? This is an important question to answer. Scholars of Mindanao and the MNLF war have written extensively about the influence of complex historical, cultural, and sociological grievances against the Philippine state in precipitating conflict.[41] These domestic factors certainly matter:

using my theoretical framework, those grievances help explain the availability of proxies for subversion. Moreover, Mindanao's geographic distance from the political center, its size, its independence during Spanish colonial rule, and its unique status under U.S. colonial rule also contributed to the challenge of state consolidation.[42]

While important, these static historical and geographic factors cannot explain the timing or process through which Manila's authority collapsed in Mindanao. International involvement in the form of Malaysian subversion helps make sense of when and why Moro resistance to state administration and control took the form that it did in the early 1970s—and why the effects on state authority were so significant and persisted for so long compared to previous uprisings. These long-running effects can largely be understood as the result of Malaysia's empowerment of the MNLF, which made it possible for the Moros to translate their grievances into an open contestation of Philippine authority.

To appreciate the importance of the MNLF, one must first understand the political landscape of the southern Philippines. The Moros who temporarily united to fight against the state in 1973 represented disparate regions and ethnic groups. As a proportion of population, the three largest ethnic groups were the Tausug from the Sulu Archipelago and the Zamboanga Peninsula in western Mindanao, the Maranao from the Lanao region of central Mindanao, and the Maguindanao from the Cotabato region of central Mindanao. Although Islam was the religion of all three groups, ethnic identity was at least as important as religious identity, and coordinated political behavior predicated on a common religion was not necessarily a given. Several factors elevated Islam as a unifying social cleavage. The Corregidor Affair helped cement the idea that the Philippine state was hostile to all Muslims. So too did attacks on Muslim communities in central Mindanao by Christian bandits known as the *ilaga* (rats). The ongoing attacks and the pervasive sense that Manila had engineered them or at least tolerated them helped raise the profile of religious identity, but did not themselves promote political coordination or cooperation. As an example, consider the behavior of voluntary armed Muslim bands that formed to deal with the *ilaga*. These bands were organized provincially and around the ethnic groups: the Black Shirts in Cotabato, the Barracudas in Lanao, and the Green Guards on the Zamboanga Peninsula. Although they shared a common goal, they acted independently of one another and did not actually provide much security to the Muslim communities of the South.[43]

Malaysian support helped the MNLF overcome the divisions of ethnicity and region and consolidated the disparate forces into a semicoherent organization, if only for a few critical years. According to Wan Kadir Che Man, a respected scholar of the Moro conflict, such organization would not have been possible without external assistance, including the involvement of foreign leaders like Tun Mustapha.[44] Indeed, in Che Man's view, this coordination was the principal contribution of the MNLF in the ongoing Moro struggle.[45] The First 90 who traveled to Malaysia included a majority of Maranaos, as well as some Maguindanaos and Tausugs. Under the tutelage of their Malaysian trainers and in the year they spent together training against a common enemy, they learned to stop thinking of themselves as members of their respective ethnic groups and instead as soldiers united against the (Christian) Philippine state.[46] The MNLF's founders, who conceived of the MNLF from the safety of their camp on Malaysian soil, represented the principal ethnic groups: Dimas Pundato was a Maranao, Hashim Salamat was a Maguindanao, and Nur Misuari was a Tausug.[47]

Malaysian training and assistance also helped create a viable fighting force capable of taking on the battle-hardened AFP. In the past, the Moro struggle against external oppression had been characterized by values that gave primacy to individualized acts of heroism and the personal glory of martyrdom. Translated into battlefield tactics, these values did not lend themselves well to coordination, efficiency, or effectiveness. The post-1968 struggle represented a radical break with the past. Samuel Tan, a Filipino historian specializing in the study of Southeast Asia's Muslims, credits the adoption of modern-day guerrilla tactics and the emphasis on mobility and coordination as important factors that made the Moro struggle in the postcolonial period difficult to control and eliminate.[48] Instruction on these tactics came from Malaysian operatives who ran the training camps.[49] The First 90 spent more than a year in Malaysia learning the art of guerrilla war. Subsequent waves of recruits also traveled to Malaysia for training. After his return to the Philippines, Misuari augmented his growing force with new local recruits from Sulu, where he established his own training camps.[50] Other MNLF fighters were trained in Pakistan and Libya, but the MNLF intelligence chief, Abdul Sahrin, who had been to camps in all three countries, described those in Malaysia as the best.[51]

Malaysia's provision of cash, arms, and ammunition also played a pivotal role in generating persistent weak state authority in the southern Philippines. Compared to the AFP, the MNLF was well supplied and able to keep up the pressure on the state. According to an Associated Press story, Manila said it had evidence that since 1972, Malaysia had supplied the MNLF with more than 200,000 rounds of ammunition and 5,407 weapons, including grenades, machine guns, and antiaircraft guns, as well as 750,000 Philippine pesos ($112,500 in U.S. dollars) for the recruitment of young men.[52] Abdul Sahrin, the MNLF intelligence chief, recounted Malaysian assistance to the MNLF: "They gave us all sorts of guns. Our trainers were British-trained. We used Belgian-made rifles, carbines, armalites, AK-47s, anti-tank weapons, everything."[53] The arms and ammunition were enormously helpful in allowing the MNLF to sustain the fight against the state. According to a retired AFP officer, more than the safe havens on Malaysian territory or the training, the externally provided large firearms made a difference on the battlefield and helped the MNLF gain the upper hand early in the conflict.[54] In a March 1973 assessment, AFP chief of staff General Romeo Espino described the external assistance in the form of money, arms, and ammunition as "very adequate" and linked the "offers of the secessionists and their foreign supporters of a gun and P2,000 per rebel" to the "swelling of the ranks of the rebels in the last two years."[55] Since economic underdevelopment was pervasive in the southern Philippines, the promise of P2,000 (funds for which came from external sources) would have been a very attractive incentive to take up arms against the state.[56] Espino also attributed the MNLF's ability to go on the offensive to their external support.[57]

Manila fought back against this externally supported challenge to its authority, but the MNLF quickly gained the upper hand in the war thanks to the flood of external assistance from Malaysia. Unlike the MNLF, the AFP found itself facing critical supply shortages. At one early stage in the war, the AFP ran out of ammunition and had to pressure Taiwan in order to procure more.[58] Espino noted that the rebels had the advantage in manpower (16,900 against the government's 9,600), and that a significant number of the government forces consisted of men from the Philippine Constabulary who were tied down in garrison or police duties.[59] The U.S. embassy noted that the AFP's limited resources constituted a serious barrier to the reestablishment of state administration and control in the South.[60] Espino also reported that although the rebels did not threaten the territorial integrity or stability of the Philippines as a whole, their activities made "possible the sequestration of Philippine territory and the exercise of extraneous sovereignty over Filipinos and others living therein."[61] In other words, Espino perceived the MNLF challenge to be limited to the contestation of Philippine authority and domestic authority within the juridical boundaries of the state, rather than an existential threat to the state itself. Although the MNLF's expressed demands included independence, the characterization of the conflict's impact on Philippine domestic authority as limited comports with Kuala Lumpur's interest in supporting the MNLF as a means to harass and distract the Philippines rather than as a means to dismember it.[62]

Evidence that Malaysian subversion played a major role in the collapse of state authority in the South can also be found in Manila's attempts to shut off Malaysian assistance. In June 1973, when the war with the MNLF was going particularly poorly for the government, the Philippines apparently considered Malaysian involvement to be significant enough that it offered to drop the Sabah claim in return for Malaysia cutting off external assistance to the MNLF. This deal represented a reversal of the government's earlier position on the Sabah issue; President Marcos himself had stated previously that trading Sabah for the cessation of assistance would be an unacceptable sign of weakness.[63] Any backpedaling on the Sabah claim risked serious domestic political consequences for Marcos. Although U.S. diplomatic personnel speculated that Marcos held no personal attachment to the claim, Marcos had exploited the Sabah issue for electoral gain during the 1967 congressional elections and the 1969 presidential elections.

Legal matters also raised the political costs of dropping the Sabah claim. Marcos had signed legislation in 1968 that referenced the Philippines' dominion and sovereignty over Sabah, and despite his attempts to clarify that such language did not establish sovereignty so much as reserve the right to do so in the future, the legislation hardened the Philippine position on the claim. Moreover, the 1973 constitution, which came into effect in January, formally defined the national territory of the country to include the Philippine archipelago, its islands and waters therein, and all other territories belonging to the country by right and historic title. The article defining the national territory is noteworthy not only because it differed from the language of the 1935 constitution (which used the wording "as at present defined by law"), but also because it contained the clause about historic right, which could be interpreted to include Sabah.[64] Any attempt to drop the Sabah claim or settle it in favor of Malaysia could therefore be painted as a violation of the constitution and exploited for domestic political purposes. Nonetheless, at a high-level meeting with Indonesia and Malaysia in Hong Kong in June 1973, Marcos indicated through his representatives his willingness to drop the claim.[65]

Unfortunately for the Philippines, the conditions in 1973 and 1974 were not ripe for a resolution of the Sabah claim. At that time, the principal objection to the Philippine offer was the linkage between Malaysian support and the disturbances in the South. Kuala Lumpur has never publicly admitted its official involvement in undermining Philippine state authority in the South. Even when Malaysia first hinted at a quid pro quo on Sabah, it was careful to cast Mustapha as the bogeyman who could be reined in only once the Philippines removed his source of legitimacy. By the mid-1970s, Malaysian support to the MNLF dwindled, and may have stopped altogether, and in 1977, Marcos announced that he would take steps to formally renounce the Sabah claim.[66] Perhaps because of the timing—some years into the martial law period (which would last from 1972 to 1981) and the ongoing war in the South—press and popular reaction was largely supportive. Those in favor pointed to the practical dividends that renunciation of the claim would bring to the country and its bilateral relations with Malaysia. Ultimately, Marcos did not formally drop the claim and instead simply stopped pursuing it. The claim remains unresolved today, though it no longer threatens Philippine-Malaysian relations.

The cessation of centrally directed Malaysian assistance to the MNLF did not bring about an end to conflict in the southern Philippines or the restoration of state authority. Far from it: even today, the Mindanao conflict remains one of the longest-running conflicts in the world. Libya replaced Malaysia as an external source of financial and diplomatic support, and under the auspices of the Organization of the Islamic Conference, Libya helped the MNLF negotiate a peace agreement in 1976. The 1976 Tripoli Agreement was highly controversial within the MNLF. It not only led to a rift in the MNLF that resulted in the emergence of a splinter group called the Moro Islamic Liberation Front (MILF), but also quickly collapsed following disagreements over implementation between the MNLF and the state. The MNLF went back to war. So too did the MILF. The MNLF eventually signed a final peace agreement with Manila under the administration of President Fidel V. Ramos in 1996. From that point on, the MILF and its splinter groups became the main armed actor prosecuting the conflict over land, cultural rights, identity, and autonomy in Muslim Mindanao.

The Collapse of State Authority

The case of the southern Philippines is useful in several respects for understanding the politics of subversion and subversion's effects on state authority. First, the case helps improve on the statistical analysis from chapter 3 by directly tracing the effect of Malaysian subversion on Philippine state authority. The in-depth qualitative analysis allowed me to show the degradation of state authority and the uneven patterns of state consolidation in Mindanao in the 1970s, and to link state weakness to Malaysian subversion. Temporal and regional comparisons demonstrated that the state authority penalty manifested not only as an outbreak of violence, but also as unevenness in the state's physical presence. Though mundane, infrastructure and government bureaucrats are essential for state administration and governance, and their deficiencies in Muslim Mindanao point to a lack of state consolidation in those areas.

Second, the case illustrates a theoretical proposition about when states use subversion, thereby complementing the analysis of the post-Soviet space in chapter 4. That chapter focused on assessing the role of policy incompatibility (motivation) and proxy availability (means) in conditioning the use of subversion. An additional implication from the theoretical discussion in chapter 2 held that states should also be more willing to engage in subversion when other policy instruments, like conventional force, are more costly. This case supports that claim. Malaysia contemplated using conventional force against the Philippines, but Manila's alliance with the United States and Malaysia's weak military capabilities made that course of action unattractive. Moreover, direct force would have threatened the existence of ASEAN, an organization that Malaysia had helped found with the Philippines and other states in the region. Similarly, domestic politics also made peaceful options for resolving the Sabah dispute prohibitively costly. In that context, subversion offered a solution: it could impose pain on Manila useful for extracting bargaining leverage and preoccupying Manila's attention with domestic trouble.

Third, the case helps make sense of the central puzzle of this book: why some states fail to exercise authority throughout their territories. The Philippines is a well-institutionalized state with a considerable degree of state presence in much of its territory—no small feat for an archipelago state of more than 2,000 inhabited islands. Yet Muslim Mindanao escaped strong state authority, even relative to the rest of the southern Philippines. My claim is not that subversion explains the origins of state weakness in Mindanao; to understand origins, we should look to the role of other factors, including the history and politics of state formation. But subversion does help explain why that state weakness persisted and worsened in an otherwise capable country that made state consolidation gains elsewhere in the South. Malaysian involvement helped a disparate set of dissident groups coalesce into a fighting force capable of asserting control over parts of the southern Philippines and repelling the AFP. This involvement helps explain the timing of the conflict's outbreak. It also helps explain why the state failed to prevent this swelling of Moro discontent from escalating into a war, despite previous successes at neutralizing Moro uprisings like the Kamlon Rebellion.

A final lesson of this case lies in its policy implications. What can U.S. policymakers learn from a case of subversion between two non-great-power states that occurred during the 1970s? Southeast Asia was a region of geopolitical confrontation during the Cold War; the rise of China and its growing assertiveness toward the region suggests that Southeast Asia will again become a zone of great power confrontation in the coming decades. The United States prefers that its partners and allies in the region are strong, stable, and more consolidated. All else equal, it especially values those characteristics in states located in geopolitically important or contested regions. State weakness in the Philippines thus poses a challenge to U.S. policymakers as well as to authorities in Manila. Yet to read current problems in Mindanao as purely internal in cause, or to dismiss them because they do not directly involve a great power rival, would be a mistake. Malaysia's role in subverting the Philippines teaches us that one does not need to be a great power to meddle in the affairs of an adversary, and that non-great-power subversion can still exact far-reaching harm on state authority. Policymakers seeking to understand and address the problems of weak state authority should therefore pay attention not only to the activities of their great power adversaries, as chapter 4 shows, but also to the behavior of other states in regions of interest.

UNDERMINING STATE AUTHORITY IN CAMBODIA

This chapter continues chapter 5's close investigation of how subversion imposes costs on the exercise of state authority and undermines state consolidation, again with the goal of illustrating the role of foreign interference in impeding state consolidation. I examine the case of Thailand's subversion against Cambodia during the Vietnamese occupation of 1979–89. In December 1978, the Vietnamese invaded Cambodia, then called Democratic Kampuchea, and overthrew the incumbent Khmer Rouge regime.[1] It renamed the country the People's Republic of Kampuchea (PRK), installed a friendly regime, and oversaw much of Cambodian state administration. Regime change radically altered the geopolitical alignment of the country in favor of Vietnam, which plunged Cambodia's relations with neighboring Thailand into crisis. Because Thailand's preference for a friendly or nonaligned Cambodia was fundamentally at odds with the PRK's and Vietnam's preferences, Thailand sought to prevent the PRK from consolidating control over Cambodian territory. It cooperated with the Khmer Rouge, now a resistance group, to subvert the PRK. Thailand's efforts were profoundly successful at blocking state consolidation.

Thailand's involvement in Cambodia offers methodological advantages that prompted its selection as a case. Perhaps the most distinctive feature of this case is the tabula-rasa-like state of the country at the time the PRK assumed power in Phnom Penh. Prior to the Vietnamese invasion, the Khmer Rouge ruled Cambodia from 1975 to 1979 under the leadership of Pol Pot, a Marxist-Leninist educated in Paris. The choice of the term "ruled" is not accidental: the Khmer Rouge did not govern the country so much as devastate it completely. As a foreign-installed regime supported by an occupying power, the PRK confronted the monumental task of establishing state control and projecting state authority throughout the country. The fact that the Khmer Rouge dismantled, destroyed, or laid waste to state infrastructure during its rule and its subsequent flight after its overthrow made this task even more daunting for the PRK. Although the humanitarian consequences of the Khmer Rouge's policies were staggering, the situation confronting the PRK presents a useful analytic opportunity for assessing the effects of subversion on state authority. Since the PRK did not exercise meaningful authority outside Phnom Penh, it had to project authority everywhere. The historian Michael Vickery describes the challenge bluntly: "There was no state for them to take over. They had to create it anew."[2] This feature of the case mitigates the inferential challenge of assessing whether subversion contributed to incomplete state consolidation or whether prior levels of weak state authority were instead responsible. My claim is not that history began anew in January 1979. Rather, my claim is more modest: the abrupt change in regime and the complete absence of state authority in the country provide useful analytic leverage for understanding why state consolidation proceeded so unevenly in the 1980s.

The case also addresses concerns of reverse causality. Previous chapters handled this threat to inference in two different ways. In chapter 3, I used regression to compare levels of state authority within the same province over time, exploiting variation in rivalry, my measure of policy incompatibility. In chapter 5, I used process tracing to show how Malaysian subversion weakened state authority and impeded state consolidation. In this chapter, I utilize elements of both approaches. Vietnam's sudden invasion of Cambodia and the toppling of the Khmer Rouge abruptly altered the geopolitical orientation of the country in a way detrimental to Thailand's interests. Subversion began because Bangkok's policy preferences regarding Cambodia's alignment were no longer congruent with the preferences of the regime in Phnom Penh. In other words, it was not the case that existing levels of state weakness over territory in Cambodia caused incompatible policy preferences with Thailand or prompted Thailand's choice to subvert.

This chapter also illustrates arguments from my theory. First, the case exemplifies the use of subversion for the purposes of tie-down. By keeping the Khmer Rouge alive to fight, harass, and annoy the PRK, Thailand could increase the likelihood that the PRK would reallocate resources toward dealing with the insurgency rather than using those resources to threaten Thailand's sovereignty and territorial integrity. I also continue the previous chapter's focus on two non-great-power states to reinforce the claim that subversion is a tool not confined to the arsenals of the world's strongest states. In fact, Thailand was militarily weaker than Vietnam, which exacerbated Bangkok's fears of being attacked and constrained its options for dealing with Cambodia. Additionally, the analysis reinforces the theoretical point that proxies need not share identity-based or ideological ties with the sponsor state. The Khmer Rouge shared little in common with Thailand except a desire to see the PRK overthrown and the Vietnamese gone. Finally, the chapter demonstrates the mechanisms through which subversion damages state authority: the Khmer Rouge destroyed state infrastructure and scattered bureaucrats from their posts.

Because of the country's devastation, Cambodia had limited capacity to collect and publish official statistics about state presence during the 1980s. For that reason, the kind of detailed statistical reports that informed my analysis of Philippine state authority in Mindanao are not available here. The evidence for this chapter therefore relies on a combination of scholarly literature, reports from humanitarian and development agencies, accounts from journalists, and some official Thai government documents. Together, these sources paint a picture of a country struggling to assert authority over the northwestern parts of its territory near Thailand, even as it improved state presence elsewhere.

Cambodia's Geopolitical Realignment

The issue of Cambodia's foreign policy alignment has been relevant for its neighbors Thailand and Vietnam for centuries. For much of its history as a modern state, Cambodia acted as a neutral buffer between Thailand and Vietnam.[3] When Cambodia received its independence from France in 1953, it again played this role, alongside Laos. For Thailand in particular, a friendly or at least nonaligned Cambodia was essential to Thai security. Vietnam was Thailand's traditional enemy and rival. In previous eras, both states competed for regional hegemony, influence, and suzerainty over neighboring kingdoms in Southeast Asia. In the contemporary period, Cambodia's position in between Thailand and Vietnam provided a kind of strategic depth for Bangkok that mitigated the likelihood of an armed attack from Vietnam.[4] Neither state could menace the other one directly as long as Laos and Cambodia remained under the control of nonaligned governments.

Cambodia's geopolitical status was especially urgent during the Cold War. Thailand had been one of the few states to escape colonial rule, and during the Cold War it aligned itself with the United States. Its geographic location in mainland Southeast Asia, however, meant that it could not avoid involvement in the region's struggle against Communism. Communist movements in Thailand, Laos, Cambodia, and South Vietnam challenged incumbent governments, and they enjoyed assistance from North Vietnam, itself under Communist control. In 1975, South Vietnam, Laos, and Cambodia all fell to Communists. North Vietnam absorbed South Vietnam to form a single state, and in neighboring Laos it established a significant military presence in the form of "advisers" to the government.

While Laos was firmly aligned with Vietnam, Cambodia's situation was more complicated—but in ways that benefited Thai interests. The Khmer Rouge, Cambodia's Communist regime, was led by the French-educated Pol Pot, a Marxist-Leninist whose revolutionary training occurred under French Communist influence rather than Vietnamese influence. Hanoi and the Khmer Rouge also espoused different visions for Communism in Cambodia. Khmer Communism had a nationalist character. In the 1960s, to emphasize this point, the party changed its name from the Khmer People's Revolutionary Party to the Communist Party of Kampuchea.[5] In contrast, the Vietnamese model of Communism was very much internationalist in character.[6] Vietnam depicted itself as the "elder brother" in charge of the revolution in Indochina regardless of national identity. The Khmer Rouge chafed under Vietnamese efforts to dominate the Communist struggle and political affairs in the region. In an act of defiance, they aligned themselves with China at a time when the Sino-Vietnamese (and Sino-Soviet) gulf was widening.

Tensions also escalated over a territorial dispute between Vietnam and Cambodia concerning the Mekong River delta. Unwilling to negotiate or to moderate their irredentist objectives, Pol Pot's forces launched a series of cross-border attacks into Vietnam. Inside Cambodia, the Khmer Rouge expelled some of the Vietnamese population and slaughtered the rest. Purges within the Pol Pot clique removed any potential friends who would have been sympathetic to Vietnam.[7] Hanoi decided that the Khmer Rouge had to go.

On Christmas Day 1978, Vietnam invaded Cambodia. The Khmer Rouge were no match for the Vietnamese forces. Within days of the invasion, the Vietnamese captured Cambodia's provincial nerve centers in rapid succession: Kratie on December 30, Stung Treng on January 3, Neak Luong on January 5, and Kompong Cham on January 6. Pol Pot seriously erred in his calculations of Vietnamese strength and the Khmer Rouge's ability to repel the advancing Vietnamese military, evacuating Phnom Penh only at the last minute. The Vietnamese captured the capital on January 7. Having dispatched the Khmer Rouge, the Vietnamese declared an end to Democratic Kampuchea, renamed the country the People's Republic of Kampuchea, and installed what amounted to a puppet regime. The Kampuchean United Front for National Salvation (FUNSK, the abbreviation for its French name), a patchwork resistance organization that preinvasion Phnom Penh had derided as "a Vietnamese political organization with a Khmer name," was nominally placed in control of the PRK.[8] FUNSK president and Khmer Rouge defector Heng Samrin took up the presidency of the new regime.

Regime change immediately and mechanically reoriented Cambodia's foreign policy toward Vietnam. Thai authorities correctly perceived that the new regime in Phnom Penh was not independent. Indeed, the degree to which Hanoi exerted authority over the PRK was considerable and near total.[9] The Vietnamese dominated the coercive apparatus of the new state. As the FUNSK was hastily organized, it lacked robust armed forces of its own to confer on the new regime. On the eve of the invasion, the FUNSK had just a few battalions.[10] The PRK therefore relied on the Vietnamese military to provide the coercive shield it needed to survive. By 1980, nearly 200,000 Vietnamese troops were stationed inside Cambodia—four times the number known to be in neighboring Laos.[11] These forces were actively engaged in combat operations, and they remained in Cambodia until the late 1980s. In contrast, by the mid-1980s, the PRK's own military numbered only about 30,000 regulars until the introduction of conscription.[12]

The Vietnamese were also heavily involved in the administration of the state. They created two separate bureaucracies: the Party Central Committee, which over time replicated the structure of the Vietnamese Communist Party, and the Kampuchean People's Revolutionary Council, which acted as the state apparatus. To ensure that they controlled the vital matters of national defense, internal security, and diplomacy, the Vietnamese placed those issues in the hands of the party, where Hanoi could continue to exercise direct influence.[13] A defector from the Foreign Ministry claimed that fifteen Vietnamese advisers supervised the work of the Foreign Ministry's fourteen departments, and that all matters of foreign policy were handled with guidance from those advisers.[14] Dy Lamthol, a former PRK civil servant who defected in 1982, claimed that policies were initiated by the Vietnamese through a shadowy unit called B68.[15] According to Lamthol, who was interviewed for a piece in the weekly newsmagazine *Far Eastern Economic Review*, "Everything is coming from the Vietnamese."[16] Even Heng Samrin, the face of the PRK, was totally dependent on Vietnamese support and had no independent power base of his own.[17]

Bangkok regarded the occupation and the PRK regime as a clear and present danger to Thailand's security. To use the language of my theoretical argument, the PRK's alignment with (and control by) Hanoi was incompatible with Thailand's preference for a nonaligned or friendly Cambodia. Phnom Penh's geopolitical orientation threatened Thai interests in two ways. First, the invasion and occupation upset the balance of power in mainland Southeast Asia. In an address in December 1979, Thai foreign minister Uppadit Pachariyangkun outlined two objections to the situation in Cambodia: the invasion set a danger-ous precedent against noninterference and respect for sovereignty in the region, and a pro-Vietnamese regime in Cambodia upset the political balance in the region.[18]

Second, Thailand worried about Vietnam's expansionist ambitions. By invading Cambodia and setting up a friendly puppet regime, Hanoi revealed itself to be a highly aggressive state. As the invasion came only a year after the establishment of the Vietnamese "special relationship" with Laos, Bangkok worried that it might be the start of a larger drive for Vietnamese regional hegemony. The Vietnamese vision of Communism was internationalist, with Vietnam taking a leading role in Indochina. Vietnam had previously trained and supported insurgents in the Communist Party of Thailand, and the Viet-namese occupation of Cambodia and near-total control of the PRK put Hanoi in a much better position to easily resume these activities. Bangkok therefore believed that the Vietnamese were committed to aiding the revolution else-where in the region.[19]

Leaving aside Communist ideology, Thai officials worried that Vietnam had designs on Thai territory and would not be content with Cambodia.[20] In conver-sations with Thai academics that took place in 1985, the Thai Ministry of Foreign Affairs decried the violation of Cambodia's sovereignty, saying that there was no guarantee that Thailand would avoid a similar fate.[21] Interpreting Vietnamese actions through the lens of historical experience, Thai strategists considered it inevitable that Vietnam would turn on Thailand next.[22] No longer a neutral buf-fer, Cambodia could serve as a staging ground for a conventional confrontation between Vietnam and Thailand. For Bangkok, war would have been a worst-case outcome. The Vietnamese possessed superior military strength compared to the Thai. Bangkok, lying about 200 kilometers from the Cambodian border, was vulnerable to attack. Worse, Thailand's traditional regional ally, the United States, had all but pulled out of Southeast Asia, and showed no appetite to fight the Vietnamese again.

Survey evidence supports the interpretation that Vietnam and the PRK's orientation toward Vietnam fed Thailand's sense of insecurity. A 1982 survey of 2,000 political, military, state, and intellectual elites found that the countries most likely to be named as threats to Thailand were Vietnam (97% of responses), the Soviet Union (96%), and the PRK (86%).[23] Of those who named Vietnam, 74% specified that threat as direct military aggression and 81% specified it as political subversion (support for Communism). While Thai elites agreed that the PRK was also a threat, they perceived a lower level of threat than from Vietnam. This suggests that it was not so much the PRK as an entity that Thailand opposed, but rather Vietnam and its control over the PRK.

In a 1985 conversation between Ministry of Foreign Affairs officials and Thai academics, one Thai scholar explicitly linked Vietnam's domination of neighboring Cambodia to Thai security:

> What is the implication for Thailand if Vietnam should completely dominate Kampuchea? I think it would make the Vietnamese leaders more careless and there is the possibility of greater security threats to Thailand and greater pressure along the disputed Thailand-Laos border. Under such conditions we may sacrifice certain advantages on the Thai-Kampuchea border if our bargaining position is reduced. Also, it could lead to the revival of separatist factions or insurgents who have bases in the neighboring countries. It may sound as though these developments are impossible but we must be prepared.[24]

Clearly, Cambodia's political orientation and Vietnam's heavy control of the country could not stand.

Faced with Cambodia's realignment and considerable evidence of Vietnamese aggression in the region, Thailand needed to act. However, its options for pursuing its policy interests against the PRK and Hanoi were limited. In a different international context, Thailand would have done what it had always done in the past: mount a counterinvasion of Cambodia to drive out the Vietnamese. In 1979, that option was essentially off the table. Perhaps alluding to the emerging international normative and legal regime governing armed intervention, "at a heated strategy debate in early 1979," according to Nayan Chanda, Prime Minister Kriangsak Chamanan "countered the argument for direct intervention by asking, 'In whose name do we go in? The Khmer Rouge?'"[25] Thailand could not justify a counterinvasion by claiming to act on behalf of Khmer Rouge. The international community considered the Khmer Rouge to be a vile regime, and even if the regime had been toppled by illegal means, the moral argument for returning it to power was thin.

Nor was self-defense a compelling argument. The Vietnamese had invoked that justification for their own invasion of Cambodia, but the Western powers, China, and non-Communist states rejected this line of reasoning. Because the self-defense justification failed for Vietnam, which faced a clear, ongoing threat to its peace and security, a Thai counterinvasion was not likely to be well received. If Thailand was not careful, it could find itself on the receiving end of international isolation or punishments, just as Vietnam did after its invasion of Cambodia.

An additional constraint was the probability of success. Though a conventional war fought on Thai territory was a nightmare scenario, an intervention in Cambodia to expel a militarily stronger opponent was similarly unappealing and would likely end in defeat. The Vietnamese were a battle-hardened enemy with a track record. In recent years, they had conquered South Vietnam, quelled an insurgency, prevailed against the United States, and toppled the Khmer Rouge. The dim prospects for a conventional solution to Thailand's Cambodia dilemma made subversion, with its strategic and operational advantages, all the more appealing as a foreign policy instrument.

Subversion and the Khmer Resistance

Sufficiently motivated by divergent preferences regarding Cambodia's geopolitical alignment, and with conventional action essentially off the table, Thailand decided to deal with its security problem next door by engaging in subversion. Conveniently, Bangkok found proxies who were willing to cooperate and were already encamped on the Thai side of the border. After the fall of Phnom Penh, many Cambodians fled into Thailand. Several resistance groups also took shelter on the Thai side of the border. Three main groups emerged: the Khmer Rouge; the Khmer People's National Liberation Front (KPNLF); and the National United Front for an Independent, Neutral, Peaceful, and Cooperative Cambodia (FUNCINPEC, the French acronym).[26] Although the KPNLF and FUNCINPEC were anti-Communist and therefore more ideologically appealing to Bangkok, they lacked the military and organizational capabilities of the Communist Khmer Rouge. Consequently, the Khmer Rouge became Bangkok's primary agent for subversion.

The proximate objective of subversion was tie-down. As Thailand's proxy, the Khmer Rouge could enter Cambodian territory and confront the Vietnamese and the PRK in ways that Thailand could not. By distracting and harassing the new regime, subversion would ensure that the PRK and the Vietnamese would pay high costs to establish authority over Cambodia. Although states can do more than one thing at once, resources and attention are not limitless. Preventing state consolidation would force the PRK and the Vietnamese to spend more resources on stabilization than they otherwise would—and in turn, reduce the resources available for threatening Thailand's sovereignty and security. As one Thai military thinker observed, "Having lost Cambodia as a buffer, the best Thailand could do was to sustain the fighting that in itself constituted a buffer."[27] A Thai scholar concurred with this sentiment, noting that "the border camps became effective political, economic, and military tools for Thailand, together with China and the United States, to hinder the efforts of the Vietnamese and PRK governments from rebuilding Cambodia."[28] If properly empowered and supported, perhaps the Khmer Rouge might even be able to convince the Vietnamese to abandon their Cambodian adventure, much in the way that the Vietnamese themselves had convinced the United States to abandon South Vietnam.[29] Successful subversion could achieve Thailand's goals with plausible deniability and minimal material cost.

Bangkok's strategy of subversion involved three prongs of assistance: hosting the Khmer Rouge on Thai territory, cajoling and coercing international aid groups to resuscitate the Khmer Rouge's malnourished and sickly fighters, and cooperating with China to arm the Khmer Rouge. The first prong was shelter. After their capture of Phnom Penh in January 1979, the Vietnamese spent the next four months flushing the Khmer Rouge out of the Cambodian countryside. Thailand actively permitted the Khmer Rouge and the other groups to seek refuge on Thai territory, using their sovereignty as a shield. Though the Vietnamese pursued the Khmer Rouge to the border, they generally refrained from violating Thai sovereignty. On the infrequent occasions when they did make cross-border incursions, the Thai military drove them back into Cambodia.

The encampment of the Khmer Rouge alongside civilian refugees on the Thai side of the border paved the way for the second prong of subversion: the diversion of international humanitarian assistance intended for the refugees. The refugee presence provided important political cover for Bangkok. Thailand could demand international assistance and aid for the refugees, and secretly allocate some of that aid to the Khmer Rouge. The importance of this aid as a component of Thai subversion cannot be overstated. When the Khmer Rouge fled Cambodia, they entered Thailand gravely ill and severely malnourished. They were in no state to challenge the Vietnamese to a military contest. Bangkok needed the Khmer Rouge to recover as quickly as possible to prevent the PRK and the Vietnamese from consolidating their control of Cambodia.

This was not an easy task for Bangkok. Thailand needed to resupply the Khmer Rouge. However, the United Nations Joint Mission, a group of aid agencies and organizations cooperating to alleviate the humanitarian crisis on the border, refused to deliver food aid to soldiers like the Khmer Rouge. To skirt this problem, Bangkok began diverting international food shipments intended for civilians. The UN Joint Mission estimated that up to half of its shipments went to soldiers rather than civilian refugees.[30] The Thai took control of the World Food Program's food stocks and secretly delivered a portion of that food to the Khmer Rouge in violation of the program's rules.[31] When the Joint Mission suspended food distribution to the Khmer Rouge–controlled refugee camps following a Vietnamese incursion into Thailand in June 1980, the Thai retaliated by banning all humanitarian assistance. Bangkok made it clear that the ban was punishment for the interruption of aid to the Khmer Rouge. The refugee presence thus provided politically useful leverage, as Thailand could make food distribution to the Khmer Rouge a condition of humanitarian assistance to the civilian refugees.

The third prong of subversion involved cooperation between Bangkok and Beijing to arm the Khmer Rouge. Like Bangkok, Beijing feared an expansion of Vietnamese influence in Southeast Asia. It too concluded that subversion offered a convenient, cheap, and effective means of putting the Vietnamese in their place. Beijing sought to provide material support to the Khmer Rouge, but this required using Thailand as the overland conduit for that support.[32] Because Thai authorities were willing to do what was necessary short of war to dispense with the Vietnamese threat, they showed little compunction about cooperating with the state that had once supported Thailand's own Communist insurgency.[33] Beijing and Bangkok thus put aside their differences and struck a de facto alliance to open a "Deng Xiaoping Trail" that would permit Chinese arms, ammunition, heavy weapons, food, medicine, and civilian supplies to reach the three Khmer resistance groups.[34] Thailand transported Chinese arms and supplies directly to the resistance groups as part of its strategy to block Vietnamese consolidation over Cambodia.

This three-pronged strategy of subversion transformed the Khmer Rouge from a defeated band of malnourished soldiers into a fighting force capable of meeting the Vietnamese military in battle. It is important to note that Thai assistance to the Khmer Rouge was by no means a foregone conclusion. As I argued in the theoretical discussion in chapter 2, and as I showed in chapter 4, the choice of proxy depends not on identity or ideology but on shared preferences toward the target state. The Thai–Khmer Rouge alliance of convenience is a clear illustration of this point. Bangkok had no love for the Khmer Rouge. The Communist regime had once had fraught relations with Bangkok, though an uneasy rapprochement began in 1977.[35] Moreover, the Khmer Rouge were a morally repugnant group that had exterminated a quarter of Cambodia's population during their rule. Yet national security concerns and political expediency called for putting aside Bangkok's very real disgust for the Khmer Rouge; these were the agents available for subversion. To paraphrase a Thai expression, Bangkok had to use a thorn to pull a thorn: to drive the Vietnamese from Cambodia and secure itself, Thailand would have to support the Khmer Rouge.[36] Had Thai authorities refused to permit the Khmer Rouge on their territory, it is conceivable that the Vietnamese military would have destroyed the only resistance group with the manpower to mount a significant challenge to the Vietnamese in 1979.[37] Instead, Thailand's willingness to assist the Khmer Rouge proved crucial to the group's recovery and its subsequent efforts to block the consolidation of the state in Cambodia.

Effects on the Consolidation of State Authority

What were the effects of subversion on state consolidation in Vietnamese-occupied Cambodia? To answer this question, I compare levels of state authority, control, and administration between regions of Cambodia beginning in 1979. The PRK's task when it assumed power was to project authority everywhere throughout Cambodia's territory. As a puppet regime of a foreign occupying power, the PRK had no control beyond Phnom Penh.[38] Moreover, the devastation that the Khmer Rouge wrought on the country from 1975 to 1979 meant that Cambodia lacked even the physical manifestations of state power that the PRK could have used to extend its authority. For the PRK, Cambodia was like a blank slate.

The state of ruin in the country was so total that it is hard to fathom. Hearing the story of the Khmer Rouge's excesses and seeing the country for the first time, outside observers described Cambodia as having returned to the "dark ages."[39] When Vietnamese forces and the FUNSK—that Vietnamese organization with a Khmer name—arrived in the provincial administration centers, they found the cities easy to take, as, according to Margaret Slocomb, they had been "virtually empty for three years."[40] A longtime journalist of the region described the country in 1979 as "a land without money, markets, postal system, or schools."[41] Nothing even resembling a state administration remained: no records of land ownership existed, no taxes had been collected for at least nine years, and there were no government ministry buildings even in Phnom Penh.[42] A report published by the humanitarian organization Oxfam minced no words about the state of state authority:

> The country, by 1979, had no currency, no financial institutions, and virtually no industry. The trains were not running and the roads were damaged and unrepaired. There was no postal system, no telephones, and virtually no electricity, clean water, sanitation, or education. . . . The country's infrastructure was destroyed. Of 450 doctors before 1975, only about 50 remained in the country in 1979. The rest had been murdered or escaped abroad. Of the 20,000 teachers in the early '70s only 5,000 remained. Very few trained administrators survived—those who took their place under Heng Samrin were generally very young and inexperienced.[43]

The PRK's complete lack of state authority outside Phnom Penh presents a unique opportunity for analysis. Because the PRK and its Vietnamese backers had to start from nothing, prior levels of state weakness are unlikely to threaten my ability to draw valid conclusions about the effect of subversion on state consolidation. Put differently, it is unlikely that the PRK's failure to consolidate state authority could be the result of uneven levels of state presence before the onset of subversion since there was no state presence of which to speak. For the PRK, the entirety of Cambodia outside the capital was an "ungoverned space," over which authority was to be asserted.

My theory predicts that Thai subversion would be most likely to block state consolidation in northwestern Cambodia, the part of the country nearest to the Thai border. In chapter 2, I introduced the notion of a loss-of-interference gradient, where the effect of subversion should decline with distance. I expect to observe a similar relationship here, particularly in the earliest years of Thai subversion, since those efforts involved sheltering, supporting, and supplying the Khmer Rouge from Thai territory. I therefore compare state authority between regions of Cambodia, and expect to observe greater state consolidation challenges in the Northwest than in other parts of the country.

As I did in the previous chapter, I look for evidence of weak state authority between regions and in different functional areas of state activity, beginning with the maintenance of security and order. The Vietnamese drove the Khmer Rouge out of Cambodian territory in August 1979.[44] While they succeeded in stabilizing other parts of the country, the Northwest proved difficult to pacify because of its proximity to Thailand. After resting and recuperating on Thai territory, the Khmer Rouge resumed military activities against the Vietnamese and the PRK with the 1980–81 dry season. In 1981, the Khmer Rouge gained authority and control over several areas in the Northwest, including the provinces of Battambang, Siem Reap, Oddar Meanchey, and Preah Vihear (see figure 6.1).[45] The violent contestation for territorial control also extended into southwestern Cambodia and the Cardamom Mountains.[46] For the next few years, conflict followed a seasonal cycle. In the dry season, when the terrain was amenable to the movements of a conventionally equipped army, the Vietnamese military went on the offensive and pushed west. In the rainy season, the resistance groups retook control of territory and the populations therein, and rebuilt their military camps. Although the Khmer Rouge could not easily hold territory, the state couldn't either—an indication of the Khmer Rouge's success at preventing the state from consolidating control.

Thai support for the Khmer Rouge proved crucial for events in Cambodia after an unusually long dry-season campaign in 1984–85. The Vietnamese army smashed the resistance bases inside Cambodia, including the base at Phnom Malai in Battambang Province, which had previously been firmly under the control of the Khmer Rouge.[47] That victory proved to be pyrrhic: the flight of civilians under the Khmer Rouge's control into refugee camps on the Thai side of the border was actually advantageous for the resistance. The shield of Thai sovereignty protected the civilians from attack, and the relief organizations took over the provision of food and care. This meant that the Khmer Rouge no longer had to provide for basic order and security for their civilians. Several thousand soldiers out of an estimated 25,000 to 30,000 were now freed from defense duties and could instead concentrate full time on undermining Vietnamese control of Cambodia.[48]

FIGURE 6.1. Provinces of Cambodia as of 1980. The crosshatched area indicates Tonlé Sap Lake.

The Khmer Rouge thus moved the fight against Vietnamese control further into the interior of the country. For the first time, the resistance struck against Vietnamese authority in the eastern part of the country in a meaningful way. The PRK reported that in 1984, 15,000 "enemies" operated inside Cambodia; by 1987, that number had risen to 21,000.[49] Attacks were recorded in the towns of Battambang and Siem Reap in the Northwest; Kampong Thom, Kampong Chhnang, and Oudong (in Kampong Speu Province) in the center, and Takeo south of Phnom Penh.[50] One year later, Prey Veng, Svay Rieng, and Kampong Speu in the Southeast were also hit. The spread of insecurity into previously untouched parts of Cambodia reflects the evolution of the Khmer Rouge's strategy: from defense of fixed territorial bases to guerrilla warfare. The new strategy altered the Khmer Rouge's challenge to Vietnamese authority from one of depth to one of breadth. Whereas the defense of territory produced concentrated pockets of ungoverned space outside the control of the Vietnamese and the PRK, guerrilla attacks spread insecurity well beyond the Thai border but did not result in the capture of territory. This strategy was made possible by Bangkok's willingness to allow the Khmer Rouge's civilian population to shelter on Thai soil.

The instability in the Northwest contrasts with the PRK's success in establishing order in other parts of Cambodia, particularly in the regions bordering Laos and Vietnam. Two pieces of evidence support this conclusion. First, compared to the stable areas of the country, the Northwest attracted disproportionate amounts of attention from scholars and journalists interested in covering the conflict. These accounts naturally focused on the sites where the Khmer Rouge were actively operating, and primarily concentrated on events taking place in the Northwest. The absence of reports of violence in other parts of the country thus suggests that the PRK was able to consolidate authority elsewhere.

Second, because it can be tricky to interpret absence of evidence as evidence itself, I also infer where the PRK and the Vietnamese did not exercise state authority by examining their defensive behavior within the country. Since the Khmer Rouge's guerrilla tactics undercut Vietnam's conventional superiority, the PRK began laying antipersonnel mines as a defensive strategy. The PRK focused on areas where its authority was most tenuous, and where the Khmer Rouge were most threatening. The scale of these efforts was massive: by the end of the 1984–85 dry-season campaign, the PRK laid 464,000 land mines and planned on laying another 1.6 million the next year.[51] Land mines are difficult to detect once laid, and expensive to remove, and for those reasons they are a cause of serious accidents. The location of these accidents, even decades later, indicates where the PRK thought their authority was weak at the time the mines were laid. Figure 6.2 depicts mine and unexploded ordnance accidents by province from 2005 to 2007, per 10,000 population. Consistent with my expectations, the northwestern regions have a greater density of accidents than other parts of the country. Because the data are normalized by population, the spatial distribution of accidents points toward weaker state control in the Northwest near Thailand, and stronger state control elsewhere.[52]

I also look for evidence of uneven state authority in terms of the state's physical presence. I argued in chapter 2 that subversion undermines state authority by destroying the physical means through which the state governs and projects power. The Khmer Rouge understood the centrality of physical state presence for the PRK's ability to govern, and they cut a path of destruction and lawlessness through the countryside with the aim of undermining that state presence. For example, the PRK sought to consolidate control of territory by building roads, railroads, and air, sea, and river ports. The Khmer Rouge responded with a sabotage campaign that entailed attacking local government facilities, mining roads, and highways; blowing up bridges; and disrupting the railroads.[53] Route 6, which ran from the Thai border through Siem Reap to Kompong Thom, was

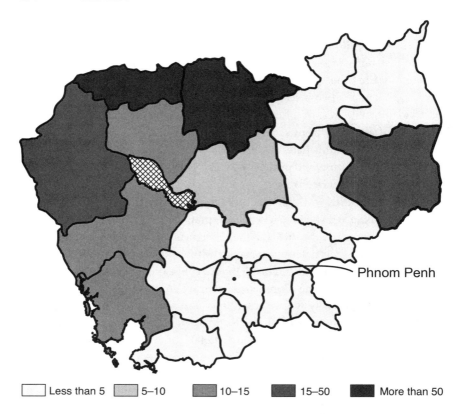

Phnom Penh

☐ Less than 5   ▨ 5–10   ▨ 10–15   ■ 15–50   ■ More than 50

FIGURE 6.2. Mine and unexploded-ordnance accidents in Cambodia, 2005–7.
Map shows accidents per 10,000 population and depicts the 1980 boundaries
of Cambodia. Accident data cover the period January 2005–December 2007.
Data are from the Cambodian Mine Action and Victim Assistance Authority
as reported in Wheeler 2008. Population data are from 2004 as reported in
National Institute of Statistics 2004, 58. Because landmines are inherently
difficult to detect, accident data are useful for revealing the location of mines laid
during the 1980s—which in turn indicates areas where the state did not exercise
effective control and authority. The crosshatched area indicates Tonlé Sap Lake.

closed to civilian traffic due to the lack of security.[54] A senior Vietnamese military observer noted that the main routes between Phnom Penh and the western border with Thailand were in a permanent state of insecurity due to the Khmer Rouge's activities.[55]

Disruption and destruction in the northwestern and southern parts of the country contrast with successful statebuilding activities elsewhere. For example, the state began repairing the river port at Phnom Penh and the seaport at Sihanoukville (Kampong Som, then located in Kampot Province), paved new asphalt roads, and restored bridges.[56] It also built new schools, hospitals, and health facilities. By the end of 1982, 80% of children were back in school, and health centers spread throughout the country.[57] The PRK placed particular emphasis on penetrating the remote and geographically challenging northeastern part of the country near Laos and Vietnam, and it offered incentives to attract teachers and technicians to work in that area.[58] By 1988, the state also constructed new agricultural development and research centers essential for the promotion of agriculture. These centers were located in the southern provinces of Kandal, Kampong Speu, Takeo, and Prey Veng; one rice research center was established in Battambang in the Northwest.[59] Thus, even though the PRK could not maintain and easily defend state infrastructure in the Northwest, it did enjoy statebuilding successes in other regions.

The failure to consolidate authority in northwestern Cambodia compared to elsewhere is also evident in the administrative difficulties that the PRK encountered in the provinces of that region. Besides being insecure, northwestern Cambodia was also a political and administrative vacuum. PRK cadres that were sent to the northwestern districts in 1985 found that the state was virtually absent in an administrative sense; in some places ordinary Cambodians had never had contact with PRK administrators at all.[60] The KPNLF, one of the militarily weaker resistance groups, undermined the PRK's civil and military bureaucracy by sending political cadres into the interior to counter the PRK cadres by delegitimizing the Vietnamese-backed regime and its authority.[61] The Khmer Rouge's attacks on local government offices in the communes and districts also impeded basic administrative activity. A report to the National Assembly expressed deep concern about the psychological effects the attacks had on the bureaucrats and other government workers, and worried that the attacks "numb their will for battle and fulfilling duties."[62]

The Khmer Rouge also used psychological warfare and propaganda to empty state offices of their bureaucrats and to redirect citizen loyalties away from the state. The Khmer Rouge attempted to convince local Cambodians to resist the authority of the PRK and their Vietnamese backers, and to avoid a situation in which Khmers fought other Khmers. Near-constant anti-Vietnamese propaganda sought to delegitimize the Vietnamese and the PRK government. The Khmer Rouge depicted the Vietnamese as foreign occupiers, and the PRK as its puppet. In that vein, the resistance movements themselves were an important symbol against perceived Vietnamese oppression.

The propaganda campaign had insidious effects on state authority. One scholar of the PRK period of Cambodia observed that the "relentless propaganda campaign waged against [the regime], particularly that of denigrating the PRK leadership as the yuon (Vietnamese) head on the Khmer body, was very difficult to combat and as corrosive as the highly effective guerrilla war."[63] This psychological warfare was particularly damaging to state authority in the northwestern part of the country near Thailand. Khmer Rouge propaganda disrupted local governance by promoting absenteeism through the allure of easy wealth obtained via gem mining. As late as 1989, for example, a PRK circular claimed that in Battambang Province in the Northwest,

> between ten and twenty percent of cadres, staff, and workers in the departments and units of the province have given up their state jobs, their military units, and district duties; the village and commune militias are lacking fighting force, some schools and hospitals have closed their doors, and they have all gone to dig for gems, creating a confused situation throughout the province.[64]

The Khmer Rouge's deleterious effects on state consolidation in Cambodia thus extended beyond the spread of disorder to include the impediment of basic government services in the Northwest.

The PRK was able to reconstitute state authority in other parts of the country. In the immediate aftermath of its victory, when there was no state to administer, the PRK encouraged local leaders like village elders and chiefs to help build state authority.[65] Later, the state took a more active role in selecting local administrators, and staffed the new bureaucratic positions in the countryside with a mix of prerevolutionary officials and respected locals. In the parts of the country that were stable, such as Koh Kong, Kampong Som, Svay Rieng, and the Northeast more generally, the PRK and the Vietnamese could afford to appoint individuals with close political ties to Cambodian leaders. In the parts of the country that were not stable, the PRK did not have this luxury. For example, Battambang in the Northwest was the site of fighting and Khmer Rouge resistance, and the Vietnamese required that a loyal cadre be installed in that strategically significant region. They sent a Khmer Communist trained in Hanoi to govern the unruly province after the previous governor defected to Thailand.[66] By 1982, the government had recruited and trained tens of thousands of new cadres, and in the district and subdistrict levels, administrative units below the province, cadres were working in Kandal, Prey Veng, Kampong Speu, and Kampong Thom.[67] The presence of state officials in the countryside meant that many parts of Cambodia were in fact governed. This did not necessarily mean that those areas were governed well. In a circular dated January 31, 1984, Acting Prime Minister Chea Soth chastised some government bureaucrats for misbehaving and abusing their authority.[68] The circular warned that this kind of malfeasance could jeopardize loyalties to the PRK. While serious, these problems of state administration paled in comparison to the situation in the Northwest, where state workers were virtually absent and state services suspended.

Just as we saw in chapter 5's case study of the Philippines, the target state linked its consolidation problems to the activities of an external sponsor. Whereas the Philippines was willing to concede in the underlying dispute with Malaysia, the PRK and the Vietnamese saw no room for bargaining with Thailand. Instead the PRK sought to shut off Thailand's support through physical means. The key to this effort was the K5 project. This project involved the construction of a massive wall along the 800-kilometer Thai-Cambodian border to deter and prevent the infiltration of resistance forces from Thai territory.[69] The human labor requirements of this project were staggering. In 1984, more than 90,000 workers were deployed; in 1985, another 26,000 were requested.[70] The K5 project also involved laying land mines, but because the state provided little instruction, the mining effort killed and maimed many of the workers sent to the Thai border. No wonder that few ordinary Cambodians volunteered to work on the project. The vast majority had to be conscripted, a practice that proved to be deeply unpopular and further undermined the Vietnamese and the PRK government's attempts to win the population. For the PRK, Thailand's role in subversion necessitated this project. That the PRK and their Vietnamese backers expended significant political and human capital on the construction of the K5 wall is a testament to their belief in the severity of Thailand's role as host to the Khmer Rouge and other resistance groups.

Blocking the Leviathan

The Cambodian case offers several lessons about the relationship between subversion and weak statehood. Like the previous chapter, this chapter's examination of two nongreat powers illustrates how one state can use subversion in lieu of conventional force to achieve its foreign policy objectives against a militarily stronger adversary. The close relationship between the PRK and Vietnam meant that Vietnam acted as the PRK's security apparatus. Thailand feared a conventional confrontation against its more capable opponent, but the strategic and operational benefits of subversion—plausible deniability, political cover, and territorial access and expertise—allowed Bangkok to prevent the PRK and the Vietnamese from consolidating control over Cambodia. While we cannot know whether Vietnam would have continued its expansion west across the Indochinese peninsula as Bangkok feared, subversion forced Hanoi and the PRK to expend considerable resources throughout the 1980s to assert authority over the Northwest.

The case also reinforces an important theoretical point about proxies and the instrumental nature of subversion. Thailand's partnership with the Khmer Rouge was not based on ethnic kinship, shared culture, religious identity, or ideological ties. To a greater degree than we have seen in the preceding empirical chapters, Bangkok and the Khmer Rouge cooperated only because the Khmer Rouge were the only viable agents on the ground. The Thai abhorred the Khmer Rouge both for their Communist ideology and for the atrocities and genocide that the regime had perpetrated on the Cambodian people, but subversion required Bangkok to hold its nose and look the other way. Indeed, subversion makes strange bedfellows: Thailand even cooperated with China, its former adversary, to help the Khmer Rouge undermine state authority against their mutual enemies in Cambodia. This suggests that either the threshold for agent suitability is small or that a lack of alternatives forces greater pragmatism between the sponsor and proxy.

Bangkok's political expediency points to an important lesson for policymakers. If actors who are otherwise adversaries will work together to subvert state authority, it will be difficult to sever the link between external interference and internal state consolidation in the face of extreme threat or policy incompatibility. Although the geopolitical backdrop of the Cold War heightened the stakes for Thailand, Bangkok's fear of Vietnam and its strong preference for a nonaligned or friendly Cambodia predated the Cold War by centuries. The inconvenient fact that the Khmer Rouge were genocidal butchers did little to deter Thailand from choosing subversion when conventional force was not a feasible alternative. Bangkok worked with the agents that were available and willing to cooperate with it. So long as agents are available and the policy disputes are sufficiently severe and irreconcilable, subversion is likely to remain a part of the foreign policy toolkit.

Conclusion

THE LEVIATHAN, CRIPPLED

Relations between states affect order within states. Subversion is a powerful foreign policy instrument, and its effects strike at the heart of what it means to be a state in the international system. The international system is essentially a club in which entry is based on recognition by other members of the club and membership is organized around the principle of formal equality. Yet formal equality does not imply similarity. Indeed, formal equality belies significant heterogeneity in the units of the system. International relations scholars already recognize that states differ in terms of their power and capabilities, and that these differences are consequential for understanding what states do and how their actions affect other states. What has received less attention is the fact that states differ on a much more fundamental level: their degree of *stateness*. Comparatively few units in the international system are fully consolidated states that exercise authority throughout their territories. Among those that fall short of this standard, the variation in state authority is considerable. This book has sought to understand and explain that variation.

I have argued that we cannot understand the problem of incomplete state consolidation as the product of domestic factors alone. Rather, a more complete picture begins with the observation that countries may have incompatible interests. In pursuit of these interests, one state can harness political subversion against the territorial authority of another state. Subversion entails the empowerment of proxies to degrade state authority in a target state. Armed and sheltered by external sponsors, proxies impose costs on the exercise of authority by eliminating the physical presence of the target state, building parallel institutions that substitute for the state, and persuading citizens to switch their loyalties to an entity claiming final authority that is not the state itself. These activities profoundly weaken the target state. They prevent state consolidation, and they allow ungoverned and partially governed spaces to persist beyond the state's reach. Violence can be a part of this process, and it features in cases where the target state fights back against externally supported challenges to its authority. Even where violence does not emerge, however, these subversive activities stunt the state itself: the leviathan remains juridically intact but effectively crippled.

Two key aspects of this book's theory and evidence will be of general interest to political scientists. International relations scholars will be most interested in the kinds of states that use subversion, an important instrument of statecraft that the IR literature has not previously appreciated. Comparativists will be interested in the types of countries likely to be affected by subversion. More broadly, they will want to know when international factors are part of the explanation for enduring state weakness, and when we should look instead to domestic factors.

With respect to the international relations question, my theory holds that strong states and weak states alike can use subversion. The evidence is clear on this point. Russia, a great power, undermined authority in Georgia, and Malaysia and Thailand, both nongreat powers, undermined authority in the Philippines and Cambodia, respectively. Other nongreat powers beyond Malaysia and Thailand have also dirtied their hands with subversion. Syria, Mozambique, and Uganda also engaged in subversion, and it remains a key instrument of Iranian statecraft today. Even Pakistan, a nuclear state that fought conventional wars against India, engaged in subversion. Means and motive structure when states are likely to engage in subversion, but conditional on those two factors being met, there appears to be little limit to the kinds of states that can add this tool to their foreign policy toolkit. The generalizability of my findings to strong and weak states alike thus points to this book's powerful lesson about the hidden and covert nature of interstate conflict in the contemporary period.

With respect to the question of when subversion explains state weakness, the evidence points to three answers. Because my sample of states includes observations before and after 1989, subversion is not an instrument of statecraft confined to the Cold War period. My sample's coverage of all world regions except the West also indicates that subversion's harmful effects on state authority are not limited to one particular region. Together, these first two answers point to the generalizability of my findings across regions and time, at least since 1960. Subversion remains a source of state weakness for many countries even today.

Beyond space and time, this book makes a valuable contribution by studying states that occupy the middle range of the sovereignty spectrum. These are states that are neither fully consolidated nor totally failed. Because they constitute the majority of the countries in the international system, the middle-range cases are also important in their own right as objects of study. This book shows that these are the states where subversion will contribute meaningfully to weak state authority. Strong states are more likely to counter the damage dealt to the exercise of authority. Failed states are too disordered for subversion to inflict much more chaos. This does not mean that sponsor states will not try to target adversaries that occupy the ends of the sovereignty spectrum—only that in these places it is unlikely that subversion imposes large costs on state authority. For the middle-range states, subversion is a powerful impediment to state consolidation. No wonder, then, that these states continue to compose the greatest expanse of ungoverned and partially governed space across the world.

The International Roots of Weak Statehood

States have always faced the challenge of consolidating their authority over territory, but the 9/11 terror attacks imbued this problem with new urgency. U.S. policymakers now recognized that weak states might be sources of international security threats. They also realized that the weak state challenge was not only the lack of strong state institutions, but also the failure of the state to exert effective authority throughout its territory. The problem of ungoverned and partially governed space looms large on the U.S. and Western foreign policy agendas. Even as voices in Washington call for U.S. foreign policy to refocus itself on an assertive China and resurgent Russia, policymakers still characterize weak statehood and its security externalities as threats to U.S. interests. This conviction is clear in the securitization of development and remains a justification for state- and nationbuilding.[1] The United States no longer uses those terms to describe such activities, instead preferring the euphemism of "stabilization." Nevertheless, the core mission remains the same. If the problem in some parts of the developing world is that there is not enough state in not enough places, the solution that the security and development communities have converged on is to expand the state's authority.

In confronting this problem, this book calls us to understand incomplete state consolidation through the lens of international politics. Once we recognize the role of subversion in undermining the state, we can no longer treat state weakness as a solely technical or solely domestic problem. This observation may seem trivial, but it challenges existing practices in foreign assistance and externally led statebuilding. These practices often rest on the implicit or explicit assumption that state weakness stems from scarce fiscal resources, a lack of technical knowledge and expertise, and malformed institutions. In other words, the reason why states do not exercise effective authority over their territory is that it is simply too expensive to do so—or that states do not know how to do it effectively. In some cases, this worldview may correctly characterize the problem. The physical challenges of projecting authority over long distances and difficult geographies certainly influence the extent to which states govern their territories. So too do fiscal constraints, which make it harder to maintain an adequate bureaucratic presence in peripheral areas.

When external policymakers and international organizations recognize the political dimensions of state authority, they tend to treat it as a purely domestic issue. In one version of this perspective, the problem is a lack of political will. In a second version, the problem is a lack of legitimacy. The off-the-shelf solution to both problems is to improve performance legitimacy by delivering goods and services. Increasing service provision brings the state into closer contact with its population and improves human welfare. To the extent that external actors and states focus their efforts on ungoverned and partially governed spaces, greater service provision should reduce the unevenness in state authority. Here the implicit bias toward technical interventions rears its head again, since the service-provision problem can be reduced to one of fiscal constraint and technical expertise.

This book shows that the statebuilding challenge is not so simple. Its findings demand that policymakers confront the inherently political and international nature of state development. By demonstrating that incomplete state consolidation has international roots stemming from difficult, severe, and sometimes intractable political disputes, this book suggests that there is a limit to what states can achieve with development funds, capacity-building projects, and technical-assistance programs in the absence of political interventions. Technical solutions by their very nature avoid the messy issues of politics. They miss an important contributor to the state weakness problem—the political incentives for states to disrupt governance and state authority in their adversaries. While there are often good reasons why states and international organizations pursue technical solutions, we should be clear-eyed about their limits. At best, such interventions are bandages on bullet wounds.

What can policymakers do to mitigate the problem of weak state authority? To be clear, this book does not advocate statebuilding by external imposition, an ethically nebulous practice with limited success.[2] My argument suggests a more modest approach: sever the link between subversion and weak state authority. My theory holds that states use subversion when they are sufficiently motivated (by policy disputes) and when the means to do so (proxies) are available. This implies three options for states seeking to break the link between subversion and weak state authority: (1) reduce the sponsor's motive, (2) deprive the sponsor of means, and (3) increase the costs of subversion.

The first option calls for addressing the underlying policy disputes that lead states to seek to undermine authority. In principle it is possible to find an agreeable settlement that the disputants should prefer over destructive attempts to undermine authority. Third parties might offer their good offices and mediation services, help enforce and guarantee negotiated deals, or condition rewards on the resolution of disputes. In the Malaysia-Philippines case, the United States refused to involve itself in the territorial dispute over Sabah, but it could have pressured Manila to back away from the Sabah claim. However, we should be skeptical about the prospects of resolving long-running antagonisms. Psychological factors and domestic political strategies of leadership survival can inflame interstate tensions, amplify insecurities, and create the perception of issue indivisibilities. Leaders may fear the reputational repercussions of appearing to back down in the face of an intransigent adversary. Although third parties might be able to design confidence-building and face-saving measures that mitigate some of these problems, these efforts will likely yield only marginal reductions in tensions between states.

Barring a resolution of the issues under dispute, a second possible option is to deprive the sponsor of the means of subversion by addressing the underlying grievances that make agents available. What made possible Malaysian meddling in the Philippines and Russian meddling in Georgia were domestic state policies that produced disaffected, politically marginalized populations willing to cooperate with international sponsors to subvert state authority. Interventions that could address or at least mitigate some of the underlying grievances of these groups could weaken their susceptibility to foreign influence. To the extent that some of these grievances stem from inequalities between groups, development programs and investments may be helpful. However, a political solution will be necessary to fully address and rectify the state policies that created the pool of available agents. Leaders of target states will have to make real political compromises with disaffected populations. External powers could increase the likelihood of a compromise by offering rewards and pressuring target state leaders and local groups to resolve their political differences peacefully.

Neither of the aforementioned policy options will be easy to pursue. It is precisely because policy disputes are so intractable and proxies so disenchanted that states turn to subversion in the first place. Policymakers should thus consider a third option: increase the costs of subversion. Part of the attractiveness of subversion as a form of statecraft is that it is cheap to use. It is cheap in a relative sense, in that to be effective it requires less investment in military capability than conventional force. It is also cheap in an absolute sense, in that subversion costs the state little to host proxy groups, provide diplomatic coverage, funnel military and financial assistance, or offer psychological support. To reduce foreign meddling, powerful states should punish the states that attempt to degrade state authority. Imposing economic sanctions and reducing development aid and military assistance are two possible ways of inflicting costs. Suspending sponsor states from international organizations and international agreements is another.

Fixing the world's unconsolidated states will not be easy. Statebuilding is a decades-long process. External efforts to build and consolidate states often fail; internal efforts have succeeded, but with great bloodshed. This book does not advocate statebuilding as a policy. That decision requires weighing both political and ethical factors. It also requires a clear-eyed reckoning with the political obstacles to state development. Those actors that seek to bring ungoverned and partially governed spaces under the authority of the state will find that there is no silver-bullet solution to the problem of weak statehood. Recognizing that problem's international dimensions, as this book urges, represents an important first step in the process of statebuilding. Only then can we begin to comprehensively address the challenge of ungoverned space.

War by Other Means

One of the most important developments in contemporary international relations is the decline of interstate war. In human welfare terms, that is a normatively good thing. However, this book demonstrates that to view the decline of visible and extreme violence between states as evidence of a decline of conflictual international politics would be a mistake. Conflict is alive. So too are the underlying disputes that give rise to it.

What has changed in the decades following 1945 is not so much the existence of conflict but the preferred method through which states prosecute conflict. Rather than resort to war, states resort to subversion. Subversion is powerful, insidious, and invisible. It can be wielded by the strong. It can be deployed by the weak. It disrupts state authority and blocks state consolidation. As a policy instrument, it also works, as Russian meddling in the post-Soviet space makes abundantly clear. By outsourcing the dirty business to nonstate proxies, subversion allows states to pursue their policy objectives without firing a single shot. To paraphrase Clausewitz, if war is politics by other means, then subversion is war by other means.

This political reality challenges the traditional interstate understandings of conflict that are dominant in the security community. Subversion is complex and messy. When states engage in war, policymakers, analysts, and military strategists understand the threat and how to defeat it. The details vary from case to case, but the basic framework of interstate conflict still applies. When states engage in subversion, it is not obvious that the state-to-state models are relevant. Today's "gray-zone conflicts" and "hybrid wars" bear little resemblance to the traditional forms of interstate contestation on the battlefield. A distinguishing feature of these threats is the blurring of the international and domestic, and the state and nonstate. Subversion is all of these things at once. A state actor empowers a nonstate actor. Political interference originates from an international source but operates through a domestic channel. The causes are external but the consequences are internal.

The traditional division between the domestic and the international leaves policymakers poorly equipped to grapple with interstate relations involving foreign subversion. If we focus only on the interstate dimension, then we fail to see how the empowerment of nonstate proxies acts as an extension of state power and state interests. If we focus only on the intrastate dimension, then we fail to appreciate how international actors sustain weak statehood, protect violent nonstate groups, and perpetuate ungoverned space. This book shows that such strong distinctions between domestic and international politics are unsustainable in analyses of statecraft and conflict in the contemporary period. Those that adhere to a model of foreign policy where interstate politics and domestic politics occupy separate realms operate with a handicap. Their analyses will be flawed, and their policy recommendations will be ineffective or counterproductive. Even worse, they may overlook the emergence of new threats altogether.

Grappling with hybrid threats does not require disposing of international relations theory or existing policymaking models. Rather, our understanding of interstate relations must be enlarged in order to accommodate the evolving ways that states pursue their interests. This book offers policymakers a framework for making sense of today's threats by bringing analytic clarity to the haze of modern conflict. If we think of subversion as a tool that states deploy in their relations with other states, then we return to a world of interstate relations familiar to the policy community. Subversion is a kind of limited unconventional warfare, where the proximate objective is to disrupt but not necessarily overthrow, to divide but not necessarily rule. By offering a rigorous analytical framework backed by scientific evidence, this book illuminates the politics underlying the use of subversion as an instrument of modern statecraft.

Rethinking the Artificiality of States

Understanding subversion as war by other means also demands that we reevaluate the idea that states that did not form through interstate warfare are somehow artificial and thus politically deficient. Many scholars have argued that a unique process of state formation in sub-Saharan Africa is responsible for conflict, economic underperformance, political underdevelopment, and weak state consolidation in that region.[3] According to this literature, former colonial powers created "artificial" borders by drawing straight lines on a map without regard to topography or the identities and interests of the people on the ground. As a result, African states encompass some groups with little desire to live together and partition other groups across international borders. Because international norms prohibit changes to the territorial status quo, these borders are here to stay.[4] The so-called African tragedy is thus twofold: external powers gave Africa inappropriate borders and then prevented Africa from fixing them.

To conclude that bad borders produce bad political outcomes, however, is too simplistic. Focusing on artificial borders as the cause of Africa's woes puts us on the wrong analytic track. It assumes that ethnic identity is politically salient and that individuals prefer to live with their own ethnic kin and cannot abide being governed by non-kin. Even if those assumptions hold, grievance does not automatically produce conflict and weak state authority. This book's theory and evidence reveal a more complicated relationship between political demography and conflict—one mediated by external state adversaries actively seeking to undermine state authority. My argument speaks to the political consequences of partitioned ethnic groups by considering not just the incentives of such actors to resist the state but also their prospects for doing so successfully. External sponsors materially alter those prospects. Just as sponsors need proxies to weaken the target state, so too do proxies require external empowerment to effectively resist central state authority and carve out alternative governance arrangements. This is not to say that ethnic minorities never rise up against state authority on their own—only that the artificial states literature mischaracterizes this process by failing to account for the role of international actors.

Getting the causal story right is important. The artificial states literature points to different policy implications for state consolidation than the ones that arise from my argument. If Africa's ungoverned spaces are the product of externally imposed boundaries, there can be little hope of improving state authority in a world of border fixity. If, however, incomplete state consolidation results from the interaction of international adversaries and partitioned groups, then there are clear entry points for policymakers interested in solving the state weakness problem. That is not the case if we attribute state weakness solely to decisions made at a particular moment in history.

This book also challenges the artificial states literature to reconsider its understanding of state formation and its consequences for governance. The literature implies that there is a "normal" pattern of state development and an "abnormal" pattern of state development. Normal state development refers to the European experience, where European states fought each other to establish topographically natural borders. Abnormal state development refers to the African experience, where African states received artificial straight-line borders and had to live with them. If only African countries had had the opportunity to develop "normally"—waging bloody wars against each other and killing millions of people along the way, as Europeans did—then they would have had better economic and political outcomes and exert greater authority over their territory.

The implications of the artificial states literature are normatively unsustainable. This book shows that they are also empirically wrong. Conflict has not gone away; it merely adopted the guise of subversion. Conflict today does not contest state borders—it contests authority within those borders, with disruptive and insidious consequences for state consolidation. My claim that foreign subversion weakens the state rests on a wealth of scientific evidence drawn from multiple parts of the world and multiple empirical approaches. The conclusions we can draw from that evidence are strong and clear. Greater conflict between states will not be a panacea for the problem of undergovernance. It will not give Africa natural borders. It will not build consolidated states.

Statebuilding and Subversion, Past and Present

The changing practices with respect to the use of force also have implications for understanding statebuilding and state consolidation over the course of the twentieth century. The systemic shift that occurred in 1945 fundamentally altered the relationship between conflictual international politics and internal political development by changing the calculations of states with respect to how they manage their interstate relations. In the early modern period and the 19th century, states that could not peacefully resolve their disputes went to war with their adversaries. For the states that survived, war had beneficial effects for state institutionalization and consolidation. States built institutions, and they devised ways to govern their territories. As a result, these two processes were intimately connected.

The international system of the post-1945 era is one in which the use of force is both materially costly and legally proscribed. While war has certainly not disappeared, the system-level shift changed the way that states restrict, limit, and make costly the use of force, increasing the appeal of weakening state authority for foreign policy gain. Subversion is a form of power, but that power is all the more important when the other tools of statecraft are so costly that they remain in the toolbox. States degrade and cripple governance in their adversaries, and they do so because sovereignty-undermining strategies are attractive and help achieve state objectives. Consequently, the link between state institutionalization and state consolidation has been severed.

By conceptually separating institutionalization and consolidation, it becomes possible to see how the conventional wisdom about conflict and statebuilding is misleading. Many scholars have argued that interstate conflict builds stronger states.[5] This book offers a correction to the bellicist literature. Far from being helpful for state consolidation, conflictual international relations produces profound state weakness. The failure to account for conflictual international politics, and how it might operate differently in the post-1945 world, risks misunderstanding the process of state consolidation and the obstacles to the successful extension of state authority over territory in the contemporary period.

But what if we have misunderstood the process of state consolidation in early modern and 19th-century Europe? The European experience is the baseline for much of the literature on state formation and state development. In those accounts, Europe's strong states emerged due to the exigencies of near-constant warfare and competition between states. As with the scholarship on state consolidation in the contemporary period, subversion is largely absent from that story—but not because subversion did not happen. Rather, scholars have not looked for it in the European experience or considered its consequences for state development. This book shows that once we account for subversion, we understand why state weakness persists in so many places outside Europe. In turn, this suggests an intriguing possibility for reassessing the conventional wisdom of European statebuilding by examining subversion in that context.

Three brief examples drawn from different eras of European history and different parts of the continent point to patterns of international relations and state consolidation similar to those described in this book. First consider the example of British support for the Principality of Catalonia during the War of the Spanish Succession that began in 1701. The war concerned who would rule Spain: Philip V, the Duke of Anjou and a member of the French Bourbons, or Archduke Charles, a member of the Austrian Habsburgs. The Catholic Bourbons were Protestant Britain's enemies and economic rivals, and Britain sought to diminish French power in Europe. Inside Spain, Catalonia was in turmoil. Catalans detested Bourbon France, an absolutist and centralizing state with little respect for minorities. They also resented the local Bourbon administration, which governed the principality in a heavy-handed and brutal way.[6] Thus, the Catalans and the British shared a common interest in thwarting Bourbon state authority in Spain.[7] The Treaty of Genoa of 1705 committed the British to military support and to uphold Catalonia's separate constitution. In return, the Catalans agreed to recognize the Archduke. Together, they ousted the local Bourbon authorities and captured Barcelona for the Archduke, who landed in August 1705. Barcelona became the capital of a parallel court under Habsburg authority, complete with the institutions and governance structures of a real state administration.[8]

Another example of foreign interference is Russian involvement in the Serbian Revolution. The revolution began in the Belgrade Pashalik, an administrative division of the Ottoman Empire. Although Sultan Selim III had promised autonomous rights to the Serbs, conflict between the Porte and the empire's powerful and rebellious slave-soldiers known as janissaries resulted in the suspension of those rights. In 1804, the Serbs rose up in defense of their rights, and they succeeded in gaining control of the pashalik in 1805.[9] Foreign interference shaped the course of this struggle. When the Serbs looked to Russia for support in 1804, Russia demurred. Russia and the Ottomans shared good relations due to their alliance against Napoleonic France, and St. Petersburg encouraged the Serbs to open direct negotiations with the Porte.[10] By 1806, however, the Ottoman Empire had switched sides to ally with France against Russia, provoking war with Russia and altering Russian calculations regarding the Serbs. Russia began supporting the Serb cause, and it provided money, munitions, and naval assistance in an effort to punish the Ottomans.[11] This involvement proved to be so significant that it prolonged the revolution. Russian support encouraged the Serbs to strive not just for autonomy—their original demand and a request the Porte was willing to grant—but for real independence.[12] Importantly, Russian assistance was forthcoming only when Russian and Ottoman interests were at odds; when their interests were aligned, Russia abandoned the Serbs.

A third example comes from Prussia's interference in Schleswig and Holstein, two duchies that formed part of the Kingdom of Denmark. Holstein was German speaking and a member of the German Confederation. Schleswig was Danish speaking and was never a part of either the German Confederation or the Holy Roman Empire, the confederation's predecessor. In the 1840s, tensions escalated between Germans and Danes over language policies and other nationality issues, and came to a head over a succession crisis that threatened to cleave Holstein from its historical association with Schleswig.[13] These events spawned a movement known as Schleswig-Holsteinism, which claimed that the two duchies were a single state that would seek admission into the German Confederation. When Danish liberals known as Eiderdanes pushed the king to assert greater authority over Schleswig, the Schleswig-Holsteiners rebelled and established their own government for the duchies. In Germany, liberals and conservatives alike supported the cause, citing both the need to defend the duchies' German nationality and the revolutionary danger from the liberal Eiderdanes.[14] Prussia, a member of the confederation, intervened on behalf of the Schleswig-Holsteiners. This intervention allowed the fledgling government to survive for a few years until international pressure forced a Prussian withdrawal. Without the advantage of foreign support, the Schleswig-Holsteiners were decisively defeated in 1850.[15]

In all of these examples, foreign interference played an important role in undermining state authority in the target polity. France, Russia, and Prussia all helped to foment internal disorder in the territories of their Spanish, Ottoman, and Danish adversaries. These efforts rendered Catalonia, the Belgrade Pashalik, and Schleswig-Holstein ungovernable from the perspective of central authorities. Yet this interference took a somewhat different form than subversion as I describe it in this book. Subversion in the contemporary period involves empowering, arming, training, and protecting nonstate proxies, almost always without direct armed intervention on the part of the sponsor. Foreign interference in early modern and 19th-century Europe involved the use of force in order to protect nonstate actors seeking to govern in lieu of central state authorities. That foreign interference played out differently before the world wars is not surprising. The international state system was a more fluid place, where borders were not fixed, territorial nation-states existed alongside empires and confederations, and military force was a normal and legitimate means for pursuing foreign policy aims. In other words, subversion-like activities did occur, but they took on a different form that made sense for that time.

The fact that the great powers intervened to protect and support nonstate entities when it suited their foreign policy interests is an important missing piece in the story of European statebuilding. Bourbon Spain, the Ottoman Empire, and the Kingdom of Denmark are not exceptional in European history. Their adversaries' efforts to sow internal dissent and to prop up alternative governance arrangements are examples of a form of statecraft that states deployed throughout the continent. These examples constitute part of a broader systematic pattern driving international relations and state consolidation. Just as scholars have failed to appreciate the role of subversion in the contemporary period, so too have they overlooked subversion in earlier times.

The findings of this book suggest that it is time to correct that oversight. I have demonstrated the power of foreign interference for obstructing state consolidation in the contemporary period. Once we recognize subversion's role in explaining the persistence of state weakness, it becomes untenable to ignore the possibility that foreign interference may have played a similar role in Europe. State consolidation in Europe was a violent, bloody, and painful process that unfolded over centuries. European wars forced states to build institutions and govern and defend their territories. Foreign interference, in its early modern form of armed intervention in support of nonstate actors, would have worked against these pressures by making it harder for targets to exercise state authority. In turn, that may explain why state consolidation took so long in Europe. Scholars of European statebuilding must confront this book's arguments by revisiting the European experience through the lens of subversion.

The story of state consolidation is a story of international relations. Subversion is a timeless state practice. We have seen countries deploy subversion against their adversaries in the post-1945 period and the post-9/11 period, but also in the early modern period and the long 19th century. It is a practice that knows no bounds. From Africa to Asia, from the old world to the new, subversion undermines the state. I have shown that state weakness has international roots. These roots run wider than we thought; they are deeper than we knew. Scholars who follow these roots and take up this line of inquiry may well uncover a landscape littered with crippled leviathans.

DATA AND STATISTICS

Details about the Myers Index

I operationalize state weakness as the state's access to accurate information about its population. My measure captures the accuracy of age data in national population censuses, and I rely on a technique called the Myers Index to quantify the degree of age accuracy. This section provides further details on this technique.[1] Recall that in a natural population, without accounting for mortality, there should be a uniform distribution of population with ages ending in each terminal digit (zero through nine). That is, 10% of the population should have ages ending in 0, 10% should have ages ending in 1, and so on. Mortality skews this distribution such that the lower terminal digits each have greater than the expected 10% of population, and the higher terminal digits each have lower than the expected 10%. To see this intuition, consider ages 10–89. There should be fewer 89-year-olds than 88-year-olds, and fewer 88-year-olds than 87-year-olds. Starting the age bin at a different terminal digit, as in the case of ages 15–94, only shifts the problem to a different set of terminal digits.

To correct for the effect of mortality, Robert Myers developed a technique of creating a "blended" population that will return each terminal digit 10% of the time, assuming that the true ages are correctly recorded. Since beginning a bin at any given digit overstates the relative frequency of that digit, Myers's technique does "complete justice" to each digit by starting at each one in turn. For example, to calculate a Myers score for the population aged 10–89, the frequencies of each terminal digit are first tabulated 10 times, starting from each terminal digit. The 10 counts are summed and converted into a percentage of the grand population total. The resulting Myers Index ranges from 0, representing no heaping on any digit, to 90, representing the case where all ages were reported at a single terminal digit.

Measuring state weakness over territory with the Myers Index offers a number of advantages. Besides being a theoretically and conceptually appropriate measure, as I describe in chapter 3, it is also available for a large number of countries and subnational units over time, and therefore improves on existing measures where spatial and temporal coverage is much more limited. Still, those existing measures are useful for validating the Myers Index. Table A.1 presents correlations between the Myers Index and the national-level measures of state weakness. Table A.2 presents correlations between the Myers Index and subnational-level measures of state weakness. The Myers Index is signed so that higher values indicate greater state weakness. In both tables, all correlations have the predicted sign.

Data sources for the indicators in Tables A.1 and A.2 are as follows.

Bertelsmann Transformation Index (BTI)

The Bertelsmann Transformation Index is a subjective evaluation of countries in terms of their progress toward achieving democracy and a market economy. The index total as well as an indicator on stateness appear in the main text in table 1.1.

TABLE A.1   National-level validity checks for Myers Index

INDICATOR	OBS.	DECADES	CORR.	SIGNIFICANT?
GDP per capita	250	1960–2010	−0.423	$p < .01$
Infant mortality	149	1990–2010	0.631	$p < .01$
Adult literacy	151	1990–2010	−0.731	$p < .01$
Primary school enrollment	173	1990–2010	−0.659	$p < .01$
ICRG: Index total	172	1980–2010	−0.479	$p < .01$
ICRG: Internal conflict	172	1980–2010	−0.413	$p < .01$
ICRG: Bureaucratic quality	172	1980–2010	−0.321	$p < .01$
WGI: Government effectiveness	149	1990–2010	−0.401	$p < .01$
WGI: Political stability	149	1990–2010	−0.391	$p < .01$
WGI: Rule of law	149	1990–2010	−0.318	$p < .01$
WGI: Regulatory quality	149	1990–2010	−0.387	$p < .01$
WGI: Control of corruption	149	1990–2010	−0.376	$p < .01$
FSI: Index total	95	2000–2010	0.487	$p < .01$
FSI: Public services	95	2000–2010	0.546	$p < .01$
FSI: Security	95	2000–2010	0.354	$p < .01$
BTI: Index total	90	2000–2010	−0.377	$p < .01$
BTI: Stateness	90	2000–2010	−0.488	$p < .01$

Notes: All correlations have the predicted sign. ICRG: International Country Risk Guide; WGI: Worldwide Governance Indicators; FSI: Fragile States Index; BTI: Bertelsmann Transformation Index.

TABLE A.2   Subnational-level validity checks for Myers Index

INDICATOR	COUNTRY	YEARS	OBS.	CORR.	SIGNIFICANT?
Gross domestic product per capita	Brazil	1980, 1991, 2000, 2010	107	−0.264	p < .01
Gross domestic product per capita	China	1982, 1990, 2000, 2010	121	−0.455	p < .01
Gross domestic product per capita	Indonesia	2005, 2010	58	−0.265	p < .05
Gross domestic product per capita	Turkey	1985, 1990, 2000	183	−0.700	p < .01
Net domestic product per capita	India	1981, 1983, 1991, 1993, 1999	126	−0.313	p < .01
Infant mortality rate	China	1982, 1990, 2000	89	0.414	p < .01
Infant mortality rate	India	1961, 1981	52	0.405	p < .01
Infant mortality rate	Turkey	2000	61	0.451	p < .01
Birth registration	Multiple[a]	Multiple[a]	394	−0.441	p < .01
Post offices per 10 villages	Indonesia	2010	33	−0.438	p < .05
Road density	China	1982, 1990, 2000, 2010	121	−0.379	p < .01
Villages connected to roads	India	1991, 1993, 1999	86	−0.456	p < .01
Perceptions of security	Indonesia	2010	33	−0.308	p < .10
Teacher–student ratio	China	1982, 1990, 2000, 2010	120	−0.383	p < .01
Illiteracy rate	Brazil	1980, 1991, 2000, 2010	107	0.488	p < .01
Literacy rate	India	1981, 1991, 1999, 2001	124	−0.247	p < .01
Literacy rate	Turkey	2000	61	−0.839	p < .01

Notes: All correlations have the predicted sign. Recall that higher values on the Myers Index reflect worse levels of state authority.

[a] Armenia 2001, Bangladesh 2011, Burkina Faso 2006, Cambodia 1998, Cambodia 2008, Cameroon 2005, Colombia 2005, Ethiopia 2007, Ghana 2000, Haiti 2003, Honduras 2001, India 2011, Indonesia 2000, Indonesia 2010, Kenya 1999, Kenya 2009, Maldives 2006, Mozambique 2007, Nepal 2001, Nepal 2011, Niger 2001, Nigeria 2006, Pakistan 1998, Senegal 2011, Sierra Leone 2004, Swaziland 2007, Tanzania 2002, Tanzania 2012, Uganda 2002, Zambia 2010.

Experts rank countries on the stateness indicator according to their performance on the monopoly of force, the existence of administrative structures, legitimacy, and the freedom of interference from religious entities. Data are from the Bertelsmann Foundation.[2] Higher values for the BTI and its components indicate better state capacity or state authority.

Birth Registration

Birth registration is a form of civil registration with the state. Birth registration is generally an automatic process when births occur in a state facility or a hospital. In other cases, parents must register the birth of the child with state administrative authorities in a separate process. In some cases the state will also issue a birth certificate, but this is not yet standard practice across the world. Subnational data on birth registration are from the Demographic and Health Surveys, a series of nationally representative surveys conducted in developing countries around the world.[3] The birth registration variable that appears in Table A.2 is defined as the percentage of children under the age of 5 whose births were registered with the state at the time the survey was conducted. Since the likelihood of birth registration is much higher when the degree of state administration is greater—either because birth registration is an automatic administrative process or because state privileges and rights incentivize registration with the state—higher rates of birth registration suggest greater levels of domestic sovereignty.

Fragile States Index (FSI)

The Fragile States Index, previously known as the Failed States Index, ranks countries on several components indicative of fragile statehood. The FSI aggregates data across 12 social, economic, and political indicators, such as uneven economic development, state legitimacy, and group grievances. The data-generation process underlying the 12 indicators is proprietary and opaque, so it is unclear how the individual measures are constructed. In addition to the overall index score, table 1.1 also includes two components closely related to domestic sovereignty: the provision of public services and the security apparatus's monopoly on force. Higher values on the FSI indicate weaker states. Data are from the Fund for Peace.[4]

GDP per Capita

National GDP data are from the Penn World Table and are expressed in constant terms.[5] GDP data reported at the subnational level are scarce, but are available for Brazil, China, Indonesia, and Turkey.[6] Net domestic product data are available for India.[7] For the subnational data, all data are reported in local currencies as constant values.

Infant Mortality

Infant mortality rates are a proxy for state authority because infant mortality is sensitive to a number of factors related to state administration and control. High infant mortality rates are indicative of state failure.[8] The rate of infant mortality is defined as the number of infants, per 1,000 live births, who die before their first birthday. National data come from the Institute for Health Metrics and Evaluation.[9] Subnational data are available for China, India, and Turkey.[10] Higher values indicate worse levels of infant mortality.

International Country Risk Guide (ICRG)

The International Country Risk Guide provides a set of ratings of a country's economic, political, and financial risk. The index contains several components, each with their own subindicators, that contribute to the overall country ranking. The components include bureaucratic quality, internal conflict, law and order, and government stability, among others. Table 1.1 includes the correlation between Myers and the ICRG index as a whole, as well as the internal conflict component and the bureaucratic quality component. The ICRG is produced through subjective expert assessments of each country along each component. Higher values on the index indicate a state facing fewer economic, political, and financial risks, which some analysts consider to be a proxy for state capacity, so I expect to observe a negative correlation. Data are from Political Risk Services.[11] Higher values on the ICRG and its components indicate stronger state authority.

Literacy

An important function of the state is to provide public goods and services. In the era of universal mass education, primary education falls under the purview of the state, and literacy rates can therefore serve as a proxy for the presence of public schools (and, more generally, the state's administrative apparatus). Literacy appears in both the national and subnational correlation validity checks for the Myers Index. National-level data are from the World Bank's World Development Indicators.[12] The World Development Indicators define adult literacy as the percentage of people aged 15 and above who can, with understanding, read and write a short, simple statement on their everyday life. Literacy generally encompasses numeracy. Subnational data for Brazil (as illiteracy rate), India, and Turkey are from the Brazilian Institute for Applied Economic Research (Instituto de Pesquisa Econômica Aplicada), the Indian Planning Commission (now known as the National Institute for Transforming India), and the Turkish Statistical Institute.[13] Higher literacy rates (lower illiteracy rates) suggest better state administration.

Perceptions of Security

Providing for security and public order is one of the most important functions of the state, and thus is an important component of domestic sovereignty. Subjective perceptions data on security are available at the subnational level for Indonesia and are from Statistics Indonesia (Badan Pusat Statistik).[14] Higher values indicate more positive perceptions of security.

Post Offices per 10 Villages

The number of post offices per 10 villages is a proxy for the presence of the state's administrative apparatus in a particular territory. A higher density of post offices per 10 villages suggests a higher density of state administrative activities, offices and personnel, or functions. Data are available for Indonesia and are from Statistics Indonesia (Badan Pusat Statistik).[15]

Primary School Enrollment and Teacher-Student Ratio

Primary enrollment (net percentage) is the ratio of children of official school age who are enrolled in school to the population of the corresponding official school age. National-level data are from the World Development Indicators.[16] As no subnational data on school enrollments are available, table 1.2 in the main text instead uses data from the China Data Center on teacher-student ratio to proxy for state administration.[17] In both cases, higher values indicate greater state authority.

Road Density and Villages Connected to Roads

The presence of transportation infrastructure suggests a greater degree of state administration and control, as infrastructure is often provided by the state in developing countries. To proxy for transportation infrastructure, I use subnational measures of road density from the China Data Center and the percentage of villages connected to roads from the Indian Planning Commission.[18] A greater density of roads and greater levels of village-road connectivity should be associated with greater state authority.

Worldwide Governance Indicators (WGI)

The Worldwide Governance Indicators are one of the more commonly used national-level indicators of state capacity. Five of six of the WGI measures appear in table 1.1; these indicators in principle capture separate components of state administration and control, but in practice are highly correlated with each other. The sixth indicator from the WGI, called "voice and accountability," is conceptually closer to a measure of the regime than a measure of the state, and I therefore do not include it in table 1.1. The source data for the WGI are primarily perceptions data from citizens, businesses, and experts.[19] Higher values on the WGI indicate greater state authority.

Country-Years in the Sample

TABLE A.3   List of countries and years in the sample

COUNTRY	YEARS
Algeria	1966
Argentina	1970, 1980, 1991, 2001, 2010
Armenia	2001, 2011
Bangladesh	1981, 1991, 2001, 2011
Belarus	1999
Belize	2000
Benin	1979, 1992, 2002
Bhutan	2005
Bolivia	1976, 1992, 2001, 2012
Brazil	1970, 1980, 1991, 2000, 2010
Burkina Faso	1985, 1996, 2006
Burma	1983
Burundi	1979, 1990
Cambodia	1962, 1998, 2008
Cameroon	1976, 1987, 2005
Chile	1960, 1970, 1982, 1992, 2002
China	1982, 1990, 2000, 2010
Colombia	1964, 1973, 1985, 1993, 2005
Congo-Brazzaville	1974, 1984, 2007
Costa Rica	1963, 1973, 1984, 2000, 2011
Croatia	2011
Ecuador	1962, 1974, 1982, 1990, 2001, 2010
Egypt	1996, 2006
El Salvador	1992, 2002
Estonia	2001, 2011
Ethiopia	1994, 2007
Gambia	1983, 1993
Ghana	1960, 1970, 1984, 2000, 2010
Guatemala	1994, 2002
Guinea	1983, 1996
Guinea-Bissau	1991
Haiti	1982, 2003
Honduras	1988, 2001
India	1961, 1971, 1981, 1991, 2001, 2011
Indonesia	1971, 1980, 1990, 2000, 2010
Iran	1966, 1976, 1986, 1996, 2006
Iraq	1965, 1997
Jordan	1994, 2004
Kenya	1969, 1979, 1989, 1999, 2009
Kyrgyzstan	1999, 2009
Liberia	1974
Lithuania	2001, 2011
Malawi	1987, 1998, 2008
Malaysia	1970, 1980, 1991, 2000
Mali	1976, 1987, 1998, 2009
Mauritania	1988

(Continued)

TABLE A.3   (Continued)

COUNTRY	YEARS
Mexico	1960, 1970, 1990, 1995, 2000, 2005, 2010
Mongolia	1989, 2000
Morocco	1982, 1994, 2004
Mozambique	1997, 2007
Nepal	1961, 1981, 2001
Nicaragua	1963, 1971, 1995, 2005
Niger	1977, 2001
Nigeria	2006
Pakistan	1973, 1981, 1998
Panama	1960, 1970, 1980, 1990, 2000, 2010
Papua New Guinea	1980, 1990, 2000
Paraguay	2002
Peru	1961, 1972, 1981, 1993, 2007
Romania	1977, 1992, 2002
Rwanda	1978, 1991, 2002
Senegal	1976, 1988, 2002
Sierra Leone	2004
Slovenia	2002, 2011
Somalia	1975
South Africa	1970, 1980, 1991, 1996, 2001, 2007
South Korea	1960, 1970, 1980, 1985, 1990, 2000
Sudan	1993, 2008
Swaziland	1976, 1986, 1997, 2007
Syria	1960, 1970
Tanzania	1978, 1988, 2002, 2012
Thailand	1960, 1970, 1980, 1990, 2000
Togo	1981
Turkey	1975, 1985, 1990, 2000
Uganda	1991, 2002
Uruguay	1963, 1975, 1985, 1996, 2006
Venezuela	1971, 1981, 1990, 2001, 2011
Vietnam	1989, 1999, 2009
Zambia	1969, 1980, 1990, 2000, 2010

Data Sources and Description: Independent Variables

Split Ethnic Groups

I adapt the procedure used by Stelios Michalopoulos and Elias Papaioannou to code, by province, the presence of an ethnic group that is split across a national boundary.[20] To identify ethnic homelands, I use geospatial data from the Geo-referencing of Ethnic Groups (GREG) dataset.[21] Then, following Michalopoulos and Papaioannou, I intersect the GREG data with a layer of national boundaries from the Global Administrative Areas database (GADM).[22] Because the GREG and GADM GIS data are likely drawn with some error, I identify a split group as any group in which at least 10% of its total surface area belongs to more than one country.

To identify split groups by province, I intersect the GREG data with the subnational boundary data used in this project. Again due to concerns about measurement error, I drop any group whose total surface area within a given *province* represents less than 10% of the total surface area occupied by all ethnic groups (as the GREG data code some areas as occupied by no group). I then code the split groups variable as whether the predominant ethnic group in the province is split across a national border; I operationalize this as the group that has at least a plurality in the province. The ethnic groups must be contiguous with the group across the national border. For this calculation, the underlying data are projected into Cylindrical Equal Area (world) projection to minimize distortions to area.

Terrain Ruggedness

For each province in the sample, I calculate the average "slopedness" of the region in percent rise using world topography data from the U.S. Geological Survey and modified by Tom Patterson.[23] The topography data provide the average elevation for each cell in a raster image file of the world. Following a procedure similar to the one deployed by Nathan Nunn and Diego Puga and using spatial software, I first calculate the maximum change in elevation between each cell and its eight neighboring cells.[24] This process identifies the steepest downhill descent from that cell. Then I calculate the average change in elevation of all the cells contained in each province. The resulting value is a measure of slopedness that approximates the average ruggedness of the physical terrain, where slopedness is reported as the average percent rise. For this calculation, the underlying boundary data are projected into the Cylindrical Equal Area (world) projection to minimize distortions to area.

Distance from the Capital

Ideally, I would like to calculate distance between the national capital and the provincial capital, or from the national capital to the largest populated area in each province. However, due to harmonization issues (requiring the merging of some provinces into superunits to obtain time-consistent units) and lack of data, it is not possible to utilize either of these methods of calculation. I therefore first determine the geographic centroid of the province and then calculate the distance between this point and the national capital. Distances are given as kilometers. For this calculation, the underlying boundary data are projected into the Azimuthal Equidistance (world) projection to minimize distortions to distance.

Population Density

For each province, I use the population counts that underlie the Myers calculation to generate a total population size, and then divide population by the province's area in square kilometers to obtain population density. For this calculation, the underlying boundary data are projected into the Cylindrical Equal Area (world) projection to minimize distortions to area.

Economic Development: Land Suitability

Land suitability is the average land quality for cultivation. The underlying geospatial data are drawn from an index developed by Navin Ramankutty and coauthors that is the product of two components reflecting the climatic and soil suitability for cultivation.[25] For this calculation, data are projected into the Cylindrical Equal Area (world) projection to minimize distortions to area.

Natural Resources

For each province, I calculate the percentage of territory containing known oil and gas deposits using geospatial data from PRIO's Petroleum Dataset.[26] For this calculation, data are projected into the Cylindrical Equal Area (world) projection to minimize distortions to area.

Additional Tables

TABLE A.4   Effect of rivalry on state weakness

	(1)	(2)
Rivalry	−0.0123	0.0180
	(0.0332)	(0.0326)
Split ethnic group	0.0610*	0.0408
	(0.0352)	(0.0349)
Rivalry × split ethnic group	0.152***	0.0986**
	(0.0472)	(0.0475)
Terrain ruggedness		0.00423
		(0.0165)
Distance from capital		0.0389**
		(0.0171)

	(1)	(2)
Population density		–0.126***
		(0.0295)
Economic development		0.0139
		(0.0114)
Natural resources		–0.0142
		(0.0113)
Constant	–0.0394**	–0.0334**
	(0.0170)	(0.0169)
Observations	2,151	2,151

Notes: OLS model. The dependent variable is state weakness, operationalized as the logged Myers Index. Higher values indicate greater state weakness. All regressors except rivalry and split ethnic group are logged. Standard errors in parentheses and clustered by country-year. All models include country-year fixed effects (intercepts suppressed).

* $p < 0.10$, ** $p < 0.05$, *** $p < 0.01$.

TABLE A.5   Effect of rivalry on state weakness over time (first-difference model)

	(1)	(2)
Δ rivalry	0.157***	0.0895*
	(0.0427)	(0.0530)
Δ population density	–0.0296	0.00920
	(0.0257)	(0.0327)
Constant	–0.216***	–0.226***
	(0.0110)	(0.00662)
Observations	1,208	1,208
Province fixed effects	No	Yes

Notes: First difference model. The dependent variable is state weakness, operationalized as the logged Myers Index. Higher values indicate greater state weakness. Population density is logged. Standard errors in parentheses and clustered by province. All time-invariant measures drop out.

* $p < 0.10$, ** $p < 0.05$, *** $p < 0.01$.

Supplementary Analyses and Robustness Checks

I conduct several additional analyses to probe the sensitivity and robustness of the results. First, I examine the robustness of the over-time results to an alternate specification in levels with province fixed effects in lieu of a first-differences approach. Although this specification is less efficient, it offers an additional robustness check against the problem of reverse causality. The first-differences approach examined how changes in rivalry affected changes in state authority. An analysis in levels with province fixed effects avoids the problem of irregular observations in the dependent variable, and trades off greater imprecision and

TABLE A.6   Effect of rivalry on state weakness over time (fixed-effects model)

	(1)	(2)
Rivalry	0.446***	0.0496
	(0.0510)	(0.0482)
Population density		−0.0242
		(0.0290)
Year		−0.0201***
		(0.00116)
Constant	−0.127***	39.98***
	(0.0145)	(2.318)
Observations	2,151	2,151

Notes: OLS model. The dependent variable is state weakness, operationalized as the logged Myers Index. Higher values indicate greater state weakness. State weakness and population density are standardized to have mean 0 and standard deviation 1. Rivalry is dichotomous. Standard errors in parentheses and clustered by province. Both models include province fixed effects, which subsume all time-invariant measures such as split ethnic group.

* $p < 0.10$, ** $p < 0.05$, *** $p < 0.01$.

less efficiency for the ability to be more confident that reverse causality is not driving my results. I report this analysis in levels using province fixed effects in table A.6. I once again exclude covariates that are time invariant, and I address the secular trend in Myers scores by including a linear time variable. As expected, the estimates are rather imprecise—rivalry is not statistically distinguishable from zero—but the estimate of the effect of rivalry remains positive. This is consistent with the predictions of the theory and with the first-differences results reported in chapter 3.

Second, I show that my statistical results are also robust to alterations to the composition of the sample and to different specifications regarding the effects of time as well. To test sample sensitivity, I rerun the analysis and in each iteration drop a different country. Figure A.1 shows the point estimates and 95% confidence intervals for the interaction term for each iteration. To test specification sensitivity with respect to time, I repeat the main analysis using country and year fixed effects (with standard errors clustered by country) instead of country-year fixed effects. The results appear in figure A.2. In both cases, the deleterious effect of the interaction of rivalry and split ethnic group is robust.

Finally, the results are robust to excluding a residual category of rivalry from the Thompson and Dreyer dataset that the authors call "interventionary" rivalry.[27] As a residual category, it is not entirely clear what counts as an interventionary rivalry. The category seems to include rivalries that are primarily about "acquiring leverage in the other state's decision making,"[28] but could also include cases in which hostilities arise due to cross-border raids. Complicating the matter is the fact that Thompson rivalries can have multiple types based on the underlying

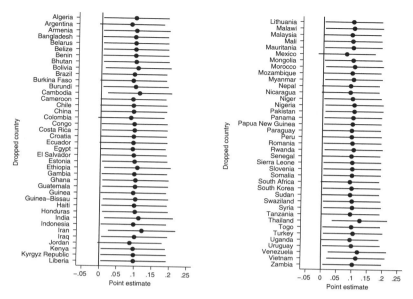

FIGURE A.1. Sample sensitivity. OLS model with country-year fixed effects and standard errors clustered by country-year. The dependent variable is state weakness, operationalized as the logged Myers Index. Higher values indicate greater state weakness. Each line in the figure refers to the estimated coefficient for the interaction of rivalry and split ethnic group when excluding the specified country from the sample. Bars refer to 95% confidence intervals.

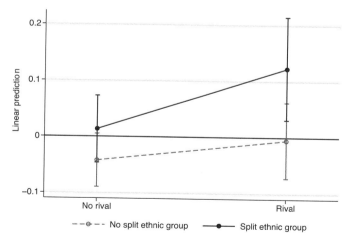

FIGURE A.2. Marginal effects on state weakness with country and year fixed effects and standard errors clustered by country. Marginal effects holding covariates at their means. The dependent variable is state weakness, operationalized as the logged Myers Index. Higher values indicate greater state weakness. Bars refer to 95% confidence intervals. Total observations: 2,151 province-years.

TABLE A.7 Effect of rivalry on state weakness, excluding interventionary rivalries

	(1)	(2)
Rival	−0.0174 (0.0374)	0.0152 (0.0367)
Split ethnic group	0.0504 (0.0379)	0.0278 (0.0374)
Rival × split ethnic group	0.200*** (0.0522)	0.125** (0.0521)
Terrain ruggedness		0.00761 (0.0171)
Distance from capital		0.0362** (0.0175)
Population density		−0.130*** (0.0308)
Economic development		0.0210* (0.0125)
Natural resources		−0.0158 (0.0116)
Constant	−0.0871*** (0.0178)	−0.0790*** (0.0176)
Observations	1,953	1,953

Notes: OLS model. The dependent variable is state weakness, operationalized as the logged Myers Index. Higher values indicate greater state weakness. All regressors except rivalry and split ethnic group are logged. Standard errors in parentheses and clustered by country-year. All models include country-year fixed effects (intercepts suppressed).

* $p < 0.10$, ** $p < 0.05$, *** $p < 0.01$.

issues. It is thus possible that one issue or type (say, territorial disputes) in fact prompts the intervention that earns the rivalry the interventionary label. For these two reasons, interventionary rivalries may or may not represent a reverse causality issue.

To be sure that this category of rivalries is not driving the results, I rerun the analysis and exclude any rivalry coded as an interventionary rivalry. Table A.7 shows the results. Since rivalries can have more than one type, this coding rule excludes some rivalries of other types, resulting in an observation loss of 198 province-years. Still, the results are robust to excluding interventionary rivalries.

Notes

INTRODUCTION

1. Krasner 1999; Jackson and Rosberg 1982.

2. Because of its spatial nature, incomplete state consolidation is similar to Guillermo O'Donnell's concept of "brown areas," Michael Mann's notion of "infrastructural power," and what Thomas Risse and colleagues call "areas of limited statehood." See Risse and Börzel, forthcoming; Risse and Stollenwerk 2018; Risse 2011; O'Donnell 1993; Mann 1984.

3. Hendrix 2011; Piazza 2008; Gleditsch 2007; Salehyan 2007.

4. Gizelis 2009; Busse and Hefeker 2007; Abadie and Gardeazabal 2003; Ghobarah, Huth, and Russett 2003; Rodrik 1999.

5. Murdoch and Sandler 2004.

6. Lemke and Crabtree 2019; Stewart 2019; Risse and Stollenwerk 2018; Florea 2017; Griffiths 2017; Arjona 2016; Huang 2016; Naseemullah and Staniland 2016; Driscoll 2015; Keister 2014; Krasner and Risse 2014; Mukhopadhyay 2014; Mampilly 2011; Marten 2012; Staniland 2012.

7. Clunan and Trinkunas 2010. Some scholars are more skeptical; see for example Patrick 2010.

8. Bureau of Democracy, Human Rights, and Labor 2007.

9. Prior to 2011, the reports were called Annual Threat Assessments. Coats 2018, 2017; Clapper 2016, 2015, 2014, 2013, 2012, 2011; Blair 2010, 2009; McConnell 2008; Negroponte 2007, 2006.

10. Iqbal and Starr 2016; Coggins 2015.

11. Lake 2016; Miller 2013; Fearon and Laitin 2004; Krasner 2004.

12. Zegart 2015; Mazarr 2014.

13. Desch 1996; Tilly 1992; Rasler and Thompson 1989; Hintze 1975; Huntington 1968.

14. Fazal 2007; Korman 1996. Recent scholarship has begun to challenge this narrative. See Acharya and Lee 2018; Abramson 2017.

15. Tilly 1992; Rasler and Thompson 1989.

16. Queralt 2019; Gennaioli and Voth 2015; Centeno 2002; Herbst 2000.

17. Atzili 2012; Hensel, Allison, and Khanani 2009; Fazal 2007; Mueller 2004; Zacher 2001. Interestingly, recent work by Dan Altman suggests that conquest still occurs but takes a form that is less war prone. See Altman (forthcoming).

18. Herbst 2000.

19. Lustick 1997; Jackson and Rosberg 1982.

20. Gartzke 2007; Oneal and Russett 1997.

21. Brooks 2007; Bearce 2003.

22. Kisangani and Pickering 2014; Gibler 2012; Lektzian and Prins 2008; Thies 2007, 2005, 2004.

23. Acemoglu and Robinson 2012; Lange 2004; Mahoney 2003; Acemoglu, Johnson, and Robinson 2001; Mamdani 1996; Migdal 1988.

24. Michalopoulos and Papaioannou 2016; Englebert, Tarango, and Carter 2002.

25. Tollefsen and Buhaug 2015; Hendrix 2011; Scott 2009; Fearon and Laitin 2003; Herbst 2000.

26. Soifer 2015; Saylor 2014; Kurtz 2013; Slater 2010; Boone 2003; Hechter 2001; Levi 1988; Migdal 1988.

27. Iqbal and Starr 2016; Cederman, Weidmann, and Gleditsch 2011; Østby 2008; Montalvo and Reynal-Querol 2005; Collier and Hoeffler 2004.

28. Vogt 2018.

29. Although there is a literature on foreign support for rebels and terrorists, it has not examined the implications of that support for state consolidation or state development more generally. See San-Akca 2016; Borghard 2014; Bapat 2012; Carter 2012; Findley, Piazza, and Young 2011; Salehyan, Gleditsch, and Cunningham 2011; Byman and Kreps 2010; Byman 2005.

30. Other forms of political interference, such as cyberwarfare and election meddling, are relatively recent innovations and are not tools available to or relevant for the vast majority of today's states. The territorial and covert aspects of subversion also distinguish it from the practice of foreign-imposed regime change. See Downes and Monten 2013; Peic and Reiter 2011; Owen 2002.

31. Nor is the existence of a proxy the result of weak state consolidation. I discuss proxy availability and concerns about endogeneity in greater depth in chapters 2, 3, and 4.

32. Even the literature on external peacebuilding and statebuilding has not typically distinguished between the construction of institutions and the state's reach over its territory, or has focused exclusively on the former. See Barma, Levy, and Piombo 2017; Matanock 2017; Barma 2016; Lake 2016; Zürcher et al. 2013; Fortna 2008; Walter 2002.

33. Gibler 2012; Thies 2005, 2004.

34. Hathaway and Shapiro 2017; Goertz, Diehl, and Balas 2016; Goldstein 2011; Pinker 2011; Lacina, Gleditsch, and Russett 2006; Lacina and Gleditsch 2005; Mueller 1989. Some scholars dispute the claim that war is declining. See Fazal 2014; Braumoeller 2013; Gohdes and Price 2013.

35. Herbst 2000; Lustick 1997. Weinstein 2005 makes a related argument about war, statebuilding, and international intervention.

36. Lee and Zhang 2017.

1. THE STATE OF STATE AUTHORITY

1. Rubongoya 2007.

2. Eastern African Department Infrastructure Operations Division 1992, 4.

3. MacDonald 2010.

4. Lee, Walter-Drop, and Wiesel 2014; Zürn and Leibfried 2005; Fukuyama 2004; de Swaan 1988.

5. Mampilly 2011.

6. Iqbal and Starr 2016.

7. Of course, Somalia is somewhat of an extreme example, as the state cannot govern if no one controls the state.

8. Krasner 1999, 11.

9. Lindvall and Teorell 2016; Hanson 2014; Hendrix 2010.

10. In previous work, I called this "state centralization." See Lee 2018.

11. See Herbst 2000; O'Donnell 1993; Mann 1984.

12. Lee and Platas Izama 2015; Lake and Fariss 2014; Goldstone et al. 2000.

13. D'Arcy and Nistotskaya 2017; Lee and Zhang 2017; Scott 1998.

14. In general, the official statistical yearbooks report subnational data at the regional level, the highest administrative unit in Georgia. Abkhazia is an example of a region. In contrast, the breakaway territory of South Ossetia is formally part of the region of Shida Kartli, so it is not typically possible to see the same region-level patterns of missingness in

the yearbooks that we observe for Abkhazia. When data for cities are reported, however, Tskhinvali, the capital of the self-proclaimed Republic of South Ossetia, is usually missing.

15. Queralt 2018; Onorato, Scheve, and Stasavage 2014; Hanson and Sigman 2013; Soifer 2013; Centeno 2002.

16. Lee and Zhang 2017.

17. This distinction is crucial. As I will argue in chapter 2, sponsors and their proxies undermine the target state's authority by supplanting its institutions. This is a key mechanism through which subversion weakens the state.

18. Kansakar 1977, 19.

19. Census administrators generally have a rough idea of how many households each enumerator is responsible for interviewing. In Uganda's 2014 census exercise, the ratio was one enumerator to about 100 households.

20. Gibril 1979; Quandt 1973.

21. Quandt 1973, 49–52.

22. Quandt 1973, 45. Emphases mine.

23. Quandt 1973, 46.

24. Lee and Zhang 2017.

25. Hobbs 2004; Raveh 1981; Myers 1976, 1940; Van de Walle 1968; Carrier 1959; Bachi 1951.

26. Details of the calculation are described in Lee and Zhang 2017 and Myers 1940.

27. See the appendix for more details on the Myers Index and the method of calculation.

28 Our data can be obtained online at https://www.statecapacityscores.org.

29. Importantly, unlike economic data, which can be politically sensitive, age data are not inherently political. This also contrasts with certain categories of population data, such as ethnicity or citizenship status. See Hollyer, Rosendorff, and Vreeland 2018; Lee and Zhang 2017; Lieberman and Singh 2017; Wallace 2016.

30. Chalk 2007.

31. Schofield 2010, 181–82.

32. Gersony 1997, 38.

33. Gersony 1997, 58.

34. Gersony 1997, 48–49.

35. Khalel and Vickery 2015.

36. Khalel and Vickery 2015.

37. World Health Organization 2006, 5.

38. World Bank 1980, 27n1.

39. World Bank 1980, 27n2, 28.

40. The World Bank was not able to obtain data from Central Mindanao, likely due to the lack of state authority in the region.

41. National Statistics Office Philippines and Macro International 1994, 97. The national average does not appreciably change if Metro Manila is dropped.

42. National Statistics Office Philippines and Macro International 1994; Madigan 1985; Engracia 1983.

43. World Bank 1984, 129.

44. Gladstone 2016.

45. Dabla 2011, 67.

46. Schofield 2010, 183.

47. World Bank 1980, 32.

48. National Population Commission and ICF Macro 2009.

49. *Press Briefing* 2012.

50. Full basic vaccination refers to BCG (Bacillus Calmette-Guérin, for tuberculosis), measles, three doses of DPT (diphtheria-pertussis-tetanus), and polio vaccine (excluding the polio vaccine given at birth).

51. Energy Commission of Nigeria 2003, 35.
52. Scott 2009.
53. Risse and Stollenwerk 2018, 105. See also Slater and Kim 2015.

2. THE STRATEGY OF FOREIGN SUBVERSION

1. Much of this literature analyzes delegation using a principal-agent framework. For a discussion of state-to-state delegation, see Berman, Lake, Padró i Miquel et al. 2019. For a discussion of delegation as it relates to controlling violence, see Padró i Miquel and Yared 2012. For a discussion of delegation between states and nonstate actors, see San-Akca 2016; Salehyan, Siroky, and Wood 2014; Bapat 2012; Salehyan, Gleditsch, and Cunningham 2011; Byman and Kreps 2010.

2. Bapat 2012. Carter 2015, however, shows that the sponsor state may encounter difficulties making good on this deal.

3. Syrian marginalization of its own Kurdish population further suggests the cynical interpretation of Syrian support for the PKK.

4. Reputation plays an important role in explaining the conflictual behavior of states. See Lupton 2018; Yarhi-Milo 2018; Weisiger and Yarhi-Milo 2015; Dafoe, Renshon, and Huth 2014; Walter 2006.

5. Swami 2004, 150.
6. James 2015, 11.
7. Sumner 2004, 2787–88; Lalonde 2002.
8. Mesfin and Beyene 2018; McGregor 2014; Nzwili 2013; BBC News 2011.
9. Salehyan 2007.
10. Metz 1986, 492.
11. Borghard 2014; Byman and Kreps 2010.

12. Even if accidents and mishaps do occur, the well-known problem of hostile attribution bias would result in states concluding that such action was purposive rather than accidental. This is particularly likely to hold in the case of states that already operate with high levels of mutual suspicion. Covert actions are attractive for these reasons. See Carson 2018; O'Rourke 2018.

13. Salehyan, Gleditsch, and Cunningham 2011, 713.
14. Vinci 2009, 106.

15. Interestingly, not all types of sovereignty are equally respected. Even as states seem to treat borders as meaningful boundaries that delineate the territorial scope of state authority, subversion itself represents a violation of Westphalian sovereignty in an effort to damage domestic sovereignty. I return to this theme in the conclusion.

16. For an extensive treatment of how states select rebel groups and how rebels select state sponsors, see San-Akca 2016.

17. Mylonas 2012.
18. Kendie 1999, 156.
19. Kendie 1999, 154.
20. Kassu 2012, 147–48.
21. San-Akca 2016; Carter 2015; Salehyan 2007.
22. San-Akca 2016; Carter 2012; Byman 2005.
23. Byman and Kreps 2010, 8.
24. Karatnycky 2015.
25. Boulding 1962, 230.
26. Atzili 2012; Hensel, Allison, and Khanani 2009; Fazal 2007; Zacher 2001; Jackson and Rosberg 1982.
27. Benson 2011; Leeds 2003; Smith 1995; Morrow 1994.
28. Slocomb 2003, 245–46.

29. Stewart 2019; Arjona 2016; Huang 2016; Staniland 2012; Mampilly 2011.

30. Marcus 2007, 182.

31. Jongerden 2007, 275.

32. Marcus 2007, 183.

33. This echoes a perspective in the literature on the state as a protection racket. See Olson 1993; Tilly 1985.

34. Taspinar 2005; Zaman 1999.

35. Marcus 2007, 192.

36. Soifer 2016, 2015.

3. HOSTILE NEIGHBORS, WEAK PERIPHERIES

1. Chapter 4 provides a useful opportunity to conduct a more nuanced analysis of the effects of the factors that condition subversion.

2. Thompson and Dreyer 2012.

3. The main alternative to Thompson and Dreyer's perceptions-based approach codes rivalry based on the density of the countries' militarized interstate disputes. The dispute-density approach flips the logic: the decision to use a particular instrument (conventional force) has already been made, thereby ruling out cases where subversion substituted for force. See Klein, Goertz, and Diehl 2006.

4. To permit appropriate over-time comparisons, I create time-consistent units, "reconstructing" provinces as they existed before new provinces were created.

5. Turkey also shares an 18-kilometer border with Azerbaijan.

6. Horowitz 1985.

7. Michalopoulos and Papaioannou 2016.

8. The medium-n analysis in the next chapter allows me to improve on the coding of both factors by leveraging the greater degree of nuance made possible by fewer cases.

9. Michalopoulos and Papaioannou 2016.

10. Weidmann, Rød, and Cederman 2010.

11. Risse and Stollenwerk 2018.

12. A tiny fraction of countries, such as Lebanon since its founding and Pakistan since 2000, choose not to conduct censuses for reasons related to domestic ethnic tensions. These are rare exceptions rather than the rule.

13. Minorities at Risk Project 2009.

14. Since neither measure perfectly captures policy incompatibility or agent availability, it is possible that subversion occurs even when my measures indicate that one or both factors are missing.

15. Fearon and Laitin 2003.

16. Tollefsen and Buhaug 2015; Hendrix 2011.

17. Patterson 2013; Nunn and Puga 2012.

18. Herbst 2000.

19. Central Statistics Agency Ethiopia 2016.

20. Datanet India Private Limited 2014.

21. Oxford Poverty and Human Development Initiative 2013.

22. Ramankutty et al. 2002.

23. Comin, Easterly, and Gong 2010; Nunn 2009; Easterly and Levine 2003; Engerman and Sokoloff 2002; Acemoglu, Johnson, and Robinson 2001, 2002.

24. See table A.4 in the appendix.

25. Indicators are from Kaufmann, Kraay, and Mastruzzi 2018; and World Bank 2018.

26. Kaufmann, Kraay, and Mastruzzi 2018.

27. Lee and Platas Izama 2015; Lake and Fariss 2014; Goldstone et al. 2000.

28. Mares and Queralt 2015; Rogers and Weller 2014; Dincecco 2011; Hendrix 2010; Lieberman 2002; Tanzi 1991; Levi 1988; Musgrave 1969.

29. Lee and Zhang 2017.

30. Scott 2009.

31. Other high-altitude capitals, such as La Paz (Bolivia) and Quito (Ecuador), do not enter my sample because they are not located in border provinces.

32. Herbst 2000.

33. See table A.5 in the appendix.

34. Compared to the fixed effects approach, the estimates reported in figure 3.3 are more precise. Both approaches yield estimates of the effect of rivals that are signed according to prediction. See tables A.5 and A.6 in the appendix.

4. THE ROOTS OF SUBVERSION

1. Lo 2015, 2002; Mankoff 2012.

2. There are numerous excellent works on Russian foreign policy, identity, and nationalism in the post-Soviet states, and the politics of integration, assimilation, and accommodation. While it is not possible to provide a comprehensive list, starting points include Lo 2015, 2002; Tsygankov 2013; Mankoff 2012; Trenin 2011; Beissinger 2002; Kolstø 2000; Laitin 1998; Melvin 1998; Brubaker 1996; and Kolstoe 1995.

3. See for example Fukuyama 1989.

4. Bugajski 2009, 9.

5. Tsygankov 2013, 58.

6. Leichtova 2014; Mankoff 2012; Oldberg 2011.

7. Lo 2002, 115.

8. Lo 2002, 117.

9. Shevtsova 2006, 313.

10. Mankoff 2012, 33.

11. Cooley 2012; Mankoff 2012; Darden 2010.

12. Kolstø 1996, 623.

13. Melvin 1998, 33.

14. *Demoscope Weekly* 2018.

15. Roeder 1999, 858.

16. Melvin 1998, 32–33.

17. Kolstoe 1995, 222, 240–41.

18. Kolstoe 1995, 147–48.

19. Roper 2001, 104–5.

20. Laitin 1998, 86.

21. King and Melvin 1999, 119.

22. Hyndle and Kutysz 2002, 55.

23. Artman 2013; Lynch 2000.

24. The founding members were Georgia, Ukraine, Uzbekistan, Azerbaijan, and Moldova. The second *U* is parenthetical because Uzbekistan later withdrew its membership.

25. Asmus 2010; Nilsson 2009.

26. Nilsson 2009, 89.

27. Asmus 2010, 57.

28. Nilsson 2009, 99.

29. Mankoff 2012, 235.

30. Ellison 2011, 351.

31. Trenin 2011, 96.

32. Ironically, Saakashvili's program of reform did not actually include meaningful democratic improvements. In fact, shortly after taking power, the government changed the constitution to increase the powers of the executive. See Nilsson 2009.

33. Mankoff 2012, 239.

34. Ozolina 2003, 206.

35. Sleivyte 2010, 127.

36. Trenin 2002, 286.

37. Bilinsky 1999, 11.

38. Donaldson, Nogee, and Nadkarni 2014, 221.

39. Blank 1998, 119.

40. Szporluk 1993, 366. Russians similarly considered Belarusians to be part of the nation.

41. Solchanyk 1996, 21.

42. Bukkvoll 2001.

43. Kuzio 2000, 84.

44. Beginning in 1996, Ukraine began exhibiting a stronger desire to join Europe. Ukrainian foreign minister Hennady Udovenko set off a diplomatic furor by floating the idea that Ukraine could seek "associated status" with NATO. President Leonid Kuchma likewise announced that Ukraine's strategic objective was integration into European "structures." One year later, Ukraine joined Georgia, Uzbekistan, Azerbaijan, and Moldova to found GU(U)AM, discussed earlier in the chapter. See Kuzio 2000; Bukkvoll 1997.

45. Wydra 2003, 116.

46. Beissinger 2002.

47. *Demoscope Weekly* 2018.

48. Toft 2003, 93.

49. Toal and O'Loughlin 2013, 136. These estimates should be taken with a grain of salt, as data on Georgia's minorities during that time period are not very reliable.

50. Zürcher 2007.

51. Sabanadze 2014, 126.

52. Sabanadze 2014, 127.

53. King 2008, 217.

54. Zürcher 2007, 126.

55. Souleimanov 2013, 160.

56. Sabanadze 2014, 127.

57. Kolstoe 1995, 133.

58. Brubaker 2011; Hogan-Brun et al. 2008; Rannut 2008.

59. The secessionist/autonomy referenda were gambits by local elites who were threatened by independence, democratization, and economic liberalization. These referenda generally lacked popular support. See Smith 2002, 97; Melvin 1995, 49.

60. Smith 1998; Park 1994.

61. Park 1994, 79.

62. Smith 1998, 10.

63. Merritt 2000.

64. Laitin 2003, 200.

65. Rose and Maley 1994, 28, 30.

66. Fein 2005, 339.

67. Fein 2005, 342.

68. Park 1994, 82.

69. Smith and Wilson 1997, 857.

70. Melvin 1995, 90.

71. Melvin 1995, 90.

72. Kuzio 1998, 87.

73. Kolstoe 1995, 177.

74. Sasse 2007; Kolstoe 1995.

75. Marples and Duke 1995, 275–76.

76. Kolstoe 1995, 181.
77. Kuzio and Meyer 1999.
78. Sasse 2007.
79. Sasse 2007, 155.
80. Sasse 2007, 156.
81. Wydra 2003; Kuzio and Meyer 1999.
82. Kuzio and Meyer 1999, 312.
83. Marples and Duke 1995, 283.
84. Sasse 2007, 160.
85. Sasse 2007, 161.
86. Lynch 2000, 133.
87. Lynch 2000, 141–42.
88. Gordadze 2009, 45.
89. The Abkhaz later issued their own, though these passports were basically worthless for travel.
90. Illarionov 2009, 55.
91. Illarionov 2009, 56.
92. Illarionov 2009, 59.
93. Rondeli 2014, 38.
94. Asmus 2010; Illarionov 2009.
95. Illarionov 2009, 59.
96. Asmus 2010, 73.
97. Illarionov 2009, 59.
98. Illarionov 2009, 60.
99. Asmus 2010, 71.
100. Trenin 2011, 97. See also Socor 2007.
101. Lo 2015, 119.
102. Bakke et al. 2018; Asmus 2010, 72.
103. Hyndle and Kutysz 2002; King and Melvin 1999.
104. Smith and Wilson 1997, 858.
105. Kolstoe 1995, 132.
106. Sleivyte 2010; Security Police of the Republic of Estonia 2005.
107. Bugajski 2009, 99.
108. Melvin 1998, 43.
109. Laruelle 2018, 67.
110. King and Melvin 1999, 124.
111. Trimbach and O'Lear 2015, 499.
112. Melvin 1995, 93.
113. Sasse 2007, 164.
114. Solchanyk 1996, 38.
115. Dawson 1998, 438.
116. Hughes and Sasse 2016, 319.
117. King 2003, 255.
118. Hill 2012, 160.
119. Trenin 2011, 92.
120. My theory predicts subversion rather than annexation. In Ukraine, we observe both outcomes. The annexation of Crimea is unique in the post-Soviet space; nowhere else has Russia claimed for itself the territory of another state, even as it subverts Georgia and Moldova by supporting their breakaway republics. The fact that Russia did not also annex Donbas but instead engaged in subversion suggests that the particularities of Crimea, including its historical association with the Russian SSR and its base for the Black Sea Fleet, drove the decision to annex rather than subvert.

121. Kolstoe 1995, 142.

122. Kolstø 2000, 120.

123. Cooley 2012.

124. Laruelle 2018.

125. Mehdiyeva 2011, 205.

126. Mehdiyeva 2011, 229.

127. Cornell 2011, 350.

128. Cornell 2011, 126.

129. Lynch 2004, 87.

130. Lo 2015, 115.

131. Anceschi 2008.

132. In any case, neither country is an attractive candidate for Western integration due to their highly authoritarian regimes and poor human rights records.

133. Laruelle 2018, 73.

134. Peyrouse 2015, 91–93.

135. Way 2005.

5. UNDERMINING STATE AUTHORITY IN THE PHILIPPINES

1. Chapter 4 shows the successful use of subversion against territorially contiguous states (Georgia and Ukraine) as well as a noncontiguous state (Moldova).

2. The text of the relevant agreements can be found in Institute of International Legal Studies 2003.

3. The original proposal included Brunei and Singapore, along with Sabah and Sarawak. Brunei declined to join the new state. Singapore joined Malaysia but left in 1965.

4. Thant 1976; Colonial Office 1962.

5. Department of Foreign Affairs 1968, 5–6.

6. Embassy Kuala Lumpur to Department of State 1968b.

7. Embassy Kuala Lumpur to Department of State 1968b.

8. Public Information Office 1968, 17–18; Embassy Bangkok to Department of State 1968.

9. Embassy Kuala Lumpur to Department of State 1967.

10. Director of Intelligence and Research 1968.

11. Embassy Manila to Department of State 1968b.

12. Arguillas 2009; Embassy Manila to Department of State 1968c.

13. Embassy Manila to Department of State 1968a.

14. Acharya 2012, 164–65.

15. Coronel-Ferrer 2005, 12. Many other scholars have written on the topic of antecedents of the conflict in the southern Philippines. See for example Tan 2010; Abinales 2000; and Che Man 1990.

16. Embassy Kuala Lumpur to Department of State 1968a.

17. Embassy Kuala Lumpur to Department of State 1968a.

18. Embassy Kuala Lumpur to Department of State 1968c. The Australian High Commission is the name of the diplomatic mission of Australia in Malaysia; both are Commonwealth countries.

19. Embassy Kuala Lumpur to Department of State 1968e.

20. The text of the legislation, Republic Act No. 5446, can be found in Institute of International Legal Studies 2003.

21. Embassy Kuala Lumpur to Department of State 1968f. It is interesting that Malaysia expected Philippine aggression to manifest as clandestine meddling in its domestic state authority rather than as a naked attempt to take Sabah by force. This expectation suggests that Kuala Lumpur did not believe that Manila had the capability to fight a conventional conflict or the ability to withstand the international costs of doing so.

22. Embassy Manila to Department of State 1968d.
23. Embassy Bangkok to Department of State 1968.
24. Embassy Kuala Lumpur to Department of State 1968g.
25. Lucman 2000, 156.
26. Galvez 1987, 20.
27. Stern 2012, 37.
28. Department of State to Embassy Kuala Lumpur 1969.
29. Embassy Manila to Department of State 1975.
30. Embassy Kuala Lumpur to Department of State 1968d.
31. Embassy Kuala Lumpur to Department of State 1973a, b, c.
32. Embassy Kuala Lumpur to Department of State 1973b.
33. Embassy Kuala Lumpur to Department of State 1973c.
34. Embassy Manila to Department of State 1974a.
35. Embassy Kuala Lumpur to Department of State 1973a.
36. One problem with subversion is that the collapse of state authority in the southern Philippines sent Filipino Muslim refugees fleeing to Sabah, where Mustapha offered them sanctuary. The influx of Muslim refugees threatened to upset a fragile ethnic balance in Sabah, which contained a sizeable non-Malay indigenous population. This is an example of blowback. See Nair 1997 for further details.
37. Contrast this contestation with the cases of Georgia and Moldova, described in chapter 4, where the state formally claims authority but does not contest control. In those cases, we observe no active violence from the state.
38. Mullenbach and Nurullayev 2018. Though Marcos declared martial law and cited recent Communist attacks in the Manila area as a justification, the AFP considered the New People's Army to be little more than a nuisance in the 1970s. It focused instead on fighting the MNLF, deploying up to 80% of its forces in that war. Ironically, this focus allowed the New People's Army to grow significantly and later launch a full-scale war in the 1980s. For more information, see Dixon and Sarkees 2016, 541.
39. Keesing's Worldwide 2018.
40. The figure excludes employees classified as casual employees. The figure looks similar when using only data on permanent employees, though there are few data points due to lack of disaggregated data in some years.
41. For good introductions written by scholars in the region, see Coronel-Ferrer 2005; Abinales 2000; Vitug and Gloria 2000; Tan 1993; Che Man 1990.
42. Abinales 2000.
43. U.S. Agency for International Development 1972. "Dealing" with the *ilaga* usually meant mounting counterattacks on Christian communities.
44. Che Man 1990, 82.
45. Che Man 1990, 80.
46. Stern 2012.
47. Perhaps not surprisingly, these leaders eventually parted ways due to their different views about the prosecution of the Moro struggle and to internal factionalism that fell along ethnocultural lines. Dimas Pundato went on to form the MNLF-Reformist group. Hashim Salamat's faction became the Moro Islamic Liberation Front. Nur Misuari was left with the rump MNLF.
48. Tan 1993.
49. Stern 2012.
50. Stern 2012.
51. Vitug and Gloria 2000, 175.
52. Embassy Manila to Department of State 1974b.
53. Quoted in Vitug and Gloria 2000, 175.

54. Retired AFP officer, interview with the author, San Juan City, the Philippines, June 18, 2014.

55. Embassy Manila to Department of State 1973a.

56. P2,000 was a considerable amount of money. In 1972, a household in Manila or its suburbs was considered to be low income if total household income was below P4,000. In 1971, the national median earnings for male farmers and fishermen was about P1,350 per year (about P26 per week), while the national median earnings overall for males was about P2,340 (about P45 per week) (data from Bureau of the Census and Statistics, *Journal of Philippine Statistics*, 1972, 16, 84). In the Sulu Archipelago and central Mindanao, which were poorer and more underdeveloped than the rest of the country, local median incomes would have been lower than the national median. It is also worth noting that the recruits training for Operation Merdeka were promised P50 per month in 1968. P2,000 would therefore have been quite an attractive offer for a prospective rebel from the South.

57. Embassy Manila to Department of State 1973a.

58. Cal 1997, 122.

59. Embassy Manila to Department of State 1973a. Although the Philippine Constabulary was at that time a branch of the AFP, it functioned mainly as a national police force.

60. Embassy Manila to Department of State 1973b.

61. Embassy Manila to Department of State 1973a.

62. Vitug and Gloria 2000.

63. Embassy Kuala Lumpur to Department of State 1973b.

64. The relevant articles of the 1935 and 1973 constitutions can be found in Institute of International Legal Studies 2003.

65. Embassy Jakarta to Department of State 1973.

66. Embassy Manila to Department of State 1977. Even though Malaysia more or less stopped actively targeting state authority in the southern Philippines, the MNLF acquired a new external patron in the form of Libya, which provided significant financial support.

6. UNDERMINING STATE AUTHORITY IN CAMBODIA

1. Cambodia has changed its name several times since it received independence. For ease of exposition, I refer to it as Cambodia.

2. Vickery 1990, 440–41.

3. Chanda 1986, 380.

4. Indochina Studies Program 1985a, 73.

5. Goscha 2006, 162–63.

6. Goscha 2006.

7. Quinn-Judge 2006, 212.

8. Evans and Rowley 1990, 109.

9. The degree to which the PRK could act independently of the Vietnamese, particularly in the first half of the 1980s, was the subject of considerable debate among scholars and regional observers. The evidence is clear, however, that the PRK was not free to make policy in the domains of security and foreign affairs; the matter of its geopolitical alignment was certainly not up for debate. The Polity IV project, which codes the regime characteristics of states, designates the 1980s in Cambodia as a period of foreign occupation ("interruption"). See Marshall, Gurr, and Jaggers 2017.

10. Carney 1987, 187.

11. Evans and Rowley 1990, 160.

12. Evans and Rowley 1990, 163.

13. Gottesman 2003, 48.

14. Quinn-Judge 1983, 155.

15. McBeth 1982.

16. McBeth 1982.

17. Gottesman 2003, 45.

18. Tongdhammachart 1982, 78. Neither Vietnam nor Cambodia was a member of ASEAN, the regional organization founded on the principles of noninterference and respect for sovereignty.

19. Rungswasdisab 2006.

20. Niksch 1981.

21. Ministry of Foreign Affairs 1985, 2–3.

22. Chanda 1986, 381. Singapore, which also held hard-liner views, expressed a similar concern. At a June 1979 meeting in Bali, Singapore's foreign minister, Sinnathamby Rajaratnam, noted, "The Cambodians have already been on the list of those who are going to die. . . . Why not Thailand tomorrow, and Malaysia, Singapore, and others who stand in the way of Vietnam's dreams?" See Evans and Rowley 1990, 185.

23. Tongdhammachart et al. 1983.

24. Indochina Studies Program 1985b, 53.

25. Chanda 1986, 381.

26. Former Cambodian prime minister Son Sann led the KPNLF. Prince Norodom Sihanouk, a member of the Khmer royal family and a former prime minister, led FUNCINPEC. Under international pressure, the three resistance groups banded together as the Coalition Government of Democratic Kampuchea, which held Cambodia's seat at the United Nations.

27. Chanda 1986, 381.

28. Rungswasdisab 2006, 91.

29. By the end of the decade, Vietnam unilaterally withdrew from Cambodia.

30. Unger 2003, 37.

31. Unger 2003, 40.

32. Thomas 1986, 20. Because of the geopolitical alignments in the Indochinese peninsula at this time, supplies destined for the Khmer Rouge had to travel through Thailand.

33. China shut down support to the Communist Party of Thailand on the grounds that the Communist insurgency would render Thailand vulnerable to Vietnamese territorial aggression. See Thomas 1986.

34. Chanda 1986, 381.

35. Oesterheld 2014.

36. Robinson 2000, 26.

37. Bangkok did have a choice in this matter, and the Thai had no qualms about turning Cambodians away from the border. At one point in 1979, the Thai military rounded up nearly 40,000 refugees, bused them to the Cambodian border near the temple at Preah Vihear, and marched them at gunpoint down the cliffs into a minefield in Cambodia. For further details see Unger 2003, 30.

38. Slocomb 2003, 53.

39. Bull 1983, 8.

40. Slocomb 2003, 53.

41. Chanda 1986, 371.

42. Gottesman 2003, 50; Vickery 1990, 439.

43. Bull 1983, 8.

44. Slocomb 2003, 53.

45. Slocomb 2003, 156; Carney 1987, 202.

46. Carney 1982, 78–79.

47. Schier 1986, 140.

48. Schier 1986, 140.

49. Gottesman 2003, 224.

50. Schier 1986, 141.

51. Gottesman 2003, 236.

52. Although the accident data date from a period twenty-five years following the end of the Khmer Rouge's conflict with the PRK, new land mines were not laid after the end of the conflict. After the conflict, the UN established the United Nations Transitional Authority in Cambodia (UNTAC), whose mandate included mine clearance and mine-awareness training. If these efforts emphasized some regions over others, then the accident data could present a biased picture of state authority deficits in the 1980s. UNTAC likely focused its mine-clearance operations on provinces with a greater density of landmines. If so, then the accident data likely underreport the severity of the state authority differences between provinces.

53. Carney 1987, 206; Director of Central Intelligence 1985, 10.

54. Quinn-Judge 1983, 161.

55. Tatu 1987, 271.

56. Mysliwiec 1988; Chufrin 1984. The remote Northeast generally lagged behind less geographically difficult parts of the country in terms of improvements to state presence.

57. Bull 1983, 12.

58. Mysliwiec 1988, 40.

59. Mysliwiec 1988, 144n7.

60. Huxley 1987, 163.

61. Carney 1982, 79, 84.

62. Slocomb 2003, 245.

63. Slocomb 2003, 157.

64. Circular No. 04SR for the Council of Ministers, quoted in Slocomb 2003, 246.

65. Gottesman 2003, 55.

66. Gottesman 2003, 54.

67. Kiernan 1982, 172.

68. Slocomb 2003, 89.

69. Gottesman 2003, 321.

70. Slocomb 2003, 236.

CONCLUSION

1. The linkages between security and political and economic development have been a boon for development practitioners seeking an increase in foreign aid. See Natsios 2011; Adelman 2007.

2. Matsuzaki 2019; Lake 2016.

3. Michalopoulos and Papaioannou 2016; Alesina, Easterly, and Matuszeski 2011; Thies 2009; Englebert, Tarango, and Carter 2002; Herbst 2000. For a similar argument in the Middle East, see Lustick 1997.

4. Atzili 2012; Fazal 2007; Zacher 2001.

5. Queralt, forthcoming; Chowdhury 2018; Gennaioli and Voth 2015; Thies 2005; Centeno 2002; Herbst 2000; Desch 1996; Tilly 1992; Rasler and Thompson 1989.

6. Elliott 2018, 81.

7. Balcells 1996, 15.

8. Alcoberro 2010, 77.

9. Initially the Serbs wanted the Porte to exercise greater authority and rein in the janissaries. By 1805, however, the Serbs switched goals and rose up against the sultan. See Anderson 1966, 48.

10. Jelavich and Jelavich 1977, 32.

11. Shaw 1976, 272; Anderson 1966, 48–49.

12. Jelavich and Jelavich 1977, 33.

13. Langer 2014.

14. Carr 1991, 39.

15. Carr 1991, 40.

APPENDIX

1. For a more technical discussion, see Lee and Zhang 2017; Myers 1940.

2. Bertelsmann Stiftung 2014.

3. Demographic and Health Surveys Program 2015.

4. Fund for Peace 2014.

5. Feenstra, Inklaar, and Timmer 2013.

6. Institute of Applied Economic Research 2014; China Data Center 2014; Badan Pusat Statistik 2014; Turkish Statistical Institute 2014.

7. Planning Commission 2002.

8. Goldstone et al. 2000.

9. Institute for Health Metrics and Evaluation 2011.

10. Bignami-Van Assche 2005; Planning Commission 2002; Turkish Statistical Institute 2014.

11. PRS Group 2014.

12. World Bank 2018.

13. Institute of Applied Economic Research 2014; Planning Commission 2002; Turkish Statistical Institute 2014.

14. Badan Pusat Statistik 2014.

15. Badan Pusat Statistik 2014.

16. World Bank 2018.

17. China Data Center 2014.

18. China Data Center 2014; Planning Commission 2002.

19. Kaufmann, Kraay, and Mastruzzi 2018.

20. Michalopoulos and Papaioannou 2016.

21. Weidmann, Rød, and Cederman 2010.

22. Available at http://www.gadm.org/.

23. Patterson 2013.

24. Nunn and Puga 2012.

25. Ramankutty et al. 2002.

26. Lujala, Rød, and Thieme 2007.

27. See Thompson and Dreyer 2012.

28. Thompson and Dreyer 2012, 21.

References

Abadie, Alberto, and Javier Gardeazabal. 2003. "The Economic Costs of Conflict: A Case Study of the Basque Country." *American Economic Review* 93 (1): 113–32. https://doi.org/10.1257/000282803321455188.

Abinales, Patricio N. 2000. *Making Mindanao: Cotabato and Davao in the Making of the Philippine Nation-State.* Quezon City: Ateneo de Manila University Press.

Abramson, Scott F. 2017. "The Economic Origins of the Territorial State." *International Organization* 71 (1): 97–130. https://doi.org/10.1017/S0020818316000308.

Acemoglu, Daron, Simon Johnson, and James A. Robinson. 2001. "The Colonial Origins of Comparative Development: An Empirical Investigation." *American Economic Review* 91 (5): 1369–1401. https://doi.org/10.1257/aer.91.5.1369.

———. 2002. "Reversal of Fortune: Geography and Institutions in the Making of the Modern World Income Distribution." *Quarterly Journal of Economics* 117 (4): 1231–94. https://doi.org/10.1162/003355302320935025.

Acemoglu, Daron, and James A. Robinson. 2012. *Why Nations Fail: The Origins of Power, Prosperity, and Poverty.* New York: Crown.

Acharya, Amitav. 2012. *The Making of Southeast Asia: International Relations of a Region.* Ithaca, NY: Cornell University Press.

Acharya, Avidit, and Alexander Lee. 2018. "Economic Foundations of the Territorial State System." *American Journal of Political Science* 62 (4): 954–66. https://doi.org/10.1111/ajps.12379.

Adelman, Carol. 2007. "Foreign Aid: Effectively Advancing Security Interests." *Harvard International Review* 29 (3): 62–67. https://www.hudson.org/content/researchattachments/attachment/1419/harvard_review_adelman.pdf.

Alcoberro, Agustí. 2010. "The War of the Spanish Succession in the Catalan-Speaking Lands." *Catalan Historical Review* 3:69–86. https://doi.org/10.2436/20.1000.01.40.

Alesina, Alberto, William Easterly, and Janina Matuszeski. 2011. "Artificial States." *Journal of the European Economic Association* 9 (2): 246–77. https://doi.org/10.1111/j.1542-4774.2010.01009.x.

Altman, Dan. "The Evolution of Territorial Conquest after 1945 and the Limits of the Norm of Territorial Integrity." *International Organization* 74 (forthcoming).

Anceschi, Luca. 2008. *Turkmenistan's Foreign Policy: Positive Neutrality and the Consolidation of the Turkmen Regime.* New York: Routledge.

Anderson, M. S. 1966. *The Eastern Question, 1774–1923: A Study in International Relations.* New York: St. Martin's.

Arguillas, Carolyn O. 2009. "Q and A with Jibin Arula: 41 Years after the Jabidah Massacre." MindaNews, March 15, 2009. http://www.mindanews.com/top-stories/2009/03/q-and-a-with-jibin-arula-%E2%80%9Csana-wala-nang-gulo-sa-mindanao%E2%80%9D-4/.

Arjona, Ana. 2016. *Rebelocracy: Social Order in the Colombian Civil War.* New York: Cambridge University Press.

Artman, Vincent M. 2013. "Documenting Territory: Passportisation, Territory, and Exception in Abkhazia and South Ossetia." *Geopolitics* 18 (3): 682–704. https://doi.org/10.1080/14650045.2013.769963.

Asmus, Ronald D. 2010. *A Little War That Shook the World: Georgia, Russia, and the Future of the West.* New York: Palgrave Macmillan.

Atzili, Boaz. 2012. *Good Fences, Bad Neighbors: Border Fixity and International Conflict.* Chicago: University of Chicago Press.

Bachi, Roberto. 1951. "The Tendency to Round Off Age Returns: Measurement and Correction." *Bulletin of the International Statistics Institute* 33:195–221.

Badan Pusat Statistik. 2014. *Badan Pusat Statistik.* Jakarta: Republik Indonesia.

Bakke, Kristin M., Andrew M. Linke, John O'Loughlin, and Gerard Toal. 2018. "Dynamics of State-Building after War: External-Internal Relations in Eurasian De Facto States." *Political Geography* 63:159–73. https://doi.org/10.1016/j.polgeo.2017.06.011.

Balcells, Albert. 1996. *Catalan Nationalism: Past and Present.* New York: Palgrave.

Bapat, Navin A. 2012. "Understanding State Sponsorship of Militant Groups." *British Journal of Political Science* 42 (1): 1–29. https://doi.org/10.1017/S000712341100007x.

Barma, Naazneen H. 2016. *The Peacebuilding Puzzle: Political Order in Post-Conflict States.* New York: Cambridge University Press.

Barma, Naazneen H., Naomi Levy, and Jessica Piombo. 2017. "Disentangling Aid Dynamics in Statebuilding and Peacebuilding: A Causal Framework." *International Peacekeeping* 24 (2): 187–211. https://doi.org/10.1080/13533312.2016.1252677.

BBC News. 2011. "Are Kenyans Seeking a Buffer Zone in Somalia?" October 28, 2011. https://www.bbc.com/news/world-africa-15499534.

Bearce, David H. 2003. "Grasping the Commercial Institutional Peace." *International Studies Quarterly* 47 (3): 347–70. https://doi.org/10.1111/1468-2478.4703003.

Beissinger, Mark R. 2002. *National Mobilization and the Collapse of the Soviet State.* New York: Cambridge University Press.

Benson, Brett V. 2011. "Unpacking Alliances: Deterrent and Compellent Alliances and Their Relationship with Conflict, 1816–2000." *Journal of Politics* 73 (4): 1111–27. https://doi.org/10.1017/S0022381611000867.

Berman, Eli, David A. Lake, Gerard Padró i Miquel, and Pierre Yared. 2019. "Introduction: Principals, Agents, and Indirect Foreign Policies." In *Proxy Wars: Suppressing Violence through Local Agents*, edited by Eli Berman and David A. Lake, 1–27. Ithaca, NY: Cornell University Press.

Bertelsmann Stiftung. 2014. *The Bertelsmann Stiftung's Transformation Index.* Gütersloh: Bertelsmann Stiftung.

Bignami-Van Assche, Simona. 2005. "Province-Specific Mortality in China, 1990–2000." Paper presented at the Annual Meeting of the Population Association of America, Philadelphia, March 31–April 2, 2005. https://paa2005.princeton.edu/papers/50710.

Bilinsky, Yaroslav. 1999. *Endgame in NATO's Enlargement: The Baltic States and Ukraine.* Westport, CT: Praeger.

Blair, Dennis C. 2009. *Annual Threat Assessment of the Intelligence Community for the Senate Select Committee on Intelligence.* Office of the Director of National Intelligence. February 12, 2009. https://www.dni.gov/files/documents/Newsroom/Testimonies/20090212_testimony.pdf.

——. 2010. *Annual Threat Assessment of the U.S. Intelligence Community for the Senate Select Committee on Intelligence.* Office of the Director of National Intelligence.

February 2, 2010. https://www.dni.gov/files/documents/Newsroom/Testimonies/20100202_testimony.pdf.

Blank, Stephen. 1998. "Russia, NATO Enlargement, and the Baltic States." *World Affairs* 160 (3): 115–25. https://www.jstor.org/stable/20672519.

Boone, Catherine. 2003. *Political Topographies of the African State: Territorial Authority and Institutional Choice*. New York: Cambridge University Press.

Borghard, Erica Dreyfus. 2014. "Friends with Benefits? Power and Influence in Proxy Warfare." PhD diss., Columbia University. https://doi.org/10.7916/D8Q81B7Z.

Boulding, Kenneth E. 1962. *Conflict and Defense: A General Theory*. New York: Harper.

Braumoeller, Bear F. 2013. "Is War Disappearing?" Paper presented at the Annual Meeting of the American Political Science Association, Chicago, August 29–September 1, 2013.

Brooks, Stephen G. 2007. *Producing Security: Multinational Corporations, Globalization, and the Changing Calculus of Conflict*. Princeton, NJ: Princeton University Press.

Brubaker, Rogers. 1996. *Nationalism Reframed: Nationhood and the National Question in the New Europe*. New York: Cambridge University Press.

——. 2011. "Nationalizing States Revisited: Projects and Processes of Nationalization in Post-Soviet States." *Ethnic and Racial Studies* 34 (11): 1785–1814. https://doi.org/10.1080/01419870.2011.579137.

Bugajski, Janusz. 2009. *Dismantling the West: Russia's Atlantic Agenda*. Washington, DC: Potomac Books.

Bukkvoll, Tor. 1997. "Ukraine and NATO: The Politics of Soft Cooperation." *Security Dialogue* 28 (3): 363–74. https://doi.org/10.1177/0967010697028003009.

——. 2001. "Off the Cuff Politics: Explaining Russia's Lack of a Ukraine Strategy." *Europe-Asia Studies* 53 (8): 1141–57. https://doi.org/10.1080/09668130120093165.

Bull, David. 1983. *The Poverty of Diplomacy: Kampuchea and the Outside World*. Oxford: Oxfam.

Bureau of Democracy, Human Rights, and Labor. 2007. *2006 Country Reports on Human Rights Practices: Moldova*. U.S. Department of State, March 6, 2007. https://www.state.gov/j/drl/rls/hrrpt/2006/78828.htm.

Bureau of the Census and Statistics. Multiple years. *Census of the Philippines*. Manila: Republic of the Philippines.

Bureau of the Census and Statistics. Multiple years. *Journal of Philippine Statistics*. Manila: Republic of the Philippines.

Busse, Matthias, and Carsten Hefeker. 2007. "Political Risk, Institutions and Foreign Direct Investment." *European Journal of Political Economy* 23 (2): 397–415. https://doi.org/10.1016/j.ejpoleco.2006.02.003.

Byman, Daniel. 2005. *Deadly Connections: States That Sponsor Terrorism*. New York: Cambridge University Press.

Byman, Daniel, and Sarah E. Kreps. 2010. "Agents of Destruction? Applying Principal-Agent Analysis to State-Sponsored Terrorism." *International Studies Perspectives* 11 (1): 1–18. https://doi.org/10.1111/j.1528-3585.2009.00389.x.

Cal, Ben. 1997. *FVR through the Years, Part II*. Quezon City: Philippine Academy for Continuing Education and Research.

Carney, Timothy. 1982. "Kampuchea in 1981: Fragile Stalemate." *Asian Survey* 22 (1): 78–87. https://doi.org/10.2307/2643712.

——. 1987. "The Heng Samrin Armed Forces and the Military Balance in Cambodia." In *The Cambodian Agony*, edited by David A. Ablin and Marlowe Hood, 180–212. Armonk, NY: M. E. Sharpe.

Carr, William. 1991. *The Origins of the Wars of German Unification*. New York: Routledge.

Carrier, N. H. 1959. "A Note on the Measurement of Digital Preference in Age Record-ings." *Journal of the Institute of Actuaries* 85 (1): 71–85. https://doi.org/10.1017/S0020268100037835.

Carson, Austin. 2018. *Secret Wars: Covert Conflicts in International Politics*. Princeton, NJ: Princeton University Press.

Carter, David B. 2012. "A Blessing or a Curse? State Support for Terrorist Groups." *International Organization* 66 (1): 129–51. https://doi.org/10.1017/S0020818311000312.

———. 2015. "The Compellence Dilemma: International Disputes with Violent Groups." *International Studies Quarterly* 59 (3): 461–76. https://doi.org/10.1111/isqu.12192.

Cederman, Lars-Erik, Nils B. Weidmann, and Kristian Skrede Gleditsch. 2011. "Hor-izontal Inequalities and Ethnonationalist Civil War: A Global Comparison." *American Political Science Review* 105 (3): 478–95. https://doi.org/10.1017/S0003055411000207.

Centeno, Miguel Angel. 2002. *Blood and Debt: War and the Nation-State in Latin America*. University Park, PA: Pennsylvania State University Press.

Central Statistics Agency Ethiopia. 2016. *CountryStat Ethiopia*. Addis Ababa: Central Statistics Agency Ethiopia. http://ethiopia.countrystat.org/home/en/.

Chalk, Peter. 2007. "Case Study: The East Africa Corridor." In *Ungoverned Territories: Understanding and Reducing Terrorism Risks*, edited by Angel Rabasa, Steven Boraz, Peter Chalk, Kim Cragin, Theodore W. Karasik, Jennifer D. P. Moroney, Kevin A. O'Brien, and John E. Peters, 147–72. Santa Monica, CA: RAND Corpo-ration. https://www.jstor.org/stable/10.7249/mg561af.17.

Chanda, Nayan. 1986. *Brother Enemy: The War after the War*. San Diego: Harcourt Brace Jovanovich.

Che Man, W. K. 1990. *Muslim Separatism: The Moros of the Southern Philippines and the Malays of Southern Thailand*. Singapore: Oxford University Press.

China Data Center. 2014. *China Data Online*. Ann Arbor, MI: China Data Center.

Chowdhury, Arjun. 2018. *The Myth of the International Order: Why Weak States Persist and Alternatives to the State Fade Away*. New York: Oxford University Press.

Chufrin, Gennady I. 1984. "Five Years of the People's Revolutionary Power in Kam-puchea: Results and Conclusions." *Asian Survey* 24 (11): 1143–50. https://doi.org/10.2307/2644148.

Clapper, James R. 2011. *Statement for the Record on the Worldwide Threat Assess-ment of the U.S. Intelligence Community for the Senate Select Committee on Intelligence*. Office of the Director of National Intelligence. February 16, 2011. https://www.dni.gov/files/documents/Newsroom/Testimonies/20110216 testimony sfr.pdf.

———. 2012. *Unclassified Statement for the Record on the Worldwide Threat Assessment of the U.S. Intelligence Community for the Senate Select Committee on Intelligence*. Office of the Director of National Intelligence. January 31, 2012. https://www.dni.gov/files/documents/Newsroom/Testimonies/20120131 testimony ata.pdf.

———. 2013. *Statement for the Record: Worldwide Threat Assessment of the U.S. Intel-ligence Community; Senate Select Committee on Armed Services*. Office of the Director of National Intelligence. April 18, 2013. https://www.dni.gov/files/documents/Intelligence%20Reports/UNCLASS_2013%20ATA %20SFR%20FINAL%20for%20SASC%2018%20Apr%202013.pdf.

———. 2014. *Statement for the Record: Worldwide Threat Assessment of the U.S. Intelligence Community; Senate Select Committee on Intelligence.* Office of the Director of National Intelligence. January 29, 2014. https://www.dni.gov/files/documents/Intelligence%20Reports/2014%20WWTA%20%20 SFR_SSCI_29_Jan.pdf.

———. 2015. *Statement for the Record: Worldwide Threat Assessment of the U.S. Intelligence Community; Senate Armed Services Committee.* Office of the Director of National Intelligence. February 26, 2015. https://www.dni.gov/files/documents/Unclassified_2015_ATA_SFR_-_SASC_FINAL.pdf.

———. 2016. *Statement for the Record: Worldwide Threat Assessment of the U.S. Intelligence Community; Senate Select Committee.* Office of the Director of National Intelligence. February 9, 2016. https://www.dni.gov/files/documents/SASC_Unclassified_2016_ATA_SFR_FINAL.pdf.

Clunan, Anne L., and Harold A. Trinkunas, eds. 2010. *Ungoverned Spaces: Alternatives to State Authority in an Era of Softened Sovereignty.* Palo Alto, CA: Stanford University Press.

Coats, Daniel R. 2017. *Statement for the Record: Worldwide Threat Assessment of the U.S. Intelligence Community; Senate Select Committee on Intelligence.* Office of the Director of National Intelligence. May 11, 2017. https://www.dni.gov/files/documents/Newsroom/Testimonies/SSCI%20Unclassified% 20SFR%20-%20 Final.pdf.

———. 2018. *Statement for the Record: Worldwide Threat Assessment of the U.S. Intelligence Community.* Office of the Director of National Intelligence. February 13, 2018. https://www.dni.gov/files/documents/Newsroom/Testimonies/2018-ATA---Unclassified-SSCI.pdf.

Coggins, Bridget L. 2015. "Does State Failure Cause Terrorism? An Empirical Analysis (1999–2008)." *Journal of Conflict Resolution* 59 (3): 455–83. https://doi.org/10.1177/0022002713515403.

Collier, Paul, and Anke Hoeffler. 2004. "Greed and Grievance in Civil War." *Oxford Economic Papers* 56 (4): 563–95. https://doi.org/10.1093/oep/gpf064.

Colonial Office. 1962. *Report of the Commission of Enquiry, North Borneo and Sarawak, 1962.* London: Her Majesty's Stationery Office.

Comin, Diego, William Easterly, and Erick Gong. 2010. "Was the Wealth of Nations Determined in 1000 BC?" *American Economic Journal: Macroeconomics* 2 (3): 65–97. https://doi.org/10.1257/mac.2.3.65.

Cooley, Alexander. 2012. *Great Games, Local Rules: The New Great Power Contest in Central Asia.* Oxford: Oxford University Press.

Cornell, Svante E. 2011. *Azerbaijan since Independence.* New York: M. E. Sharpe.

Coronel-Ferrer, Miriam. 2005. "The Philippine State and Moro Resistance: Dynamics of a Persistent Conflict." In *The Mindanao Conflict*, edited by Kamarulzaman Askandar and Ayesah Abubakar, 1–31. Penang, Malaysia: Southeast Asian Conflict Studies Network.

Dabla, Bashir Ahmad. 2011. *Social Impact of Militancy in Kashmir.* New Delhi: Gyan.

Dafoe, Allan, Jonathan Renshon, and Paul Huth. 2014. "Reputation and Status as Motives for War." *Annual Review of Political Science* 17:371–93. https://doi.org/10.1146/annurev-polisci-071112-213421.

D'Arcy, Michelle, and Marina Nistotskaya. 2017. "State First, Then Democracy: Using Cadastral Records to Explain Governmental Performance in Public Goods Provision." *Governance* 30 (2): 193–209. https://doi.org/10.1111/gove.12206.

Darden, Keith A. 2010. *Economic Liberalism and Its Rivals: The Formation of International Institutions among the Post-Soviet States*. New York: Cambridge University Press.

Datanet India Private Limited. 2014. *IndiaStat*. New Delhi: Datanet India Private Limited. https://www.indiastat.com/.

Dawson, Jane. 1998. "Ethnicity, Ideology and Geopolitics in Crimea." *Communist and Post-Communist Studies* 30 (4): 427–44. https://doi.org/10.1016/S0967-067X(97)00013-5.

de Swaan, Abram. 1988. *In Care of the State*. New York: Oxford University Press.

Demographic and Health Surveys Program. 2015. Rockville, MD: ICF. http://www.dhsprogram.com/.

Demoscope Weekly. 2018. "All-Union Population Census of 1989: The National Composition of the Population in the Republics of the USSR." http://www.demoscope.ru/weekly/ssp/sng_nac_89.php.

Department of Foreign Affairs. 1968. *Position Paper on the Philippine Claim to Sabah*. Pasay City: Republic of the Philippines.

Department of State to Embassy Kuala Lumpur. 1969. Telegram 199087, November 27, 1969. Central Files 1963–1973, Subject-Numeric File, RG 59, General Records of the Department of State, U.S. National Archives, College Park, MD.

Desch, Michael C. 1996. "War and Strong States, Peace and Weak States?" *International Organization* 50 (2): 237–68. https://doi.org/10.1017/S0020818300028551.

Dincecco, Mark. 2011. *Political Transformations and Public Finances: Europe, 1650–1913*. New York: Cambridge University Press.

Director of Central Intelligence. 1985. *Cambodia: Vietnamese Strategy and the New Realities*. Langley, VA: Central Intelligence Agency. https://www.cia.gov/library/readingroom/docs/CIA-RDP87T00495R001001040001-4.pdf.

Director of Intelligence and Research. 1968. Intelligence Note 27, January 10, 1968. Central Files 1963–1973, Subject-Numeric File, RG 59, General Records of the Department of State, U.S. National Archives, College Park, MD.

Dixon, Jeffrey S., and Meredith Reid Sarkees. 2016. *A Guide to Intra-state Wars*. Thousand Oaks, CA: CQ Press.

Donaldson, Robert H., Joseph L. Nogee, and Vidya Nadkarni. 2014. *The Foreign Policy of Russia: Changing Systems, Enduring Interests*. 5th ed. Armonk, NY: M. E. Sharpe.

Downes, Alexander B., and Jonathan Monten. 2013. "Forced to Be Free: Why Foreign-Imposed Regime Change Rarely Leads to Democratization." *International Security* 37 (4): 90–131. https://doi.org/10.1162/ISEC_a_00117.

Driscoll, Jesse. 2015. *Warlords and Coalition Politics in Post-Soviet States*. New York: Cambridge University Press.

Easterly, William, and Ross Levine. 2003. "Tropics, Germs, and Crops: How Endowments Influence Economic Development." *Journal of Monetary Economics* 50 (1): 3–39. https://doi.org/10.1016/S0304-3932(02)00200-3.

Eastern African Department Infrastructure Operations Division. 1992. *Staff Appraisal Report: Republic of Uganda Northern Construction Project*. Washington, DC: World Bank.

EFA Global Monitoring Report Team. 2015. *Investing in Teachers Is Investing in Learning: A Prerequisite for the Transformative Power of Education; Background Paper for the Oslo Summit on Education for Development*, 2015/ED/EFA/MRT/BP1. Paris: UNESCO. https://unesdoc.unesco.org/ark:/48223/pf0000233897.locale=en.

Elliott, J. H. 2018. *Scots and Catalans: Union and Disunion*. New Haven, CT: Yale University Press.

Ellison, Brian J. 2011. "Russian Grand Strategy in the South Ossetia War." *Demokrati-zatsiya* 19 (4): 343–66. http://demokratizatsiya.pub/archives/19_4_0367216M621448T3.pdf.

Embassy Bangkok to Department of State. 1968. Telegram 16650, June 26, 1968, 1968BANGKO16650. Central Files February 1963–1973, Subject-Numeric File, RG 59, General Records of the Department of State, U.S. National Archives, College Park, MD.

Embassy Jakarta to Department of State. 1973. Telegram 07498, June 23, 1973, 1973JAKART07498. Central Files February 1963–1973, Subject-Numeric File, RG 59, General Records of the Department of State, U.S. National Archives, College Park, MD.

Embassy Kuala Lumpur to Department of State. 1967. Telegram 00588, August 18, 1967, 1967KUALA00588. Central Files February 1963–1973, Subject-Numeric File, RG 59, General Records of the Department of State, U.S. National Archives, College Park, MD.

———. 1968a. A0511, April 10, 1968. Central Files February 1963–1973, Subject-Numeric File, RG 59, General Records of the Department of State, U.S. National Archives, College Park, MD.

———. 1968b. Airgram A0748, August 23, 1968. Central Files February 1963–1973, Subject-Numeric File, RG 59, General Records of the Department of State, U.S. National Archives, College Park, MD.

———. 1968c. Telegram 03734, April 11, 1968, 1968KUALA03734. Central Files February 1963–1973, Subject-Numeric File, RG 59, General Records of the Department of State, U.S. National Archives, College Park, MD.

———. 1968d. Telegram 04240, May 28, 1968, 1968KUALA04240. Central Files February 1963–1973, Subject-Numeric File, RG 59, General Records of the Department of State, U.S. National Archives, College Park, MD.

———. 1968e. Telegram 04555, June 15, 1968, 1968KUALA04555. Central Files February 1963–1973, Subject-Numeric File, RG 59, General Records of the Department of State, U.S. National Archives, College Park, MD.

———. 1968f. Telegram 05559, September 4, 1968, 1968KUALA05559. Central Files February 1963–1973, Subject-Numeric File, RG 59, General Records of the Department of State, U.S. National Archives, College Park, MD.

———. 1968g. Telegram 05770, September 22, 1968, 1968KUALA05770. Central Files February 1963–1973, Subject-Numeric File, RG 59, General Records of the Department of State, U.S. National Archives, College Park, MD.

———. 1973a. Telegram 00280, January 23, 1973, 1973KUALA00280. Central Files February 1963–1973, Subject-Numeric File, RG 59, General Records of the Department of State, U.S. National Archives, College Park, MD.

———. 1973b. Telegram 00739, February 24, 1973, 1973KUALA00739. Central Files February 1963–1973, Subject-Numeric File, RG 59, General Records of the Department of State, U.S. National Archives, College Park, MD.

———. 1973c. Telegram 01109, March 19, 1973, 1973KUALA01109. Central Foreign Policy Files, 1973–1979, Electronic Telegrams, RG 59, General Records of the Department of State, U.S. National Archives, College Park, MD.

Embassy Manila to Department of State. 1968a. Telegram 07479, February 21, 1968, 1968MANILA07479. Central Files February 1963–1973, Subject-Numeric File, RG 59, General Records of the Department of State, U.S. National Archives, College Park, MD.

———. 1968b. Telegram 08608, March 22, 1968, 1968MANILA08608. Central Files February 1963–1973, Subject-Numeric File, RG 59, General Records of the Department of State, U.S. National Archives, College Park, MD.

——. 1968c. Telegram 08721, March 26, 1968, 1968MANILA08721. Central Files February 1963–1973, Subject-Numeric File, RG 59, General Records of the Department of State, U.S. National Archives, College Park, MD.

——. 1968d. Telegram 12253, June 29, 1968, 1968MANILA12253. Central Files February 1963–1973, Subject-Numeric File, RG 59, General Records of the Department of State, U.S. National Archives, College Park, MD.

——. 1973a. Telegram 02769, March 9, 1973, 1973MANILA02769. Central Foreign Policy Files, 1973–1979, Electronic Telegrams, RG 59, General Records of the Department of State, U.S. National Archives, College Park, MD.

——. 1973b. Telegram 05831, May 19, 1973, 1973MANILA05831. Central Foreign Policy Files, 1973–1979, Electronic Telegrams, RG 59, General Records of the Department of State, U.S. National Archives, College Park, MD.

——. 1974a. Telegram 02559, March 5, 1974, 1974MANILA02559. Central Foreign Policy Files, 1973–1979, Electronic Telegrams, RG 59, General Records of the Department of State, U.S. National Archives, College Park, MD.

——. 1974b. Telegram 03106, March 15, 1974, 1974MANILA03106. Central Foreign Policy Files, 1973–1979, Electronic Telegrams, RG 59, General Records of the Department of State, U.S. National Archives, College Park, MD.

——. 1975. Telegram 02817, March 6, 1975, 1975MANILA02817. Central Foreign Policy Files, 1973–1979, Electronic Telegrams, RG 59, General Records of the Department of State, U.S. National Archives, College Park, MD.

——. 1977. Telegram 12624, August 12, 1977, 1977MANILA12624. Central Foreign Policy Files, 1973–1979, Electronic Telegrams, RG 59, General Records of the Department of State, U.S. National Archives, College Park, MD.

Energy Commission of Nigeria. 2003. *National Energy Policy*. Abuja: Federal Republic of Nigeria.

Engerman, Stanley, and Kenneth Sokoloff. 2002. "Factor Endowments, Inequality, and Paths of Development among New World Economies." *Economia* 3 (1): 41–109. https://doi.org/10.3386/w9259.

Englebert, Pierre, Stacy Tarango, and Matthew Carter. 2002. "Dismemberment and Suffocation: A Contribution to the Debate on African Boundaries." *Comparative Political Studies* 35 (10): 1093–18. https://doi.org/10.1177/001041402237944.

Engracia, Luisa T. 1983. "Infant and Child Mortality and Health Service in the Rural Philippines." Paper presented at the Sixth National Population Welfare Congress, Manila, November 17, 1983.

Evans, Grant, and Kelvin Rowley. 1990. *Red Brotherhood at War: Vietnam, Cambodia, and Laos since 1975*. New York: Verso.

Fazal, Tanisha M. 2007. *State Death: The Politics and Geography of Conquest, Occupation, and Annexation*. Princeton, NJ: Princeton University Press.

——. 2014. "Dead Wrong? Battle Deaths, Military Medicine, and Exaggerated Reports of War's Demise." *International Security* 39 (1): 95–125. https://doi.org/10.1162/ISEC_a_00166.

Fearon, James D., and David D. Laitin. 2003. "Ethnicity, Insurgency, and Civil War." *American Political Science Review* 97 (1): 75–90. https://doi.org/10.1017/S0003055403000534.

——. 2004. "Neotrusteeship and the Problem of Weak States." *International Security* 28 (4): 5–43. https://doi.org/10.1162/0162288041588296.

Feenstra, Robert C., Robert Inklaar, and Marcel P. Timmer. 2013. *The Next Generation of the Penn World Table*. Groningen: University of Groningen. https://doi.org/10.3386/w19255.

Fein, Lisa C. 2005. "Symbolic Boundaries and National Borders: The Construction of an Estonian Russian Identity." *Nationalities Papers* 33 (3): 333–44. https://doi.org/10.1080/00905990500193196.

Findley, Michael G., James Piazza, and Joseph K. Young. 2011. "Games Rivals Play: Terrorism in International Rivalries." *Journal of Politics* 74 (1): 235–48. https://doi.org/10.1017/S0022381611001551.

Florea, Adrian. 2017. "De Facto States: Survival and Disappearance (1945–2011)." *International Studies Quarterly* 61 (2): 337–51. https://doi.org/10.1093/isq/sqw049.

Fortna, Virginia Page. 2008. *Does Peacekeeping Work? Shaping Belligerents' Choices after Civil War*. Princeton, NJ: Princeton University Press.

Fukuyama, Francis. 1989. "The End of History?" *National Interest* (16): 3–18. http://www.jstor.org/stable/24027184.

———. 2004. *State-Building: Governance and World Order in the 21st Century*. Ithaca, NY: Cornell University Press.

Fund for Peace. 2014. *Fragile States Index*. Washington, DC: Fund for Peace. http://fundforpeace.org/fsi/.

Galvez, Joe. 1987. "A Peace Process That May Lead to War." *Mr. and Ms. Special Edition* 4 (21): 19–22.

Gartzke, Erik. 2007. "The Capitalist Peace." *American Journal of Political Science* 51 (1): 166–91. https://doi.org/10.1111/j.1540-5907.2007.00244.x.

Gennaioli, Nicola, and Hans-Joachim Voth. 2015. "State Capacity and Military Conflict." *Review of Economic Studies* 82 (4): 1409–48. https://doi.org/10.1093/restud/rdv019.

Gersony, Robert. 1997. *The Anguish of Northern Uganda: Results of a Field-Based Assessment of the Civil Conflict in Northern Uganda*. Kampala: USAID Mission Kampala.

Ghobarah, Hazem Adam, Paul Huth, and Bruce Russett. 2003. "Civil Wars Kill and Maim People—Long after the Shooting Stops." *American Political Science Review* 97 (2): 189–202. https://doi.org/10.1017/S0003055403000613.

Gibler, Douglas M. 2012. *The Territorial Peace*. New York: Cambridge University Press.

Gibril, M. A. 1979. *Evaluating Census Response Errors: A Case Study for the Gambia*. Paris: Development Centre of the Organisation for Economic Co-operation and Development.

Gizelis, Theodora-Ismene. 2009. "Wealth Alone Does Not Buy Health: Political Capacity, Democracy, and the Spread of AIDS." *Political Geography* 28 (2): 121–31. https://doi.org/10.1016/j.polgeo.2009.01.005.

Gladstone, Rick. 2016. "Conflicts Keep 24 Million Children Out of School, Unicef Report Finds." *New York Times*, January 11, 2016. https://www.nytimes.com/2016/01/12/world/conflicts-keep-24-million-children-out-of-school-unicef-report-finds.html.

Gleditsch, Kristian Skrede. 2007. "Transnational Dimensions of Civil War." *Journal of Peace Research* 44 (3): 293–309. https://doi.org/10.1177/0022343307076637.

Goertz, Gary, Paul F. Diehl, and Alexandru Balas. 2016. *The Puzzle of Peace: The Evolution of Peace in the International System*. New York: Oxford University Press.

Gohdes, Anita, and Megan Price. 2013. "First Things First: Assessing Data Quality before Model Quality." *Journal of Conflict Resolution* 57 (6): 1090–108. https://doi.org/10.1177/0022002712459708.

Goldstein, Joshua S. 2011. *Winning the War on War: The Decline of Armed Conflict Worldwide*. New York: Plume.

Goldstone, Jack A., Ted Robert Gurr, Barbara Harff, Marc A. Levy, Monty G. Marshall, Robert H. Bates, David L. Epstein, Colin H. Kahl, Pamela T. Surko, John C. Ulfelder Jr., and Alan N. Unger. 2000. *State Failure Task Force Report: Phase III Findings*. McLean, VA: Science Applications International Corporation. https://sites.hks. harvard.edu/fs/pnorris/Acrobat/stm103%20articles/StateFailureReport.pdf.

Gordadze, Thornike. 2009. "Georgian-Russian Relations in the 1990s." In *The Guns of August 2008: Russia's War in Georgia*, edited by Svante E. Cornell and S. Frederick Starr, 28–48. New York: M. E. Sharpe.

Goscha, Christopher E. 2006. "Vietnam, the Third Indochina War, and the Meltdown of Asian Internationalism." In *The Third Indochina War: Conflict between China, Vietnam and Cambodia, 1972–79*, edited by Odd Arne Westad and Sophie Quinn-Judge, 152–86. New York: Routledge. https://doi.org/10.4324/9780203968574.

Gottesman, Evan. 2003. *Cambodia after the Khmer Rouge: Inside the Politics of Nation Building*. New Haven, CT: Yale University Press.

Griffiths, Ryan D. 2017. "Admission to the Sovereignty Club: The Past, Present, and Future of the International Recognition Regime." *Territory, Politics, Governance* 5 (2): 177–89. https://doi.org/10.1080/21622671.2016.1265463.

Hanson, Jonathan K. 2014. "Forging Then Taming Leviathan: State Capacity, Constraints on Rulers, and Development." *International Studies Quarterly* 58 (2): 380–92. https://doi.org/10.1111/isqu.12122.

Hanson, Jonathan K., and Rachel Sigman. 2013. "Leviathan's Latent Dimensions: Measuring State Capacity for Comparative Political Research." Unpublished paper, September 2013. http://www-personal.umich.edu/~jkhanson/resources/hanson_sigman13.pdf.

Hathaway, Oona A., and Scott J. Shapiro. 2017. *The Internationalists: How a Radical Plan to Outlaw War Remade the World*. New York: Simon and Schuster.

Hechter, Michael. 2001. *Containing Nationalism*. New York: Oxford University Press.

Hendrix, Cullen S. 2010. "Measuring State Capacity: Theoretical and Empirical Implications for the Study of Civil Conflict." *Journal of Peace Research* 47 (3): 273–85. https://doi.org/10.1177/0022343310361838.

———. 2011. "Head for the Hills? Rough Terrain, State Capacity, and Civil War." *Civil Wars* 13 (4): 345–70. https://doi.org/10.1080/13698249.2011.629863.

Hensel, Paul R., Michael E. Allison, and Ahmed Khanani. 2009. "Territorial Integrity Treaties and Armed Conflict over Territory." *Conflict Management and Peace Science* 26 (2): 120–43. https://doi.org/10.1177/0738894208101126.

Herbst, Jeffrey. 2000. *States and Power in Africa: Comparative Lessons in Authority and Control*. Princeton, NJ: Princeton University Press.

Hill, William H. 2012. *Russia, the Near Abroad, and the West: Lessons from the Moldova-Transdniestria Conflict*. Washington, DC: Woodrow Wilson Center Press.

Hintze, Otto. 1975. "Military Organization and State Organization." In *The Historical Essays of Otto Hintze*, edited by Felix Gilbert, 178–215. New York: Oxford University Press.

Hobbs, Frank B. 2004. "Age and Sex Composition." In *The Methods and Materials of Demography*, edited by Jacob S. Siegel and David A. Swanson, 125–74. London: Elsevier Academic.

Hogan-Brun, Gabrielle, Uldis Ozolins, Meilutė Ramonienė, and Mart Rannut. 2008. "Language Politics and Practices in the Baltic States." *Current Issues in Language Planning* 8 (4): 469–631. https://doi.org/10.2167/cilp124.0.

Hollyer, James R., B. Peter Rosendorff, and James Raymond Vreeland. 2018. *Information, Democracy, and Autocracy: Economic Transparency and Political (In)stability*. New York: Cambridge University Press.

Horowitz, Donald L. 1985. *Ethnic Groups in Conflict*. Berkeley: University of California Press.

Huang, Reyko. 2016. *The Wartime Origins of Democratization: Civil War, Rebel Governance, and Political Regimes*. New York: Cambridge University Press.

Hughes, James, and Gwendolyn Sasse. 2016. "Power Ideas and Conflict: Ideology, Linkage and Leverage in Crimea and Chechnya." *East European Politics* 32 (3): 314–34. https://doi.org/10.1080/21599165.2015.1124091.

Human Security Report Program. 2013. *Human Security Report 2013: The Decline in Global Violence; Evidence, Explanation, and Contestation*. Vancouver: Human Security.

Huntington, Samuel P. 1968. *Political Order in Changing Societies*. New Haven, CT: Yale University Press.

Huxley, Tim. 1987. "Cambodia in 1986: The PRK's Eighth Year." *Southeast Asian Affairs*, 161–73. https://www.jstor.org/stable/27908574.

Hyndle, Joanna, and Miryna Kutysz. 2002. *Lithuania, Latvia, and Estonia's Aspirations to Integrate with NATO and the EU in the Context of These Countries' Relations with Russia*. Warsaw: Center for Eastern Studies.

Illarionov, Andrei. 2009. "The Russian Leadership's Preparation for War, 1999–2008." In *The Guns of August 2008: Russia's War in Georgia*, edited by Svante E. Cornell and S. Frederick Starr, 49–84. New York: M. E. Sharpe.

Indochina Studies Program. 1985a. "Interview with Dr. Khien Theeravit on the Kampuchean Problem." In *The Kampuchean Problem in Thai Perspective: Positions and Viewpoints Held by Foreign Ministry Officials and Thai Academics*, 63–95. Bangkok: Chulalongkorn University, Institute of Asian Studies.

———. 1985b. "Thailand and the Kampuchean Problem: Discussion between Officials of Thailand's Foreign Affairs Ministry and Thai Academics." In *The Kampuchean Problem in Thai Perspective: Positions and Viewpoints Held by Foreign Ministry Officials and Thai Academics*, 23–62. Bangkok: Chulalongkorn University, Institute of Asian Studies.

Institute for Health Metrics and Evaluation. 2011. *Child Mortality Estimates and MDG4 Attainment by Country, 1990–2011*. Seattle: Institute for Health Metrics and Evaluation.

Institute of Applied Economic Research. 2014. *IPEAData*. Rio de Janeiro: Institute of Applied Economic Research. http://www.ipeadata.gov.br/Default.aspx.

Institute of International Legal Studies. 2003. *The Philippine Claim to a Portion of North Borneo: Materials and Documents*. Quezon City: University of the Philippines Law Center.

Iqbal, Zaryab, and Harvey Starr. 2016. *State Failure in the Modern World*. Stanford, CA: Stanford University Press.

Jackson, Robert H., and Carl G. Rosberg. 1982. "Why Africa's Weak States Persist: The Empirical and the Juridical in Statehood." *World Politics* 35 (1): 1–24. https://doi.org/10.2307/2010277.

James, Laura M. 2015. *Fields of Control: Oil and (In)security in Sudan and South Sudan*. Geneva: Small Arms Survey.

Jelavich, Charles, and Barbara Jelavich. 1977. *The Establishment of the Balkan National States, 1804–1920*. Seattle: University of Washington Press.

Jongerden, Joost. 2007. *The Settlement Issue in Turkey and the Kurds: An Analysis of Spatial Policies, Modernity and War*. Leiden: Brill.

Kansakar, Vidya Bir Singh. 1977. *Population Censuses of Nepal and the Problems of Data Analysis*. Kathmandu: Center for Economic Development and Administration. http://104.236.33.185:8001/jspui/bitstream/123456789/32/1/Population%20Censuses%20of%20Nepal%20and%20the%20Problems%20of%20Data%20Analysis.pdf.

Karatnycky, Adrian. 2015. "Putin's Warlords Slip Out of Control." *New York Times*, June 10, 2015. https://www.nytimes.com/2015/06/10/opinion/putins-warlords-slip-out-of-control.html.

Kassu, Wudu Tafete. 2012. "Religion and Cold War Politics in Ethiopia." In *Religion and the Cold War: A Global Perspective*, edited by Philip Emil Muehlenbeck, 139–57. Nashville: Vanderbilt University Press.

Kaufmann, Daniel, Aart Kraay, and Massimo Mastruzzi. 2018. *Worldwide Governance Indicators*. Washington, DC: World Bank Group. http://info.worldbank.org/governance/WGI/#home.

Keesing's Worldwide. 2018. Keesing's World News Archive. http://keesings.com/index_new.php.

Keister, Jennifer. 2014. "The Illusion of Chaos: Why Ungoverned Spaces Aren't Ungoverned, and Why That Matters." *CATO Institute Policy Analysis*, no. 766, December 9, 2014. https://object.cato.org/sites/cato.org/files/pubs/pdf/pa766_1.pdf.

Kendie, Daniel. 1999. "Egypt and the Hydro-politics of the Blue Nile River." *Northeast African Studies* 6 (1): 141–69. https://doi.org/10.1353/nas.2002.0002.

Khalel, Sheren, and Matthew Vickery. 2015. "Donetsk Has Become Eastern Ukraine's Lawless City." *USA Today*, May 17, 2015. https://www.usatoday.com/story/news/world/2015/05/17/donetsk-ukraine-separatists-marauding-militias/27190647/.

Kiernan, Ben. 1982. "Kampuchea 1979–81: National Rehabilitation in the Eye of an International Storm." *Southeast Asian Affairs*, 167–95. https://www.jstor.org/stable/27908454.

King, Charles. 2003. "The Europe Question in Romania and Moldova." In *Ambivalent Neighbors: The EU, NATO, and the Price of Membership*, edited by Anatol Lieven and Dmitri Trenin, 245–68. Washington, DC: Carnegie Endowment for International Peace.

———. 2008. *The Ghost of Freedom: A History of the Caucasus*. New York: Oxford University Press.

King, Charles, and Neil J. Melvin. 1999. "Diaspora Politics: Ethnic Linkages, Foreign Policy, and Security in Eurasia." *International Security* 24 (3): 108–38. https://doi.org/10.1162/016228899560257.

Kisangani, Emizet F., and Jeffrey Pickering. 2014. "Rebels, Rivals, and Post-colonial State-Building: Identifying Bellicist Influences on State Extractive Capability." *International Studies Quarterly* 58 (1): 187–98. https://doi.org/10.1111/isqu.12042.

Klein, James P., Gary Goertz, and Paul F. Diehl. 2006. "The New Rivalry Dataset: Procedures and Patterns." *Journal of Peace Research* 43 (3): 331–48. https://doi.org/10.1177/0022343306063935.

Kolstø, Pål. 1996. "The New Russian Diaspora—An Identity of Its Own? Possible Identity Trajectories for Russians in the Former Soviet Republic." *Ethnic and Racial Studies* 19 (3): 609–39. https://doi.org/10.1080/01419870.1996.9993927.

———. 2000. *Political Construction Sites: Nation-Building in Russia and the Post-Soviet States*. Boulder, CO: Westview.

———. *See also* Kolstoe, Paul.

Kolstoe, Paul. 1995. *Russians in the Former Soviet Republics*. London: C. Hurst.

Korman, Sharon. 1996. *The Right of Conquest: The Acquisition of Territory by Force in International Law and Practice*. Oxford: Oxford University Press.

Krasner, Stephen D. 1999. *Sovereignty: Organized Hypocrisy*. Princeton, NJ: Princeton University Press.

———. 2004. "Sharing Sovereignty: New Institutions for Collapsed and Failing States." *International Security* 29 (2): 85–120. https://doi.org/10.1162/0162288042879940.

Krasner, Stephen D., and Thomas Risse. 2014. "External Actors, State-Building, and Service Provision in Areas of Limited Statehood: An Introduction." *Governance* 27 (4): 545–67. https://doi.org/10.1111/gove.12065.

Kurtz, Marcus J. 2013. *Latin American State Building in Comparative Perspective: Social Foundations of Institutional Order*. Cambridge: Cambridge University Press.

Kuzio, Taras. 1998. *Ukraine: State and Nation Building*. London: Routledge.

———. 2000. "Geopolitical Pluralism in the CIS: The Emergence of GUUAM." *European Security* 9 (2): 81–114. https://doi.org/10.1080/09662830008407453.

Kuzio, Taras, and David J. Meyer. 1999. "The Donbas and Crimea: An Institutional and Demographic Approach to Ethnic Mobilization in Two Ukrainian Regions." In *State and Institution Building in Ukraine*, edited by Taras Kuzio, Robert S. Kravchuk, and Paul D'Anieri, 297–324. New York: St. Martin's.

Lacina, Bethany, and Nils Petter Gleditsch. 2005. "Monitoring Trends in Global Combat: A New Dataset of Battle Deaths." *European Journal of Population* 21 (2–3): 145–66. https://doi.org/10.1007/s10680-005-6851-6.

Lacina, Bethany, Nils Petter Gleditsch, and Bruce Russett. 2006. "The Declining Risk of Death in Battle." *International Studies Quarterly* 50 (3): 673–80. https://doi.org/10.1111/j.1468-2478.2006.00419.x.

Laitin, David D. 1998. *Identity in Formation: The Russian-Speaking Populations in the New Abroad*. Ithaca, NY: Cornell University Press.

———. 2003. "Three Models of Integration and the Estonian/Russian Reality." *Journal of Baltic Studies* 34 (2): 197–222. https://doi.org/10.1080/01629770300000041.

Lake, David A. 2016. *The Statebuilder's Dilemma: On the Limits of Foreign Intervention*. Ithaca, NY: Cornell University Press.

Lake, David A., and Christopher Fariss. 2014. "Why International Trusteeship Varies: The Politics of External Authority in Areas of Limited Statehood." *Governance* 27 (4): 569–87. https://doi.org/10.1111/gove.12066.

Lalonde, Suzanne N. 2002. *Determining Boundaries in a Conflicted World: The Role of Uti Possidetis*. Montreal: McGill-Queen's University Press.

Lange, Matthew. 2004. *Lineages of Despotism and Development: British Colonialism and State Power*. Chicago: Chicago University Press.

Langer, Nils. 2014. "Language Policies in the Duchy of Schleswig under Denmark and Prussia." In *The Shadow of Colonialism on Europe's Modern Past*, edited by Róisín Healy and Enrico Dal Lago, 73–91. New York: Palgrave Macmillan.

Laruelle, Marlene. 2018. "Why No Kazakh Novorossiya? Kazakhstan's Russian Minority in a Post-Crimea World." *Problems of Post-Communism* 65 (1): 65–78. https://doi.org/10.1080/10758216.2016.1220257.

Lee, Melissa M. 2018. "The International Politics of Incomplete Sovereignty: How Hostile Neighbors Weaken the State." *International Organization* 72 (2): 283–315. https://doi.org/10.1017/S0020818318000085.

Lee, Melissa M., and Melina Platas Izama. 2015. "Aid Externalities: Evidence from PEPFAR in Africa." *World Development* 67:281–94. https://doi.org/10.1016/j.worlddev.2014.10.001.

Lee, Melissa M., Gregor Walter-Drop, and John Wiesel. 2014. "Taking the State (Back) Out? Statehood and the Delivery of Collective Goods." *Governance* 27 (4): 635–54. https://doi.org/10.1111/gove.12069.

Lee, Melissa M., and Nan Zhang. 2017. "Legibility and the Informational Foundations of State Capacity." *Journal of Politics* 79 (1): 118–32. https://doi.org/10.1086/688053.

Leeds, Brett Ashley. 2003. "Do Alliances Deter Aggression? The Influence of Military Alliances on the Initiation of Militarized Interstate Disputes." *American Journal of Political Science* 47 (3): 427–39. https://doi.org/10.1111/1540-5907.00031.

Leichtova, Magda. 2014. *Misunderstanding Russia: Russian Foreign Policy and the West.* Farnham, UK: Ashgate.

Lektzian, David, and Brandon C. Prins. 2008. "Taming the Leviathan: Examining the Impact of External Threat on State Capacity." *Journal of Peace Research* 45 (5): 613–31. https://doi.org/10.1177/0022343308094323.

Lemke, Douglas, and Charles Crabtree. 2019. "Territorial Contenders in World Politics." *Journal of Conflict Resolution.* First published online, May 14, 2019. https://doi.org/10.1177/0022002719847742.

Levi, Margaret. 1988. *Of Rule and Revenue.* Berkeley: University of California Press.

Lieberman, Evan S. 2002. "Taxation Data as Indicators of State-Society Relations: Possibilities and Pitfalls in Cross-National Research." *Studies in Comparative International Development* 36 (4): 89–115. https://doi.org/10.1007/BF02686334.

Lieberman, Evan S., and Prerna Singh. 2017. "Census Enumeration and Group Conflict: A Global Analysis of the Consequences of Counting." *World Politics* 69 (1): 1–53. https://doi.org/10.1017/S0043887116000198.

Lindvall, Johannes, and Jan Teorell. 2016. "State Capacity as Power: A Conceptual Framework." STANCE Working Paper Series, vol. 2016, no. 1. Lund University. http://lup.lub.lu.se/search/ws/files/10948421/2016_1_Lindvall_Teorell.pdf.

Lo, Bobo. 2002. *Russian Foreign Policy in the Post-Soviet Era: Reality, Illusion, and Mythmaking.* New York: Palgrave Macmillan.

——. 2015. *Russia and the New World Disorder.* Baltimore: Brookings Institution Press.

Lucman, Norodin Alonto. 2000. *Moro Archives: A History of Armed Conflicts in Mindanao and East Asia.* Quezon City, Philippines: FLC Press.

Lujala, Päivi, Jan Ketil Rød, and Nadia Thieme. 2007. "Fighting over Oil: Introducing a New Dataset." *Conflict Management and Peace Science* 24 (3): 239–56. https://doi.org/10.1080/07388940701468526.

Lupton, Danielle L. 2018. "Reexamining Reputation for Resolve: Leaders, States, and the Onset of International Crises." *Journal of Global Security Studies* 3 (2): 198–216. https://doi.org/10.1093/jogss/ogy004.

Lustick, Ian S. 1997. "The Absence of Middle Eastern Great Powers: Political 'Backwardness' in Historical Perspective." *International Organization* 51 (4): 653–83. https://doi.org/10.1162/002081897550483.

Lynch, Dov. 2000. *Russian Peacekeeping Strategies in the CIS: The Cases of Moldova, Georgia, and Tajikistan.* New York: St. Martin's.

——. 2004. *Engaging Eurasia's Separatist States: Unresolved Conflicts and De Facto States.* Washington, DC: United States Institute of Peace Press.

MacDonald, Lawrence. 2010. "Getting Aid Right in Northern Uganda—Interview with Julius Kiiza of Makerere University, Kampala." *Center for Global Development,* March 1, 2010. https://www.cgdev.org/blog/getting-aid-right-northern-uganda%E2%80%94interview-julius-kiiza-makerere-university-kampala.

Madigan, Francis C. 1985. *Infant Mortality by Socioeconomic Variables, Philippines, 1983.* Cagayan de Oro City: Research Institute for Mindanao Culture, Xavier University.

Mahoney, James. 2003. "Long-Run Development and the Legacy of Colonialism in Spanish America." *American Journal of Sociology* 109 (1): 51–106. https://doi.org/10.1086/378454.

Mamdani, Mahmoud. 1996. *Citizen and Subject: Contemporary Africa and the Legacy of Late Colonialism*. Princeton, NJ: Princeton University Press.

Mampilly, Zachariah Cherian. 2011. *Rebel Rulers: Insurgent Governance and Civilian Life during War*. Ithaca, NY: Cornell University Press.

Mankoff, Jeffrey. 2012. *Russian Foreign Policy: The Return of Great Power Politics*. Lanham, MD: Rowman and Littlefield.

Mann, Michael. 1984. "The Autonomous Power of the State: Its Origins, Mechanisms, and Results." *European Journal of Sociology* 25 (2): 184–213. https://doi.org/10.1017/S0003975600004239.

Marcus, Aliza. 2007. *Blood and Belief: The PKK and the Kurdish Fight for Independence*. New York: New York University Press.

Mares, Isabela, and Didac Queralt. 2015. "The Non-democratic Origins of Income Taxation." *Comparative Political Studies* 48 (14): 1974–2009. https://doi.org/10.1177/0010414015592646.

Marples, David R., and David F. Duke. 1995. "Ukraine, Russia, and the Question of Crimea." *Nationalities Papers* 23 (2): 261–89. https://doi.org/10.1080/00905999508408377.

Marshall, Monty G., Ted Robert Gurr, and Keith Jaggers. 2017. *Polity IV Project: Political Regime Characteristics and Transitions, 1800–2016*. Vienna, VA: Center for Systemic Peace.

Marten, Kimberly. 2012. *Warlords: Strong-Arm Brokers in Weak States*. Ithaca, NY: Cornell University Press.

Matanock, Aila M. 2017. *Electing Peace: From Civil Conflict to Political Participation*. New York: Cambridge University Press.

Matsuzaki, Reo. 2019. *Statebuilding by Imposition: Resistance and Control in Colonial Taiwan and the Philippines*. Ithaca, NY: Cornell University Press.

Mazarr, Michael J. 2014. "The Rise and Fall of the Failed State Paradigm." *Foreign Affairs* 93 (1): 113–21. https://www.foreignaffairs.com/articles/2013-12-06/rise-and-fall-failed-state-paradigm.

McBeth, John. 1982. "Bureaucrats from B68." *Far Eastern Economic Review*, October 15, 1982.

McConnell, J. Michael. 2008. *Annual Threat Assessment of the Intelligence Community for the Senate Select Committee on Intelligence*. Investigative Project on Terrorism. February 5, 2008. https://www.investigativeproject.org/documents/testimony/348.pdf.

McGregor, Sarah. 2014. "Kenya Eager to Return Refugees to Somalia's Jubaland Region." *Bloomberg Business*, September 22, 2014. https://www.bloomberg.com/news/articles/2014-09-21/kenya-eager-to-return-somali-refugees-wants-jubaland-settlement.

Mehdiyeva, Nazrin. 2011. *Power Games in the Caucasus: Azerbaijan's Foreign and Energy Policy towards the West, Russia, and the Middle East*. New York: I. B. Tauris.

Melvin, Neil J. 1995. *Russians beyond Russia: The Politics of National Identity*. London: Royal Institute of International Affairs.

———. 1998. "The Russians: Diaspora and the End of Empire." In *Nations Abroad: Diaspora Politics and International Relations in the Former Soviet Union*, edited by Charles King and Neil J. Melvin, 27–58. Boulder, CO: Westview.

Merritt, Martha. 2000. "A Geopolitics of Identity: Drawing the Line between Russia and Estonia." *Nationalities Papers* 28 (2): 243–62. https://doi.org/10.1080/713687468.

Mesfin, Seyoum, and Abdeta Dribssa Beyene. 2018. "The Practicalities of Living with Failed States." *Daedalus* 147 (1): 128–40. https://doi.org/10.1162/DAED_a_00479.

Metz, Steven. 1986. "The Mozambique National Resistance and South African Foreign Policy." *African Affairs* 85 (341): 491–507. https://doi.org/10.1093/oxfordjournals. afraf.a097815.

Michalopoulos, Stelios, and Elias Papaioannou. 2016. "The Long-Run Effects of the Scramble for Africa." *American Economic Review* 106 (7): 1802–48. https://doi. org/10.1257/aer.20131311.

Migdal, Joel S. 1988. *Strong Societies and Weak States: State-Society Relations and State Capabilities in the Third World.* Princeton, NJ: Princeton University Press.

Miller, Paul D. 2013. *Armed State Building: Confronting State Failure, 1898–2012.* Ithaca, NY: Cornell University Press. https://doi.org/10.7591/cornell/9780801451492. 001.0001.

Ministry of Foreign Affairs. 1985. "The Real Nature of the Kampuchean Problem." In *The Kampuchean Problem in Thai Perspective: Positions and Viewpoints Held by Foreign Ministry Officials and Thai Academics,* 1–22. Bangkok: Chulalongkorn University, Institute of Asian Studies.

Minorities at Risk Project. 2009. *Minorities at Risk Dataset.* College Park, MD: Center for International Development and Conflict Management. http://www.mar. umd.edu/mar_data.asp.

Montalvo, Jose G., and Marta Reynal-Querol. 2005. "Ethnic Polarization, Potential Conflict, and Civil Wars." *American Economic Review* 95 (3): 796–816. https:// doi.org/10.1257/0002828054201468.

Morrow, James D. 1994. "Alliances, Credibility, and Peacetime Costs." *Journal of Conflict Resolution* 38 (2): 270–97. https://doi.org/10.1177/0022002794038002005.

Mueller, John. 1989. *Retreat from Doomsday: The Obsolescence of Major War.* New York: Basic Books.

——. 2004. *The Remnants of War.* Ithaca, NY: Cornell University Press.

Mukhopadhyay, Dipali. 2014. *Warlords, Strongman Governors, and the State in Afghanistan.* New York: Cambridge University Press.

Mullenbach, Mark, and Dmitriy Nurullayev. 2018. *Dyadic Analysis of Dispute Management (DADM) Project.* http://uca.edu/politicalscience/dadm-project/.

Murdoch, James C., and Todd Sandler. 2004. "Civil Wars and Economic Growth: Spatial Dispersion." *American Journal of Political Science* 48 (1): 138–51. https://doi. org/10.1111/j.0092-5853.2004.00061.x.

Musgrave, Richard Abel. 1969. *Fiscal Systems.* New Haven, CT: Yale University Press.

Myers, Robert J. 1940. "Errors and Bias in the Reporting of Ages in Census Data." *Transactions of the Actuarial Society of America* 41 (104): 394–415.

——. 1976. "An Instance of Reverse Heaping of Ages." *Demography* 13 (4): 577–80. https://doi.org/10.2307/2060512.

Mylonas, Harris. 2012. *The Politics of Nation-Building: Making Co-nationals, Refugees, and Minorities.* New York: Cambridge University Press. https://doi.org/10.1017/ CBO9781139104005.

Mysliwiec, Eva. 1988. *Punishing the Poor: The International Isolation of Kampuchea.* Oxford: Oxfam.

Nair, Shanti. 1997. *Islam in Malaysian Foreign Policy.* New York: Routledge.

Naseemullah, Adnan, and Paul Staniland. 2016. "Indirect Rule and Varieties of Governance." *Governance* 29 (1): 13–30. https://doi.org/10.1111/gove.12129.

National Institute of Statistics. 2004. *Cambodia Inter-Censal Population Survey 2004, General Report.* Phnom Penh: Kingdom of Cambodia.

National Population Commission and ICF Macro. 2009. *Nigeria Demographic and Health Survey 2008.* Abuja: National Population Commission and ICF Macro.

National Statistics Office Philippines and Macro International. 1994. *Philippines National Demographic Survey 1993*. Calverton, MD: National Statistics Office and Macro International.

Natsios, Andrew. 2011. "Foreign Aid Programs Are Important for American National Security." *U.S. News and World Report*, October 11, 2011. https://www.usnews.com/debate-club/given-the-current-deficit-crisis-should-foreign-aid-be-cut/foreign-aid-programs-are-important-for-american-national-security.

Negroponte, John D. 2006. *Annual Threat Assessment of the Director of National Intelligence for the Senate Armed Services Committee*. Office of the Director of National Intelligence. February 28, 2006. https://www.dni.gov/files/documents/Newsroom/Testimonies/20060228_testimony.pdf.

———. 2007. *Annual Threat Assessment of the Director of National Intelligence*. January 18, 2007. Office of the Director of National Intelligence. https://www.dni.gov/files/documents/Newsroom/Testimonies/20070118_testimony.pdf.

Niksch, Larry A. 1981. "Thailand in 1980: Confrontation with Vietnam and the Fall of Kriangsak." *Asian Survey* 21 (2): 223–31. https://doi.org/10.2307/2643767.

Nilsson, Niklas. 2009. "Georgia's Rose Revolution: The Break with the Past." In *The Guns of August 2008: Russia's War in Georgia*, edited by Svante E. Cornell and S. Frederick Starr, 85–103. New York: M. E. Sharpe.

Nunn, Nathan. 2009. "The Importance of History for Economic Development." *Annual Review of Economics* 1 (2009): 65–92. https://doi.org/10.1146/annurev.economics.050708.143336.

Nunn, Nathan, and Diego Puga. 2012. "Ruggedness: The Blessing of Bad Geography in Africa." *Review of Economics and Statistics* 94 (1): 20–36. https://doi.org/10.1162/REST_a_00161.

Nzwili, Fredrick. 2013. "Kenyan Peacekeepers Accused of Creating Buffer State inside Somalia." *Christian Science Monitor*, July 5, 2013. https://www.csmonitor.com/World/Africa/2013/0705/Kenyan-peacekeepers-accused-of-creating-buffer-state-inside-Somalia.

O'Donnell, Guillermo. 1993. "On the State, Democratization, and Some Conceptual Problems: A Latin American View with Glances at Some Postcommunist Countries." *World Development* 21 (8): 1355–69. https://doi.org/10.1016/0305-750X(93)90048-E.

Oesterheld, Christian. 2014. "Cambodian-Thai Relations during the Khmer Rouge Regime: Evidence from the East German Diplomatic Archives." *Silpakorn University Journal of Social Sciences, Humanities, and Arts* 14 (2): 131–54. https://www.tci-thaijo.org/index.php/hasss/article/view/20005/17433.

Oldberg, Ingmar. 2011. "Aims and Means in Russian Foreign Policy." In *Russian Foreign Policy in the 21st Century*, edited by Roger Kanet, 30–58. New York: Palgrave Macmillan.

Olson, Mancur. 1993. "Dictatorship, Democracy, and Development." *American Political Science Review* 87 (3): 567–76.

Oneal, John R., and Bruce M. Russett. 1997. "The Classical Liberals Were Right: Democracy, Interdependence, and Conflict, 1950–1985." *International Studies Quarterly* 41 (2): 267–93. https://doi.org/10.1111/1468-2478.00042.

Onorato, Massimiliano Gaetano, Kenneth Scheve, and David Stasavage. 2014. "Technology and the Era of the Mass Army." *Journal of Economic History* 74 (2): 449–81. https://doi.org/10.1017/S0022050714000321.

O'Rourke, Lindsey A. 2018. *Covert Regime Change: America's Secret Cold War*. Ithaca, NY: Cornell University Press.

Østby, Gudrun. 2008. "Polarization, Horizontal Inequalities and Violent Civil Conflict." *Journal of Peace Research* 45 (2): 143–62. https://doi.org/10.1177/0022343307087169.

Owen, John M., IV. 2002. "The Foreign Imposition of Domestic Institutions." *International Organization* 56 (2): 375–409. https://doi.org/10.1162/002081802320005513.

Oxford Poverty and Human Development Initiative. 2013. *Multidimensional Poverty Index (MPI) Data Bank*. Oxford: Oxford Poverty and Human Development Initiative, University of Oxford.

Ozolina, Zaneta. 2003. "The EU and the Baltic States." In *Ambivalent Neighbors: The EU, NATO, and the Price of Membership*, edited by Anatol Lieven and Dmitri Trenin, 205–30. Washington, DC: Carnegie Endowment for International Peace.

Padró i Miquel, Gerard, and Pierre Yared. 2012. "The Political Economy of Indirect Control." *Quarterly Journal of Economics* 127 (2): 947–1015. https://doi.org/10.1093/qje/qjs012.

Park, Andrus. 1994. "Ethnicity and Independence: The Case of Estonia in Comparative Perspective." *Europe-Asia Studies* 46 (1): 69–87. https://doi.org/10.1080/09668139408412150.

Patrick, Stewart. 2010. *Weak Links: Fragile States, Global Threats, and International Security*. Oxford: Oxford University Press.

Patterson, Tom. 2013. *CleanTOPO2: Edited SRTM30 Plus World Elevation Data*. Shaded Relief. http://www.shadedrelief.com/cleantopo2/.

Peic, Goran, and Dan Reiter. 2011. "Foreign-Imposed Regime Change, State Power, and Civil War Onset, 1920–2004." *British Journal of Political Science* 41 (3): 453–75. https://doi.org/10.1017/S0007123410000426.

Peyrouse, Sébastien. 2015. *Turkmenistan: Strategies of Power, Dilemmas of Development*. New York: Routledge.

Piazza, James A. 2008. "Incubators of Terror: Do Failed and Failing States Promote Transnational Terrorism?" *International Studies Quarterly* 52 (3): 469–88. https://doi.org/10.1111/j.1468-2478.2008.00511.x.

Pinker, Steven. 2011. *The Better Angels of Our Nature: Why Violence Has Declined*. New York: Viking.

Planning Commission. 2002. *National Human Development Report 2001*. New Delhi: Government of India. http://www.igidr.ac.in/conf/ysp/nhd2001.pdf.

Press Briefing by the Statistician-General of the Federation/Chief Executive Officer, National Bureau of Statistics, Dr. Yemi Kale [. . .]. 2012. Abuja: National Bureau of Statistics. https://reliefweb.int/sites/reliefweb.int/files/resources/b410c26c2921c18a6839baebc9b1428fa98fa36a.pdf.

PRS Group. 2014. *International Country Risk Guide*. East Syracuse, NY: PRS Group. https://www.prsgroup.com/explore-our-products/international-country-risk-guide/.

Public Information Office, Office of the President. 1968. *The Facts about Sabah*. Manila: Bureau of Print, Republic of the Philippines.

Quandt, Anna Spitzer. 1973. "The Social Production of Census Data: Interviews from the 1971 Moroccan Census." PhD diss., University of California, Los Angeles.

Queralt, Didac. 2019. "War, International Finance, and Fiscal Capacity in the Long Run." *International Organization* 73 (4), 713–53. https://doi.org/10.1017/S0020818319000250.

Quinn-Judge, Sophie. 1983. "Kampuchea in 1982: Ploughing towards Recovery." *Southeast Asian Affairs*, 153–63. https://doi.org/10.1355/SEAA83J.

———. 2006. "Victory on the Battlefield; Isolation in Asia: Vietnam's Cambodian Decade, 1979–1989." In *The Third Indochina War: Conflict between*

China, Vietnam and Cambodia, 1972–79, edited by Odd Arne Westad and Sophie Quinn-Judge, 207–30. New York: Routledge. https://doi.org/10.4324/9780203968574.

Ramankutty, Navin, Jonathan A. Foley, John Norman, and Kevin McSweeney. 2002. "The Global Distribution of Cultivable Lands: Current Patterns and Sensitivity to Possible Climate Change." *Global Ecology and Biogeography* 11 (5): 377–92. https://doi.org/10.1046/j.1466-822x.2002.00294.x.

Rannut, Mart. 2008. "Estonianization Efforts Post-independence." In *Multilingualism in Post-Soviet Countries*, edited by Aneta Pavlenko, 149–65. Bristol, UK: Multilingual Matters. https://doi.org/10.21832/9781847690883-006.

Rasler, Karen A., and William R. Thompson. 1989. *War and State Making: The Shaping of the Global Powers*. Boston: Unwin Hyman.

Raveh, Adi. 1981. "Measurement and Correction of the Tendency to Round Off Age Returns: A Nonmetric Technique." *Genus* 37 (1/2): 99–110. https://www.ncbi.nlm.nih.gov/pubmed/12311893.

Risse, Thomas, ed. 2011. *Governance without a State? Policies and Politics in Areas of Limited Statehood*. New York: Columbia University Press.

Risse, Thomas, and Tanja A. Börzel. Forthcoming. *Governance under Anarchy? Effective and Legitimate in Areas of Limited Statehood*. New York: Cambridge University Press.

Risse, Thomas, and Eric Stollenwerk. 2018. "Limited Statehood Does Not Equal Civil War." *Daedalus* 147 (1): 104–15. https://doi.org/10.1162/DAED_a_00477.

Robinson, Courtland. 2000. "Refugee Warriors at the Thai-Cambodian Border." *Refugee Survey Quarterly* 19 (1): 23–37. https://doi.org/10.1093/rsq/19.1.23.

Rodrik, Dani. 1999. "Where Did All the Growth Go? External Shocks, Social Conflict, and Growth Collapses." *Journal of Economic Growth* 4 (4): 385–412. https://doi.org/10.1023/A:1009863208706.

Roeder, Philip G. 1999. "Peoples and States after 1989: The Political Costs of Incomplete National Revolutions." *Slavic Review* 58 (4): 854–82. https://doi.org/10.2307/2697202.

Rogers, Melissa Ziegler, and Nicholas Weller. 2014. "Income Taxation and the Validity of State Capacity Indicators." *Journal of Public Policy* 34 (2): 183–206. https://doi.org/10.1017/S0143814X1300024X.

Rondeli, Alexander. 2014. "The Russian-Georgian War and Its Implications for Georgia's State Building." In *The Making of Modern Georgia, 1918–2012: The First Georgian Republic and Its Successors*, edited by Stephen F. Jones, 35–48. New York: Routledge. https://doi.org/10.4324/9781315818207-3.

Roper, Steven D. 2001. "Regionalism in Moldova: The Case of Transnistria and Gagauzia." *Regional and Federal Studies* 11 (3): 101–22. https://doi.org/10.1080/714004699.

Rose, Richard, and William Maley. 1994. *Nationalities in the Baltic States: A Survey Study*. Glasgow: Centre for the Study of Public Policy.

Rubongoya, Joshua B. 2007. *Regime Hegemony in Museveni's Uganda: Pax Musevenica*. New York: Palgrave Macmillan. https://doi.org/10.1057/9780230603363.

Rungswasdisab, Puangthong. 2006. "Thailand's Response to the Cambodian Genocide." In *Genocide in Cambodia and Rwanda: New Perspectives*, edited by Susan E. Cook, 73–118. New Brunswick, NJ: Transaction. https://gsp.yale.edu/thailands-response-cambodian-genocide.

Sabanadze, Natalie. 2014. "Georgia's Ethnic Diversity: A Challenge to State-Building." In *The Making of Modern Georgia, 1918–2012: The First Georgian Republic and Its Successors*, edited by Stephen F. Jones, 119–40. New York: Routledge.

Salehyan, Idean. 2007. "Transnational Rebels: Neighboring States as Sanctuary for Rebel Groups." *World Politics* 59 (2): 217–42. https://doi.org/10.1353/wp.2007.0024.

Salehyan, Idean, David Siroky, and Reed M. Wood. 2014. "External Rebel Sponsorship and Civilian Abuse: A Principal-Agent Analysis of Wartime Atrocities." *International Organization* 68 (3): 633–61. https://doi.org/10.1017/S002081831400006X.

Salehyan, Idean, Kristian Skrede Gleditsch, and David E. Cunningham. 2011. "Explaining External Support for Insurgent Groups." *International Organization* 65 (4): 709–44. https://doi.org/10.1017/S0020818311000233.

San-Akca, Belgin. 2016. *States in Disguise: Causes of State Support for Rebel Groups.* New York: Oxford University Press.

Sasse, Gwendolyn. 2007. *The Crimea Question: Identity, Transition, and Conflict.* Cambridge, MA: Harvard Ukrainian Research Institute.

Saylor, Ryan. 2014. *State Building in Boom Times: Commodities and Coalitions in Latin America and Africa.* New York: Oxford University Press.

Schier, Peter. 1986. "Kampuchea in 1985: Between Crocodiles and Tigers." *Southeast Asian Affairs*, 139–61. https://doi.org/10.1355/SEAA86I.

Schofield, Victoria. 2010. *Kashmir in Conflict: India, Pakistan and the Unending War.* New York: I. B. Tauris.

Scott, James C. 1998. *Seeing like a State: How Certain Schemes to Improve the Human Condition Have Failed.* New Haven, CT: Yale University Press.

——. 2009. *The Art of Not Being Governed: An Anarchist History of Upland Southeast Asia.* New Haven, CT: Yale University Press.

Security Police of the Republic of Estonia. 2005. *Annual Review 2005.* Estonian Internal Security Service. https://www.kapo.ee/sites/default/files/public/content_page/Annual%20Review%202005.pdf.

Shaw, Stanford J. 1976. *History of the Ottoman Empire and Modern Turkey.* Vol. 1, *Empire of the Gazis: The Rise and Decline of the Ottoman Empire, 1280–1808.* New York: Cambridge University Press.

Shevtsova, Lilia. 2006. "Russia's Ersatz Democracy." *Current History* 105 (693): 307–14. https://carnegieendowment.org/files/ShevCH.pdf.

Slater, Dan. 2010. *Ordering Power: Contentious Politics and Authoritarian Leviathans in Southeast Asia.* Cambridge: Cambridge University Press. https://doi.org/10.1017/CBO9780511760891.

Slater, Dan, and Diana Kim. 2015. "Standoffish States: Nonliterate Leviathans in Southeast Asia." *TRaNS: Trans-Regional and -National Studies of Southeast Asia* 3 (1): 25–44. https://doi.org/10.1017/trn.2014.14.

Sleivyte, Janina. 2010. *Russia's European Agenda and the Baltic States.* London: Routledge.

Slocomb, Margaret. 2003. *The People's Republic of Kampuchea.* Chiang Mai: Silkworm Books.

Smith, Alastair. 1995. "Alliance Formation and War." *International Studies Quarterly* 39 (4): 405–25. https://doi.org/10.2307/2600800.

Smith, David J. 1998. "Russia, Estonia, and the Search for a Stable Ethno-Politics." *Journal of Baltic Studies* 29 (1): 3–18. https://doi.org/10.1080/01629779700000191.

——. 2002. "Narva Region within the Estonian Republic: From Autonomism to Accommodation?" *Regional and Federal Studies* 12 (2): 89–110. https://doi.org/10.1080/714004740.

Smith, Graham, and Andrew Wilson. 1997. "Rethinking Russia's Post-Soviet Diaspora: The Potential for Political Mobilisation in Eastern Ukraine and North-east Estonia." *Europe-Asia Studies* 49 (5): 845–64. https://doi.org/10.1080/09668139708412476.

Socor, Vladimir. 2007. "Georgian Declaration and Performance Underscore Commitment to NATO Membership." *Eurasia Daily Monitor* 4 (52). https://jamestown.org/program/georgian-declaration-and-performance-underscore-commitment-to-nato-membership/.

Soifer, Hillel David. 2008. "State Infrastructural Power: Approaches to Conceptualization and Measurement." *Studies in Comparative International Development* 43 (3–4): 231–51. https://doi.org/10.1007/s12116-008-9028-6.

———. 2013. "State Power and the Economic Origins of Democracy." *Studies in Comparative International Development* 48 (1): 1–22. https://doi.org/10.1007/s12116-012-9122-7.

———. 2015. *State Building in Latin America.* New York: Cambridge University Press. https://doi.org/10.1017/CBO9781316257289.

———. 2016. "Regionalism, Ethnic Diversity, and Variation in Public Good Provision by National States." *Comparative Political Studies* 49 (10): 1341–71. https://doi.org/10.1177/0010414015617965.

Solchanyk, Roman. 1996. "Ukraine, Russia, and the CIS." *Harvard Ukrainian Studies* 20:19–43. https://www.jstor.org/stable/41036683.

Souleimanov, Emil. 2013. *Understanding Ethnopolitical Conflict: Karabkh, South Ossetia, and Abkhazia Wars Reconsidered.* New York: Palgrave Macmillan.

Staniland, Paul. 2012. "States, Insurgents, and Wartime Political Orders." *Perspectives on Politics* 10 (2): 243–64. https://doi.org/10.1017/S1537592712000655.

Stern, Tom. 2012. *Nur Misuari: An Authorized Biography.* Manila: Anvil.

Stewart, Megan A. 2019. "Governing for Revolution." Unpublished book manuscript.

Sumner, Brian Taylor. 2004. "Territorial Disputes at the International Court of Justice." *Duke Law Journal* 53 (6): 1779–1812. https://scholarship.law.duke.edu/dlj/vol53/iss6/3.

Swami, Praveen. 2004. "Failed Threats and Flawed Fences: India's Military Responses to Pakistan's Proxy War." *India Review* 3 (2): 147–70. https://doi.org/10.1080/14736480049046504.

Szporluk, Roman. 1993. "Belarus', Ukraine, and the Russian Question: A Comment." *Post-Soviet Affairs* 9 (4): 366–74. https://doi.org/10.1080/1060586X.1993.10641375.

Tan, Samuel K. 1993. *Internationalization of the Bangsamoro Struggle.* Quezon City: University of the Philippines Press.

———. 2010. *The Muslim South and Beyond.* Quezon City: University of the Philippines Press.

Tanzi, Vito. 1991. *Public Finance in Developing Countries.* Aldershot: Edward Elgar.

Taspinar, Omer. 2005. *Kurdish Nationalism and Political Islam in Turkey: Kemalist Identity in Transition.* New York: Routledge.

Tatu, Frank. 1987. "National Security." In *Cambodia: A Country Study*, edited by Federal Research Division—Library of Congress, 239–304. Washington, DC: Secretary of the Army.

Thant, U. 1976. "Final Conclusions regarding Malaysia." In *Public Papers of the Secretaries General of the United Nations*, vol. 6, *1961–1964*, edited by Andrew W. Cordier and Max Harrelson, 398–403. New York: Columbia University Press.

Thies, Cameron G. 2004. "State Building, Interstate and Intrastate Rivalry: A Study of Post-colonial Developing Country Extractive Efforts, 1975–2000." *International*

Studies Quarterly 48 (1): 53–72. https://doi.org/10.1111/j.0020-8833.2004. 00291.x.

———. 2005. "War, Rivalry, and State Building in Latin America." *American Journal of Political Science* 49 (3): 451–65. https://doi.org/10.1111/j.1540-5907.2005. 00134.x.

———. 2007. "The Political Economy of State Building in Sub-Saharan Africa." *Journal of Politics* 69 (3): 716–31. https://doi.org/10.1111/j.1468-2508.2007.00570.x.

———. 2009. "National Design and State Building in Sub-Saharan Africa." *World Politics* 61 (4): 623–69. https://doi.org/10.1017/S0043887109990086.

Thomas, M. Ladd. 1986. "Communist Insurgency in Thailand: Factors Contributing to Its Decline." *Asian Affairs* 13 (1): 17–26. https://doi.org/10.1080/00927678.1986. 10553659.

Thompson, William R., and David R. Dreyer. 2012. *Handbook of International Rivalries: 1494–2010*. Los Angeles: CQ Press.

Tilly, Charles. 1985. "War Making and State Making as Organized Crime." In *Bringing the State Back In*, edited by Peter Evans, Dietrich Rueschemeyer, and Theda Skocpol, 169–87. New York: Cambridge University Press.

———. 1992. *Coercion, Capital, and European States: AD 990–1992*. Malden, MA: Wiley-Blackwell.

Toal, Gerard, and John O'Loughlin. 2013. "Inside South Ossetia: A Survey of Attitudes in a De Facto State." *Post-Soviet Affairs* 29 (2): 136–72. https://doi.org/10.1080/1 060586X.2013.780417.

Toft, Monica. 2003. *The Geography of Ethnic Violence: Identity, Interests, and the Indivisibility of Territory*. Princeton, NJ: Princeton University Press.

Tollefsen, Andreas Forø, and Halvard Buhaug. 2015. "Insurgency and Inaccessibility." *International Studies Review* 17 (1): 6–25. https://doi.org/10.1111/misr.12202.

Tongdhammachart, Kramol. 1982. "Thai Perspectives on the Conflict in Kampuchea." In *Economic, Political, and Security Issues in Southeast Asia in the 1980s*, edited by Robert A. Scalapino and Jusuf Wanandi, 75–81. Berkeley: University of California, Institute of East Asian Studies.

Tongdhammachart, Kramol, Kusuma Snitwongse, Sarasin Viraphol, Arong Suthansasna, Wiwat Mungkandi, and Sukhumbhand Paribatra. 1983. *The Thai Elite's National Security Perspectives: Implications for Southeast Asia*. Bangkok: Chulalongkorn University.

Trenin, Dmitri. 2002. *The End of Eurasia: Russia on the Border between Geopolitics and Globalization*. Washington, DC: Carnegie Endowment for International Peace.

———. 2011. *Post-imperium: A Eurasian Story*. Washington, DC: Carnegie Endowment for International Peace.

Trimbach, David J., and Shannon O'Lear. 2015. "Russians in Estonia: Is Narva the Next Crimea?" *Eurasian Geography and Economics* 56 (5): 493–504. https://doi.org/10. 1080/15387216.2015.1110040.

Tsygankov, Andrei P. 2013. *Russia's Foreign Policy: Change and Continuity in National Identity*. 3rd ed. Lanham, MD: Rowman and Littlefield.

Turkish Statistical Institute. 2014. "Gross Domestic Product by Expenditure Approach, 1987 Base." Ankara: Turkish Statistical Institute. http://www.turkstat.gov.tr/ Start.do.

Unger, Daniel. 2003. "Ain't Enough Blanket: International Humanitarian Assistance and Cambodian Political Resistance." In *Refugee Manipulation: War, Politics, and the Abuse of Human Suffering*, edited by Stephen J. Stedman and Fred Tanner, 17–56. Washington, DC: Brookings Institution Press.

U.S. Agency for International Development. 1972. Memorandum of Conversation, March 6, 1972. Central Files February 1963–1973, Subject-Numeric File, RG 59, General Records of the Department of State, U.S. National Archives, College Park, MD.

Van de Walle, Etienne. 1968. "Characteristics of African Demographic Data." In *The Demography of Tropical Africa*, edited by William Brass, 12–87. Princeton, NJ: Princeton University Press. https://doi.org/10.1515/9781400877140-006.

Vickery, Michael. 1990. "Notes on the Political Economy of the People's Republic of Kampuchea (PRK)." *Journal of Contemporary Asia* 20 (4): 435–65. https://doi.org/10.1080/00472339080000251.

Vinci, Anthony. 2009. *Armed Groups and the Balance of Power: The International Relations of Terrorists, Warlords, and Insurgents.* London: Routledge.

Vitug, Marites Dañguilan, and Glenda M. Gloria. 2000. *Under the Crescent Moon: Rebellion in Mindanao.* Quezon City: Ateneo Center for Social Policy and Public Affairs.

Vogt, Manuel. 2018. "Ethnic Stratification and the Equilibrium of Inequality: Ethnic Conflict in Postcolonial States." *International Organization* 72 (1): 105–37. https://doi.org/10.1017/S0020818317000479.

Wallace, Jeremy L. 2016. "Juking the Stats? Authoritarian Information Problems in China." *British Journal of Political Science* 46 (1): 11–29. https://doi.org/10.1017/S0007123414000106.

Walter, Barbara F. 2002. *Committing to Peace: The Successful Settlement of Civil Wars.* Princeton, NJ: Princeton University Press.

——. 2006. "Building Reputation: Why Governments Fight Some Separatists but Not Others." *American Journal of Political Science* 50 (2): 313–30. https://doi.org/10.1111/j.1540-5907.2006.00186.x.

Way, Lucan A. 2005. "Authoritarian State Building and the Sources of Regime Competitiveness in the Fourth Wave: The Cases of Belarus, Moldova, Russia, and Ukraine." *World Politics* 57 (2): 231–61. https://doi.org/10.1353/wp.2005.0018.

Weidmann, Nils B., Jan Ketil Rød, and Lars-Erik Cederman. 2010. "Representing Ethnic Groups in Space: A New Dataset." *Journal of Peace Research* 47 (4): 491–99. https://doi.org/10.1177/0022343310368352.

Weinstein, Jeremy M. 2005. "Autonomous Recovery and International Intervention in Comparative Perspective." Working Paper no. 57, Center for Global Development, April 2005. https://www.cgdev.org/sites/default/files/2731_file_WP57.pdf.

Weisiger, Alex, and Keren Yarhi-Milo. 2015. "Revisiting Reputation: How Past Actions Matter in International Politics." *International Organization* 69 (2): 473–95. https://doi.org/10.1017/S0020818314000393.

Wheeler, Carla. 2008. "GIS Technology Helps Rid Southeast Asia of Dangerous Land Mines and Unexploded Ordnance." *ArcWatch*, July 2008. https://www.esri.com/news/arcwatch/0708/feature.html.

World Bank. 1980. *Aspects of Poverty: A Review and Assessment—Philippines.* Vol. 2, *Main report with annexes and statistical appendix.* Washington, DC: World Bank. http://documents.worldbank.org/curated/en/950581468299057815/Main-report-with-annexes-and-statistical-appendix.

——. 1984. *Population, Health, and Nutrition in the Philippines: A Sector Review.* Vol. 2, *Main Report with Tables and Technical Annexes.* Washington, DC: World Bank. http://documents.worldbank.org/curated/en/491451468095972954/Main-report-with-tables-and-technical-annexes.

———. 2018. *World Development Indicators*. Washington, DC: World Bank. https:// datacatalog.worldbank.org/dataset/world-development-indicators.

World Health Organization. 2006. *Working Together for Health: The World Health Report 2006*. Geneva: World Health Organization. https://www.who.int/ whr/2006/en/.

Wydra, Doris. 2003. "The Crimea Conundrum: The Tug of War between Russia and Ukraine on the Questions of Autonomy and Self-Determination." *International Journal on Minority and Group Rights* 10 (2): 111–30. https://doi.org/10.1163/157181104322784826.

Yarhi-Milo, Keren. 2018. *Who Fights for Reputation: The Psychology of Leaders in International Conflict*. Princeton, NJ: Princeton University Press.

Zacher, Mark W. 2001. "The Territorial Integrity Norm: International Boundaries and the Use of Force." *International Organization* 55 (2): 215–50. https://doi.org/10.1162/00208180151140568.

Zaman, Amberin. 1999. "Öcalan Conducted Ruthless Offensive." *Washington Post*, February 17, 1999. https://www.washingtonpost.com/archive/politics/1999/02/17/ocalan-conducted-ruthless-offensive/ab9d2dd3-c1d6-4ce2-97ff-144646c0b990/.

Zegart, Amy. 2015. "Stop Drinking the Weak Sauce." *Foreign Policy*, February 23, 2015. https://foreignpolicy.com/2015/02/23/nuclear-cyber-cold-war-weak-states-strategy.

Zürcher, Christoph. 2007. *Post-Soviet Wars: Rebellion, Ethnic Conflict, and Nationhood in the Caucasus*. New York: New York University Press.

Zürcher, Christoph, Carrie Manning, Kristie D. Evenson, Rachel Hayman, Sarah Riese, and Nora Roehner. 2013. *Costly Democracy: Peacebuilding and Democratization after War*. Stanford, CA: Stanford University Press.

Zürn, Michael, and Stephan Leibfried. 2005. "Reconfiguring the National Constellation." In *Transformations of the State?*, edited by Stephan Leibfried and Michael Zürn, 1–36. New York: Cambridge University Press.

Author Index

Abadie, Alberto, 197n4
Abinales, Patricio N., 205n15, 206nn41–42
Abramson, Scott F., 197n14
Acemoglu, Daron, 197n23, 201n23
Acharya, Amitav, 205n14
Acharya, Avidit, 197n14
Adelman, Carol, 209n1
Alcoberro, Agustí, 209n8
Alesina, Alberto, 209n3
Allison, Michael E., 197n17, 200n26
Altman, Dan, 197n17
Anceschi, Luca, 205n131
Anderson, M. S., 209n9, 209n11
Arguillas, Carolyn O., 205n12
Arjona, Ana, 197n6, 201n29
Artman, Vincent M., 202n23
Asmus, Ronald D., 202n25, 202n27, 204n94, 204n96, 204n99, 204n102
Atzili, Boaz, 197n17, 200n26, 209n4

Bachi, Roberto, 199n25
Bakke, Kristin M., 204n102
Balas, Alexandru, 198n34
Balcells, Albert, 209n7
Bapat, Navan A., 198n29, 200n2
Barma, Naazneen H., 198n32
Bates, Robert H., 198n12, 201n27, 210n8
Bearce, David H., 197n21
Beissinger, Mark R., 202n2, 203n46
Benson, Brett V., 200n27
Berman, Eli, 200n1
Beyene, Abdeta Dribssa, 200n8
Bignami-Van Assche, Simona, 210n10
Bilinsky, Yaroslav, 203n37
Blair, Dennis C., 197n9
Blank, Stephen, 203n39
Boone, Catherine, 199n25
Borghard, Erica Dreyfus, 198n29, 200n11
Börzel, Tanja A., 197n2
Boulding, Kenneth E., 200n25
Braumoeller, Bear F., 198n34
Brooks, Stephen G., 197n21
Brubaker, Rogers, 202n2, 203n58
Bugajski, Janusz, 202n4, 204n107
Buhaug, Halvard, 197n25, 201n16

Bukkvoll, Tor, 203n42, 203n44
Bull, David, 208n39, 208n43, 209n57
Busse, Matthias, 197n4
Byman, Daniel, 198n29, 200n1, 200n11, 200nn22–23

Cal, Ben, 207n58
Carney, Timothy, 207n10, 208n46, 209n53, 209n61
Carr, William, 210nn14–15
Carrier, N. H., 199n25
Carson, Austin, 200n12
Carter, David B., 198n29, 200n2, 200nn21–22
Carter, Matthew, 197n24, 209n3
Cederman, Lars-Erik, 198n27, 201n10, 210n21
Centeno, Miguel Angel, 197n16, 199n15, 209n5
Chalk, Peter, 199n30
Chanda, Nayan, 207n3, 208n22, 208n25, 208n27, 208n34, 208n41
Che Man, W. K., 205n15, 206n41, 206nn44–45
Chowdhury, Arjun, 209n5
Chufrin, Gennady, 209n56
Clapper, James R., 197n9
Clunan, Anne L., 197n7
Coats, Daniel R., 197n9
Coggins, Bridget L., 197n10
Collier, Paul, 198n27
Comin, Diego, 201n23
Cooley, Alexander, 202n11, 205n123
Cornell, Svante E., 205nn127–28
Coronel-Ferrer, Miriam, 205n15, 206n41
Crabtree, Charles, 197n6
Cunningham, David E., 198n29, 200n1, 200n13

Dabla, Bashir Ahmad, 199n45
Dafoe, Allan, 200n4
D'Arcy, Michelle, 198n13
Darden, Keith A., 202n11
Dawson, Jane, 204n115
de Swaan, Abram, 198n4
Desch, Michael C., 197n13, 209n5
Diehl, Paul F., 198n34, 201n3
Dincecco, Mark, 202n28

Subject Index

Page references for illustrative materials (maps, tables, figures) are in *italics*.